Alternatives to Incarceration

Mass incarceration has been an ongoing problem in the United States. There have been several research studies that explain the causes and consequences of mass incarceration. A major contributor to incarceration is what happens in community supervision. In several states, many prison admissions result from technical violations from community supervision. Historically, alternatives to incarceration were developed to reduce prison populations and decrease the fiscal cost of incarceration. They were to function as a diversion away from prison. Alternatives also keep people in the community while holding them accountable and protecting community safety. Yet, given the high violations and revocations, rather than serving as an alternative to incarceration, community supervision becomes a delayed prison sentence. The book underscores the importance of ongoing research and the need for effective strategies to reduce violations and revocations. There is a clear need for more research to explore what works in reducing violations and revocations, including the factors that contribute to these issues. This ongoing exploration is crucial for the continued development and improvement of community corrections. Chapters in this book address how barriers, such as mental illness, COVID-19, and financial constraints, may impede success on supervision and highlight in the findings ways to increase success despite these barriers. Further, two chapters provide results on two commonly used strategies in community corrections: risk assessments and electronic monitoring. The chapter's findings build on previous works and provide recommendations for policy and research. This book advances knowledge on reducing violations and revocations and increasing success in community supervision. It was originally published as a special issue of *Corrections – Policy, Practice and Research.*

Ebony L. Ruhland received her Ph.D. from the School of Social Work at the University of Minnesota. Her research focuses on how criminal justice policies and practices impact individuals, families, and communities.

Alternatives to Incarceration

Opportunities and Challenges in Reducing Violations and Revocations in Community Corrections

Edited by
Ebony L. Ruhland

Routledge
Taylor & Francis Group
LONDON AND NEW YORK

First published 2026
by Routledge
4 Park Square, Milton Park, Abingdon, Oxon OX14 4RN

and by Routledge
605 Third Avenue, New York, NY 10158

Routledge is an imprint of the Taylor & Francis Group, an informa business

British Library Cataloguing in Publication Data
A catalogue record for this book is available from the British Library

ISBN13: 978-1-041-12337-8 (hbk)
ISBN13: 978-1-041-12338-5 (pbk)
ISBN13: 978-1-003-66425-3 (ebk)

DOI: 10.4324/9781003664253

Typeset in Minion Pro
by Newgen Publishing UK

Publisher's Note
The publisher accepts responsibility for any inconsistencies that may have arisen during the conversion of this book from journal articles to book chapters, namely the inclusion of journal terminology.

Contents

Citation Information

The chapters in this book were originally published in *Corrections – Policy, Practice and Research,* volume 9, issue 5 (2024). When citing this material, please use the original page numbering for each article, as follows:

Introduction

Alternatives to Incarceration: Strategies for Reducing Violations and Revocations
Ebony L. Ruhland
Corrections – Policy, Practice and Research, volume 9, issue 5 (2024), pp. 553–555

Chapter 1

An Item-Based Revalidation of the Florida Pretrial Risk Assessment Instrument
Natalie Goulette and Katherine Johnson
Corrections – Policy, Practice and Research, volume 9, issue 5 (2024), pp. 556–575

Chapter 2

Cyclical Pathways to Probation Violations: Housing, Financial Capabilities, and COVID-19
Andrea Guiffre, Kathryn Tapp, Beth M. Huebner, Kimberly R. Kras, and Lee Ann Slocum
Corrections – Policy, Practice and Research, volume 9, issue 5 (2024), pp. 576–598

Chapter 3

Reducing Community Supervision Failure for People with Mental Illness: Strategies for Promoting Success
Sarah M. Manchak, Sarah Light, Alison J. Farringer, Francesco DiRienzo, Luis Guitierrez, and Jessica Warner
Corrections – Policy, Practice and Research, volume 9, issue 5 (2024), pp. 599–617

Chapter 4

Improving Probation Outcomes for Emerging Adults: An Experiment Evaluating a Specialized Caseload in Texas
Kendra J. Clark, Jennifer Lerch, Faustino Lopez, and Faye S. Taxman
Corrections – Policy, Practice and Research, volume 9, issue 5 (2024), pp. 618–640

Chapter 5

A Rapid Review of Literature on Factors Associated with Adult Probation Revocations
Carmen L. Diaz, Staci Rising, Eric Grommon, Miriam Northcutt Bohmert, and Evan Marie Lowder
Corrections – Policy, Practice and Research, volume 9, issue 5 (2024), pp. 641–668

Chapter 6

Evaluating the Effectiveness of Electronic Monitoring with Probationers
Jeff A. Bouffard and H. Daniel Butler
Corrections – Policy, Practice and Research, volume 9, issue 5 (2024), pp. 669–687

Notes on Contributors

Miriam Northcutt Bohmert, Department of Criminal Justice, Indiana University Bloomington, Bloomington, IN, USA.

Jeff A. Bouffard, Department of Sociology, Criminal Justice at Iowa State University, Ames, IA, USA.

H. Daniel Butler, Department of Sociology, Criminal Justice at Iowa State University, Ames, IA, USA.

Kendra J. Clark, Schar School of Policy and Government, Center for Advancing Correctional Excellence, George Mason University, Fairfax, VA, USA.

Carmen L. Diaz, Department of Criminal Justice, Indiana University Bloomington, Bloomington, IN, USA.

Francesco DiRienzo, School of Criminal Justice, University of Cincinnati, Cincinnati, OH, USA.

Alison J. Farringer, School of Criminal Justice, University of Cincinnati, Cincinnati, OH, USA.

Andrea Giuffre, School of Criminology and Criminal Justice, California State University, San Bernardino, CA, USA.

Natalie Goulette, Department of Criminology and Criminal Justice, University of West Florida, Pensacola, FL, USA.

Eric Grommon, Public Policy Institute, Center for Health and Justice Research, Paul H. O'Neill School of Public and Environmental Affairs, Indiana University–Purdue University Indianapolis, Indianapolis, IN, USA.

Luis Guitierrez, School of Criminal Justice, University of Cincinnati, Cincinnati, OH, USA.

Beth M. Huebner, School of Criminology and Criminal Justice, Arizona State University, Phoenix, AZ, USA.

Kathrine Johnson, Department of Criminology and Criminal Justice, University of West Florida, Pensacola, FL, USA.

Kimberly R. Kras, School of Public Affairs, San Diego State University, San Diego, CA, USA.

Jennifer Lerch, Justice System Partners, South Easton, MA, USA.

Sarah Light, School of Criminal Justice, University of Cincinnati, Cincinnati, OH, USA.

Faustino Lopez, Hidalgo County Community Supervision and Corrections Department, Edinburg, TX, USA.

Evan Marie Lowder, Department of Criminology, Law and Society, George Mason University Fairfax, Fairfax, VA, USA.

Sarah M. Manchak, School of Criminal Justice, University of Cincinnati, Cincinnati, OH, USA.

Staci Rising, Public Policy Institute Center for Health and Justice Research, Paul H. O'Neill School of Public and Environmental Affairs, Indiana University–Purdue University Indianapolis, Indianapolis, IN, USA.

Ebony L. Ruhland, School of Criminal Justice, Rutgers University Newark, Newak, NJ, USA.

Lee Ann Slocum, Department of Criminology and Criminal Justice, University of Missouri – St. Louis, St. Louis, MO, USA.

Kathryn Tapp, School of Criminology and Criminal Justice, Arizona State University, Phoenix, AZ, USA.

Faye S. Taxman, Schar School of Policy and Government, Center for Advancing Correctional Excellence, George Mason University, Fairfax, VA, USA.

Jessica Warner, Department of Justice and Community Studies, Miami University, Hamilton, OH, USA.

Introduction – Alternatives to Incarceration: Strategies for Reducing Violations and Revocation

Ebony L. Ruhland

Community corrections are the most common criminal justice sanction used in the United States. Many more people are on probation and parole than are incarcerated in jails or prisons (Kaeble, 2024). Additionally, although we do not have precise numbers, there are thousands of people in the United States sanctioned to halfway houses, electronic monitoring, and other community-based sentences. Many community-based sanctions were developed as alternatives to incarceration with the primary purpose of reducing mass incarceration (Austin & Krisberg, 1982) and institutional correctional costs (Clear & Schrantz, 2011). Fines, community service, day reporting centers, probation, electronic monitoring, and other community programs attempted to address and respond to mass incarceration (Tonry, 2017). For over 30 years, criminal legal research and public policy have been focused on decreasing mass incarceration and identifying ways to reduce our over-reliance on prisons (and jails) in the United States (Alexander, 2010; Clear, 2009; Pattillo et al., 2004).

However, to a lesser extent, other scholars have warned us about mass probation or mass supervision (McNeill & Beyens, 2013; Phelps, 2020). In many ways, community correction has several benefits over incarceration. Community corrections can keep people in their families and communities, provide many services at lower costs than incarceration, and hold justice-involved individuals accountable while maintaining community safety. Further, research has illustrated that individuals often come out worse after a period of incarceration, and recidivism rates are high for those previously incarcerated (Cullen et al., 2011). Historically, community corrections were championed because they could improve individuals' outcomes and provide fiscally cost-effective services (Tonry, 2014). Community corrections were seen as a model that could provide individual rehabilitative services while at the same time being tough on crime (Taxman, 2012).

The aspirational goals of community corrections have yet to be fully realized. Despite the potential benefits, community supervision is often critiqued for similar reasons found in jail or prison-based sanctions. Individuals who participate in community corrections experience high violations and revocations, often due to technical violations rather than for new crimes (Clear & Austin, 2009). Technical violations are conditions that individuals must follow as requirements of their sentence; conditions are often not unlawful acts (Klingele, 2013) but legal orders because of the carceral citizenship (Miller & Stuart, 2017) an individual inherits under community corrections. Thus, community corrections may be a delayed prison sentence rather than an alternative to incarceration. There is concern that probation and community correction services have functioned as a net-widener by placing more people on these services who may not need them and placing more people in jails and prisons due to technical violations (Phelps, 2018). Several community-based programs, such as day reporting sentences and electronic monitoring, may incur high expenses. Further, the fact that many individuals ultimately end up in jails and prisons due to technical violations from community supervision ends up not being a cost-saving or a way to reduce the financial burdens of incarceration.

The purpose of this special issue is to underscore the importance of ongoing research and the need for effective strategies to reduce violations and revocations. There is a clear need for more research to explore what works in reducing violations and revocations, including the factors that contribute to these issues. This ongoing exploration is crucial for the continued development and improvement of community corrections. Articles in this special issue address how barriers, such as mental illness, COVID, and financial constraints, may impede success on supervision and highlight in the findings ways to increase success despite these barriers. Further, two articles in this issue provide results on two commonly used strategies in community corrections – risk assessments and electronic monitoring. The article's findings build on previous works and provide recommendations for policy and research. This special issue advances knowledge on reducing violations and revocations and increasing success in community supervision.

Disclosure statement

No potential conflict of interest was reported by the author(s).

References

Alexander, M. (2010). *The new Jim Crow: Mass incarceration in the age of colorblindness*. New Press.
Austin, J., & Krisberg, B. (1982). The unmet promise of alternatives to incarceration. *Crime & Delinquency*, *28*(3), 374–409. https://doi.org/10.1177/001112878202800302
Clear, T. R. (2009). *Imprisoning communities: How mass incarceration makes disadvantaged neighborhoods worse*. Oxford University Press.
Clear, T. R., & Austin, J. (2009). Reducing mass incarceration: Implications of the iron law of prison populations. *Harvard Law & Policy Review*, *3*(2), 307–324.
Clear, T. R., & Schrantz, D. (2011). Strategies for reducing prison populations. *The Prison Journal*, *91* (3_suppl), 138S–159S. https://doi.org/10.1177/0032885511415238
Cullen, F. T., Jonson, C. L., & Nagin, D. S. (2011). Prisons do not reduce recidivism: The high cost of ignoring science. *The Prison Journal*, *91*(3_suppl), 48S–65S. https://doi.org/10.1177/0032885511415224
Kaeble, D. (2024). *Probation and parole in the United States, 2022*. Bureau of Justice Statistics, https://bjs.ojp.gov/document/ppus22.pdf
Klingele, C. (2013). Rethinking the use of community supervision. *Journal of Criminal Law & Criminology*, *103*(4), 1015–1069. https://doi.org/10.2139/ssrn.2232078
McNeill, F., & Beyens, K. (2013). Introduction: Studying mass supervision. In *Offender supervision in Europe*. Palgrave Macmillan. https://doi.org/10.1057/9781137379191_
Miller, R. J., & Stuart, F. (2017). Carceral citizenship: Race, rights and responsibility in the age of Mass supervision. *Theoretical Criminology*, *21*(4), 532–548. https://doi.org/10.1177/1362480617731203
Pattillo, M., Western, B., & Weiman, D. (Eds.). (2004). *Imprisoning America: The social effects of mass incarceration*. Russell Sage Foundation.
Phelps, M. S. (2018). Ending mass probation. *The Future of Children*, *28*(1), 125–146. https://doi.org/10.1353/foc.2018.0006

Phelps, M. S. (2020). Mass probation from micro to macro: Tracing the expansion and consequences of community supervision. *Annual Review of Criminology*, *3*(1), 261–279. https://doi.org/10.1146/annurev-criminol-011419-041352

Taxman, F. S. (2012). Probation, intermediate sanctions, and community-based corrections. In J. Petersilia & K. Reitz (Eds.), *The oxford handbook of sentencing and corrections* (pp. 363–388). Oxford University Press Inc.

Tonry, M. (2014). Remodeling American sentencing: A ten-step blueprint for moving past mass incarceration. *Criminology & Public Policy*, *13*(4), 503–533. https://doi.org/10.1111/1745-9133.12097

Tonry, M. (2017). Community punishments. *Reforming criminal justice: A report of the academy for justice on bridging the gap between scholarship and reform*, *4*, 187–204.

An Item-Based Revalidation of the Florida Pretrial Risk Assessment Instrument

Natalie Goulette and Kathrine Johnson

ABSTRACT

Scholars and practitioners continue to examine the growing pretrial detainee population. These individuals have not been convicted of a crime, and yet they sit in detention, taxing jail facilities and their limited budgets. Pretrial risk assessment tools have been created to identify individuals who can be released prior to trial, without jeopardizing community safety. The current study revalidates items included in the Florida Pretrial Risk Assessment Instrument. Results suggest that most individuals on pretrial release do not commit new offenses or fail to appear for future court hearings. Similarities and differences between the original study and the revalidation are noted. The inclusion of assessing "community ties" is also explored.

Introduction

Research has shown that at any given moment, approximately two-thirds of local jail populations are pretrial detainees (Baglivio et al., 2020; Lowder, Diaz, et al., 2020; Marlowe et al., 2020; Zeng, 2018). Many are detained simply because they cannot afford bail (Cohen & Reaves, 2007; Marlowe et al., 2020; Zeng, 2018). These individuals have not been convicted of any crime (Schmalleger & Smykla, 2021). Prior research suggests that individuals who remain in pretrial detention are more likely to experience multiple negative outcomes as a result of their confinement (Goulette & Wooldredge, 2018).

Pretrial detainees can experience a number of unintended consequences that impact their physical and mental health, employment status, and overall financial well-being (Goulette & Wooldredge, 2018). Those individuals who are detained prior to trial face a greater likelihood of conviction, and are often sentenced more harshly in comparison to those who were not detained (T. Cadigan & Lowenkamp, 2011; Cohen et al., 2018; Dobbie et al., 2018; Goldkamp & White, 2006; Heaton et al., 2017; Saks & Ackerman, 2014; Wooldredge et al., 2017). By using a pretrial risk assessment tool, criminal justice personnel can estimate the probability of an individual engaging in further criminal activity and showing up to future court hearings (Scurich & Krauss, 2020). Knowing this probability helps criminal justice professionals make decisions about pretrial release or detention. Allowing low-risk individuals to obtain pretrial release ensures that these individuals are able to continue to provide for their families and themselves without jeopardizing the safety of the general public (Lowenkamp et al., 2008).

While pretrial risk assessments should not be used as the only tool to determine release or detention, they should be incorporated to make a well-fit decision on a case-by-case basis (Baglivio et al., 2020). According to previous research, when risk assessments are used in concert with judicial discretion, the result is more offenders are released, the conditions of release are less stringent, and there are no increases in failure to appear or re-arrest (Austin et al., 1985; Barno et al., 2020; T. P. Cadigan et al., 2012; Goldkamp & White, 2006; Terranova et al., 2020). This is important to consider as jurisdictions continue to grapple with an increasing pretrial detention population, stretching already overtaxed budgets even further (Baglivio et al., 2020; Goulette & Wooldredge, 2018). Lowder and Foudray (2021) suggest that organizations across the country have supported a variety of bail reform and other strategies to encourage pretrial release. By providing non-financial release options, "promoting the use of pretrial risk assessments to guide pretrial decision-making, and increasing community supervision of pretrial defendants" (Lowder & Foudray, 2021, p. 1766), jail populations will decrease and arrestees will avoid the negative impact of detention.

Predictors of pretrial misconduct

Prior research has identified a number of factors that impact an individual's risk of committing a new offense or failing to appear for a future court hearing (Austin & Murray, 2009; Bechtel et al., 2017; Latessa et al., 2009; VanNostrand, 2003). Many of these predictors are included in pretrial risk assessment instruments, including the Florida Pretrial Risk Assessment Instrument. Some of the strongest predictors identified continue to be the legal factors of current offense type and prior criminal history (Bechtel et al., 2011; Kennedy et al., 2013). Current offense type is not only located in the U.S. Federal Pretrial Services Risk Assessment Instrument (Federal PTRA) (Cohen & Lowenkamp, 2018) but also in the Public Safety Assessment (PSA) that is used in at least 38 states and a number of local jurisdictions (DeMichele et al., 2018). Current offense type is also included in risk assessment tools used in Texas (Debora & Meils, 2019), Florida (Austin et al., 2011), Indiana (Lowder, Lawson, et al., 2020), Mississippi (Marlowe et al., 2020), and Minnesota (Duwe & Rocque, 2019). Intuitively, it makes sense why the current offense is noted in pretrial risk assessments. If public safety is a concern, individuals charged with more serious offenses may be perceived as a greater danger to the community (Steffensmeier et al., 1998). In contrast, however, other risk assessment tools view individuals with more serious charges as less of a risk, with the exception of violent offenders (T. P. Cadigan et al., 2012). While no substantive argument is given for this logic, it is clear that the current offense type is included in most, if not all, risk assessment tools.

The majority of pretrial risk assessments include the individual's prior record as well, including the Ohio Risk Assessment System-Pretrial Assessment Tool (ORAS-PAT), Virginia Pretrial Risk Assessment Instrument-Revised (VPRAI-R), the Correctional Offender Management Profiling for Alternative Sanctions (COMPAS), and the PSA (Bechtel et al., 2011; Desmarais & Lowder, 2019). However, there is wide variation when observing the weight that prior criminal history carries in the overall assessment score (Konig & Krafft, 2021). While some risk assessments incorporate both misdemeanors and felonies (ORAS-PAT, PSA, Static Risk Assessment (SRA)), others only factor in felonies, with no attention given to misdemeanors (COMPAS, VPRAI-R, Federal PTRA). Certain states differentiate even further and assign points only for convictions or minimum time spent in jail as opposed to the number of arrests (Konig & Krafft, 2021).

Many pretrial risk assessment instruments also consider how enmeshed an individual is in their community (T. P. Cadigan et al., 2012). Since the earliest work of The Vera Institute, it has been argued that individuals who are well connected to the community (e.g., employment status, home ownership, time at current residence, marital status, etc.) are less likely to uproot their lives in order to flee from the jurisdiction (VanNostrand & Keebler, 2009). For example, the Federal PTRA places emphasis specifically on employment status and residential ownership (Cohen & Lowenkamp, 2018), showing that community ties have a correlation to the probability of an individual recidivating or failing to appear for court hearings. However, many scholars argue that community ties are often considered because of their face validity and research results no longer support their inclusion in risk assessment instruments (T. P. Cadigan et al., 2012; Goldkamp & Vilcica, 2009).

Another predictor considered in certain risk assessments, but excluded from others, is substance use. The Federal PTRA, the Nevada Pretrial Risk (NPR), and the Florida Pretrial Risk Assessment Instrument all take this variable into consideration when determining if an individual should be eligible for pretrial release, however, numerous states do not include any mention of substance use or drugs (Austin et al., 2011; Konig & Krafft, 2021). Unfortunately, little research has been published to explain the correlation between substance use and the success of pretrial release. One study by VanNostrand and Keebler (2009) found that "defendants who abused alcohol, cannabis, and narcotics, were more likely to fail pending trial when compared to defendants who did not abuse any substances" (p. 12). This is a difficult factor to fully investigate as it requires honesty from the individual seeking pretrial release. The variation in considering substance use and other factors across multiple jurisdictions, within multiple risk assessment tools, lends support to the notion that such instruments should be created based on empirical evidence, and it is possible that the impact of such factors can change over time (T. P. Cadigan et al., 2012; VanNostrand & Keebler, 2009).

Development of the Florida pretrial risk assessment instrument

The current study aims to contribute to the growing knowledge of risk assessment tools by conducting an item-based revalidation of the Florida Pretrial Risk Assessment Instrument. This risk assessment tool was modeled after the VRAI-R and was validated by the JFI Institute in 2011 (Austin et al., 2011). The Association of Pretrial Professionals of Florida (APPF) received federal grant money from the Bureau of Justice Assistance. The goal of the project was to create an instrument that could be used across the state of Florida (Austin et al., 2011; Goulette et al., 2021).[1] Six counties participated in the original validation project and a sample of 1,757 cases were analyzed.[2] In total, 11 factors were identified to have an independent effect on predicting pretrial misconduct. Pretrial misconduct was defined as the commission of a new offense, failure to appear for court (FTA), or a combined measure including either of these outcomes (Austin et al., 2011). Validation of the 11 factors included in the Florida Pretrial Risk Assessment Instrument occurred in two stages of data analysis. First, the association between all predictor variables and the outcome measure, pretrial misconduct, were examined through bivariate analyses, using cross-tabulations. Second, all significant predictors identified in the bivariate analyses were included in a multivariate logistic regression (Austin et al., 2011). Any predictors that were significant within the bivariate analyses, but were no longer significant in the multivariate analysis, were removed.[3]

Of the 11 factors identified by Austin et al. (2011) to have a significant influence on pretrial misconduct, six were characteristics related to the suspect. An individual's age at jail admission was collapsed into three categories, 19 years or younger, 20–29 years old, and 30 years or older. Cases involving individuals ages 20–29 were predicted to have a higher probability of pretrial misconduct than the other age categories (Austin et al., 2011). Employment status (unemployed or other) was also found to be a significant predictor of pretrial misconduct. Cases involving unemployed individuals were predicted to have a higher probability of pretrial misconduct than other individuals (Austin et al., 2011). Marital status was also included as a dichotomous measure within the Florida Pretrial Risk Assessment Instrument, with cases involving a *single* individual earning a higher score than individuals with an *other* marital status (Austin et al., 2011). Another significant predictor of pretrial misconduct was telephone ownership, coded as yes or no, with cases involving individuals who did not own a phone as scoring higher on the instrument than those cases in which the individual did own a telephone or cell phone (Austin et al., 2011). Cases in which the individual had resided less than 12 months at their current residence were predicted to have a higher probability of pretrial misconduct than individuals residing 12 months or longer at their current residence (Austin et al., 2011). Finally, a series of dummy variables were included to account for cases in which individuals reported a history of substance use, mental health issues, neither, or both. Cases involving a history of both were scored higher on the Florida Pretrial Risk Assessment Instrument than cases involving substance use, mental health issues, or neither issue (Austin et al., 2011).

The remaining five items included in the Florida Pretrial Risk Assessment Instrument pertained to prior criminal history of the individual, prior failure to appear (FTA), and the current offense. Prior criminal history was found to be a significant predictor of pretrial misconduct, according to Austin et al. (2011), and included both previous adult felonies and adult misdemeanors (none or one or more). Cases involving individuals who reported one or more adult felonies were predicted to have a higher probability of pretrial misconduct than individuals with no prior adult felonies (Austin et al., 2011). Cases involving individuals with one or more previous adult misdemeanors were also scored higher than individuals with no prior adult misdemeanors (Austin et al., 2011). The number of previous times an individual failed to appear for a court hearing was found to significantly influence the probability of pretrial misconduct (Austin et al., 2011). Cases in which an individual had two or more prior FTAs were scored higher on the instrument than individuals with one prior FTA or no prior FTAs (Austin et al., 2011).

Multiple predictors were used to identify the current most serious charge at jail admission. A series of dummy variables were included to compare the probability of pretrial misconduct in cases including violent, property, drug, or other offense types. Cases in which individuals were charged with committing a property offense were scored higher on the Florida Pretrial Risk Assessment Instrument than individuals charged with committing violent, drug, or other offense types (Austin et al., 2011). A dummy measure was also included to identify cases with a current dangerous charge, as listed in Florida Statute 907.041. These offenses are considered dangerous acts against persons, including domestic violence, kidnapping, homicide, sexual battery, and roughly 20 additional crimes.

Individuals charged under Florida Statute 907.041 cannot "be granted nonmonetary release option at a first appearance; however, the court shall retain the discretion to release an accused on electronic monitoring or on recognizance bond if the findings … warrant such a release." Under the Florida Pretrial Risk Assessment Instrument, cases that did *not* include a dangerous charge were identified to have a higher probability of pretrial misconduct than cases with these dangerous charges (Austin et al., 2011).

After the 11 predictors were identified through their bivariate and multivariate analyses, Austin et al. (2011) applied weights to each of the categories. These weights were developed using "the marginal increase in pretrial misconduct risk attributable to a particular predictor. This marginal risk was measured relative to the base (or omitted category)" (Austin et al., 2011, p. 5). These weights were calculated from the multivariate analysis, controlling for all other predictors in the model. Cases could then be scored using these calculated weights. Scores ranged from 0–51 points, with higher scores associated with a higher probability of engaging in pretrial misconduct (Austin et al., 2011). Quartiles were calculated to divide the sample of cases into four groups, corresponding with their overall probability of pretrial misconduct. Cases labeled "low risk" scored 0–12 points, "low/moderate" cases scored 13–17 points, "moderate" cases scored 18–22 points, and "high moderate" cases scored more than 22 points (Austin et al., 2011). Austin et al. (2011) acknowledged that agencies might wish to alter these designations to fit their overall needs and clients, as only 13.7% of their sample of cases were noted to have committed a new offense or FTA during the six-month follow-up period.

Calls for revalidating the Florida pretrial risk assessment instrument

While risk assessment tools can help improve judicial decision-making, it is important to revalidate these instruments periodically. First, it is important to only use the most relevant and timely factors (T. P. Cadigan et al., 2012; VanNostrand & Keebler, 2009). Variables that were once considered predictive of success regarding pretrial monitoring, may become irrelevant over time. One example of this is the ownership of a phone (T. P. Cadigan et al., 2012). Second, revalidation is crucial to eliminate any biases that exist within these instruments. For example, scholars have argued that certain variables may be closely correlated to race. While the instrument itself appears unbiased, disparities are still present within it (Desmarais et al., 2021; Lawson & Lowder, 2023; Lowder et al., 2022; Picard et al., 2019; Scurich & Krauss, 2020). Continual reevaluation of these risk assessment tools can help to remove any underlying bias they may contain, and reduce subsequent negative impact on racial minorities. Finally, jurisdictions that are employing a risk assessment tool to guide decisions related to pretrial release, will want to know that the tool is appropriate for the individuals who reside within their communities. By using empirical data to revalidate their risk assessment tool, criminal justice personnel can make such decisions confidently, while still maintaining community safety and ensuring individuals will appear for future court hearings (National Association of Pretrial Services Agencies [NAPSA], 2020).

Relatedly, NAPSA accreditation recommends pretrial service agencies to "use an objective risk assessment that has been validated for the jurisdiction within the past ten years using scientific methods and/or established pretrial release criteria supported by local empirical evidence validated within the past 10 years to make an assessment of risk" (Pretrial Services Program Accreditation Standards Checklist and Guidelines, n.d.). These revisions led the APPF to revalidate the Florida Pretrial Risk Assessment Instrument.

Method and data

Data for the current project were collected in collaboration with pretrial service personnel across nine different counties within the state of Florida. The research team met with representatives from each of the counties in the spring of 2019 to discuss the overall goals of the project and potential barriers associated with data collection (Goulette et al., 2021). During this initial meeting, county officials and the research team created a code sheet for data collection, including variables that had been used within other validated risk assessment instruments and were included in the original validation study (Austin et al., 2011; Goulette et al., 2021). County representatives confirmed that each of the items listed in the code sheet would be available for data collection. A data dictionary was also created to assist pretrial service and jail personnel. This dictionary identified each variable needed and how these variables would be coded.

As shown in Table 1, the nine counties that participated in the current project provided a mix of small, medium, and large counties across the state of Florida. Austin et al. (2011) noted similar characteristics across their sample of six counties during the original validation study. During validation, county populations ranged from 247,336 to just over 1.3 million residents (Austin et al., 2011). Our sample of counties that participated in the current project reported populations ranging from 182,000 to almost 2.8 million residents (Office of Program Policy Analysis and Government Accountability, 2020). While counties in the original study supervised between 992 and 5,072 individuals that year (Austin et al., 2011), the current sample of counties supervised between 283 and 7,865 individuals in 2018. Five of the six original counties offered pretrial services found at the county level (commission, sheriff, or justice services) while one had an administrative locus in the court (Austin et al., 2011). Similarly, of the seven participating counties who reported the location of their pretrial services, five were housed at the county level, one in the Administrative Office of the Courts, and one in corrections. While two of the counties offered first appearances only once a day, six counties held first appearance hearings twice per day (Goulette et al., 2021). This information was not reported for the remaining county nor was it included the original validation study (Austin et al., 2011). The average number of interviews completed across the counties in the original validation study was just under 8,000, with one county logging 18,450 interviews (Austin et al., 2011). In the revalidation counties, the average was approximately 7,700, with two counties reporting more than 20,000 interviews. Eight of the nine counties in this revalidation study, and all six counties in the original validation study, provided supervision of defendants on pretrial release. Finally, only three of the nine counties included in the current project also participated in the original validation study conducted by Austin et al. (2011).

At the time of data collection, a total of 28 counties across the state of Florida offered pretrial services. To contextualize the characteristics of our revalidation sample and the remaining 19 Florida counties that offered pretrial services, almost all of the counties required fees to be paid for one or more services, including GPS monitoring, drug testing, curfew monitoring, and others. The average population was a bit higher for the revalidation counties (696,612) in comparison to the average population for the other Florida counties (598,624) (Office of Program Policy Analysis and Government Accountability, 2020). Average annual program budgets were similar at $1,363,646, for the revalidation sample, and $1,106,682 for the other counties that did not participate in the current project (Office

Table 1. Characteristics of nine counties.

	A	B	C	D	E	F	G	H	I
County Population	266,944	182,033	320,239	318,316	420,985	74,228	2,751,796	1,378,538	368,456
Participated in Original Validation Study	Yes	No	No	No	Yes	No	No	No	Yes
Administrative Locus	County Court Services	AOC	Sheriff's Office	Corrections Department	County Judicial Center & County Jail	BOCC	UNK	County Corrections	UNK
Program Budget (2018)	UNK	$559,171	$323,200	$810,962	$821,452	$510,601	$5,542,000	2,967,750	727,686.89
Program Fees	Yes	Yes	Yes	No	No	No	No	Yes	Yes
Provide Supervision of Defendants on PTR	Yes	Yes	Yes	Yes	UNK	Yes	Yes	Yes	Yes
Does Program Supervise Defendants who Posted Bond	Yes	Yes	Yes (rarely)	Yes	Yes	Yes	Yes	Yes	Yes
Number Supervised in 2018	387	417	283	1,119	3500+	941	7,865	2546	3021
Jail Capacity	1,148	1,074	1,312	1,400	UNK	695 (3 locations)	4,890	4107	919
Number of Annual Arrests	UNK	6,689	8,566	15,738	UNK	7,000	56,400 (booked)	37,068	11,173 (bookings)
Percentage of Pretrial vs Sentenced Offenders	UNK	75.7 vs 24.3	70 vs 30	UNK	65 vs 22 vs 13 (other)	N/A	58 vs 8	77 vs 23	UNK
Percentage of Pretrial Defendants with Felonies only vs misdemeanors only	UNK	79.8 vs 20.2	73 vs 27	UNK	91 vs 8 vs 1 (other)	N/A	78 vs 22	65 vs 35	UNK
Frequency of First Appearance	Daily w/d	Daily w/d	Daily w/d w/e & holidays	Daily w/d w/e & holidays	Daily w/d & w/e	Daily w/d & w/d	Twice daily w/d	Twice daily w/d	Not reported
Number of Individuals Attending FA Annually	UNK	6,389	6,331	7,218	8000+	N/A	24,253	UNK	UNK
Number of Individuals Interviewed for FA	2,325	6,369	6,331	909	3500+	2707	20,709	22,211	4,669
Revalidation Sample Sizes	160 (5.6%)	336 (11.7%)	439 (15.2%)	246 (8.5%)	210 (7.3%)	335 (11.6%)	350 (12.1%)	395 (13.7%)	402 (14.0%)
Collected All Cases in Nov. 2019	Yes	Yes	No	Yes	No	No	Yes	No	No

of Program Policy Analysis and Government Accountability, 2020). In 2019, between one and eight percent of cases resulted in an arrest warrant for failure to appear across all counties with pretrial services. Between one percent and eight percent of cases across the revalidation counties involved an arrest warrant for the commission of a new criminal offense. Other pretrial service counties across the state of Florida reported between one and thirteen percent of cases involved an arrest warrant issued for a new crime committed (Office of Program Policy Analysis and Government Accountability, 2020). In comparison to the other 39 counties across the state of Florida, these 28 counties with pretrial services were found to have a higher average population, a higher average daily jail population, and a higher average number of annual arrests (United States Census Bureau, 2023). These 28 counties also reported a larger number of misdemeanor and felony offenders in comparison to the entire state of Florida (United States Census Bureau, 2023).

Sample

The goal of this revalidation study was to include a representative sample of all cases involving suspects who were released on pretrial status from nine Florida counties during July, August, September, and October 2019 (Goulette et al., 2021). A goal of 350 cases for each county was selected since the original validation study only included 250 cases from six participating counties. To achieve this, a systematic random sample was used and every county was given a sampling sequence (e.g. 1 in every 7th case, 1 in every 3rd case, etc.). This sampling sequence was chosen for each county based on the number of arrests they recorded during the prior 12-month period. When six of the nine participating counties failed to meet the goal of 350 cases, they collected data on every suspect who was released on pretrial status during the month of November 2019. While three counties were able to exceed the goal of 350 cases, three counties either met or came very close to meeting the goal (see Table 1). The three remaining counties fell short of meeting their overall goal of 350 cases (Goulette et al., 2021). Once suspects obtained pretrial release, their cases were followed by court personnel for six months, or until the case was resolved, whichever occurred first, to note any type of pretrial misconduct.[4]

Measures

One binary outcome measure captured pretrial misconduct, and compared those suspects who committed a new criminal offense or failed to appear for a court hearing with suspects who did not engage in either type of pretrial misconduct (Goulette et al., 2021). This is the same measure that was used in the original validation study to identify pertinent predictors of pretrial misconduct (Austin et al., 2011). While prior research suggests that predictors may differ in predicting the commission of a new criminal offense or failing to appear for a future court hearing (Debora & Meils, 2019; Desmarais et al., 2021), we chose to replicate the work of Austin et al. (2011) as closely as possible.

A number of predictors were examined and included in the current project. Most of these measures were included in the original validation study (Austin et al., 2011) or were examined by other validation studies (T. P. Cadigan et al., 2012; Lawson & Lowder, 2023; Lowder et al., 2022). All of these predictors were recoded into dichotomous measures to aid in data analysis. Suspects' sex (male or female), race (Black, White, and other), and age (19 or younger, 20–29 years old, and 30 years or older) were included. Suspects' employment status at jail admission (unemployed or other), history of substance use or mental illness (yes or no), marital status (single or other), and whether the suspect reported having a telephone or cellphone were noted. Binary measures depicting a suspect's living situation were also examined. Suspects reported how long they had been at their current residence (under 12 months, 12 months or longer, or unknown at the time of interview).

A number of legal factors were included in the current item-based revalidation project. The type of bond release was coded as cash, surety, release on own recognizance (ROR), or other. The total number of charges at release was coded as one, two, or three or more. Prior criminal history was captured by the number of previous adult felonies and previous adult misdemeanor/municipal/or traffic citations noted in the suspect's file (Goulette et al., 2021). The number of times an individual failed to appear for a court hearing was also included in the current study (none, one, or two or more). Court and jail personnel also noted whether the current charge at jail admission fell under Florida Statute 907.041 (yes or no).

Pretrial service personnel collected additional information they wanted to examine as it related to pretrial misconduct. None of these predictors were included in the original validation study. These additional measures were recoded into dichotomous measures and were examined after revalidation of the original items included in the Florida Pretrial Risk Assessment Instrument. Pretrial services personnel wanted to examine whether homelessness, having reliable transportation, and caring for small children (yes or no) significantly influenced pretrial misconduct. Suspects were also asked if they were complying with mental health or substance use treatment at the time of jail admission (yes or no).

Statistical analysis

Data analysis for the current study occurred in two stages and followed the same process as outlined by Austin et al. (2011). Bivariate analyses were conducted using cross-tabulations to assess the association between all predictor variables and the outcome measure, pretrial misconduct. All significant predictors identified in the bivariate analyses were then included in a multivariate analysis. Multivariate logistic regression was used to analyze the relationship between the identified predictors and the probability of pretrial misconduct while holding all other predictors constant (Austin et al., 2011). Since some of the predictors naturally overlapped with one another (homelessness and time at current residence), thorough checks for multicollinearity were done, and no issues were found.[5] This multi-stage process was first done to revalidate the items included in the original validation study, and then was used again to amend the Florida Pretrial Risk Assessment Instrument using new or alternative measures not included by Austin et al. (2011).

Results

Descriptives

Table 2 presents descriptives for the cases included in the current analyses. Roughly 70% of cases included suspects who were white and male. Over half of the sample of cases included individuals between the ages of 20–39. Nearly 50% of cases included suspects who were released on a surety bond. The majority of cases did not include suspects with a history of substance use or mental illness at the time of jail admission. Nearly 70% of the sample included individuals who were single and had lived at their current address for 12 months or longer. Half of the sample reported having reliable transportation and nearly 90% reported having a telephone or cell phone. Over 80% of cases included suspects who did not have any previous FTAs or previous felony convictions. Nearly 65% of cases included suspects who did not have previous misdemeanor/municipal/or traffic citations either. Over 80% of suspects were released from custody with one or two charges and only 30% of suspects had a current charge that was listed under Florida Statute 907.041. Roughly nine percent of the sample engaged in pretrial misconduct during the six-month follow-up period. This included failing to appear for a future court hearing ($n = 146$ or 5.1%) or committing a new criminal offense ($n = 118$ or 4.1%).

Table 2. Sample characteristics.

Characteristic	N	%
Original Validation Measures		
Failure to Appear	146	5.1%
New criminal offense	118	4.1%
Male	1,826	70.6%
White	2,019	70.1%
Black	756	26.2%
19 years and younger	143	5.0%
20–29	920	31.9%
30–39	858	29.8%
40–49	473	16.4%
50–59	337	11.7%
60–69	94	3.3%
70 & older	6	0.2%
Marital status: Single	1,954	67.8%
Employment: Other	1,934	67.2%
History of substance use	466	16.2%
History of mental illness	165	5.7%
Both substance use and mental health	110	3.8%
No history of substance use or mental health	2,140	74.3%
Have a telephone/cell phone	2,527	87.7%
Current charge is 907.041	896	31.1%
Time at Current Residence		
Under 12 mos.	704	24.4%
12 mos. +	1,980	68.7%
Unknown	197	6.8%

(Continued)

Table 2. (Continued).

Characteristic	N	%
Previous Adult Felony		
None	2,308	80.1%
One	248	8.6%
2+	305	10.6%
Unknown	20	0.7%
Previous Misdemeanor/Municipal/Traffic		
None	1,865	64.7%
One	364	12.6%
2+	637	22.1%
Unknown	12	0.4%
Total Charges at Release		
Zero	3	0.1%
One	1,912	66.4%
Two	601	20.9%
Three+	354	12.3%
Most Serious Charge		
Violent	931	32.3%
Drug	719	25.0%
Property	275	9.5%
Other offenses	949	32.9%
Type of Bond Release		
Cash	332	11.5%
Surety	1401	48.6%
ROR	461	16.0%
Other	398	13.8%
New or Amended Measures		
Have reliable transportation	1,438	49.9%
Not homeless	1,052	89.2%
Complying with substance use treatment	71	2.5%
Complying with mental health treatment	275	9.5%
Caregiver of children	836	29.0%

Percentages may not equal 100% due to rounding.

Revalidation of original Florida pretrial risk assessment measures

Bivariate analyses

Table 3 presents the results from the bivariate analyses. While Austin et al. (2011) found *age at admission* to be a significant predictor in both their bivariate and multivariate analyses, it was not found to be significantly associated with pretrial misconduct using the current data set. Employment status ($\chi2 = 21.72$, $p < .05$) and marital status ($\chi2 = 8.12$, $p < .01$) were both significantly associated with pretrial misconduct. Telephone or cell phone ownership ($\chi2 = 11.46$, $p < .01$) and time at residence ($\chi2 = 4.72$, $p < .05$) were also found to significantly influence pretrial misconduct. These predictors were also found to significantly influence pretrial misconduct by Austin et al. (2011). While a history of substance use was significantly associated with pretrial misconduct ($\chi2 = 13.95$, $p < .01$), mental illness was not. These results differed from those of Austin et al. (2011). Bond type was significantly associated with pretrial misconduct ($\chi2 = 18.85$, $p < .01$). The remaining predictors included

Table 3. Bivariate analysis ($N = 2{,}881$).

	Revalidation of Florida Pretrial Risk Assessment Instrument				Validation of Alternative Items		
	n	Percent	Chi-Square		*n*	Percent	Chi-Square
Case Characteristics				Case Characteristics			
Age at admission				Caregiver of children	69	9.2%	1.34
19 or younger	7	2.7%	3.34				
20–29 years	88	33.8%		Has reliable transportation	107	8.3%	25.69**
30 years or older	165	63.5%					
				Homeless at admission	76	17.5%	35.91**
Unemployed	107	43.0%	21.72*				
Single	201	77.0%	8.12**				
No telephone or cell phone	50	18.9%	11.46**				
Under 12 months at current residence	231	87.5%	4.72*				
Substance use	75	28.4%	13.95**				
Mental health	25	9.5%	.20				
Both	15	5.7%	2.41				
Bond type							
Cash bond	20	7.8%	18.85**				
ROR	37	8.2%					
Surety bond	172	13.9%					
Other bond	30	8.7%					
Current most serious charge							
Violent	36	13.6%	69.84**				
Drug	60	22.7%					
Property	44	16.7%					
Other	124	47.0%					
Current charge is 907.041	58	22.0%	15.32**				
Previous FTAs							
None	173	65.5%	65.21**				
One	35	13.3%					
Two or more	23	8.7%					
One or more previous adult felonies	110	42.0%	91.66**				
One or more adult misdemeanors	146	55.5%	56.04**				

in the Florida Pretrial Risk Assessment Instrument, including current most serious charge, previous FTAs, adult felonies, and adult misdemeanors, were also found to significantly influence the probability of pretrial misconduct. Cases having a charge listed in Florida Statute 907.041 were found to have a significantly higher probability of pretrial misconduct than cases without these "dangerous" charges. This finding is in direct contrast to the findings of Austin et al. (2011) who found that cases *not* involving a Florida Statute 907.041 "dangerous" charge had a *higher* probability of pretrial misconduct than cases with a "dangerous" charge.

Multivariate analyses

All of the significant predictors identified in the bivariate analyses were then included in a multivariate logistic regression model. This allowed us to examine their unique influence on the probability of pretrial misconduct, while controlling for all of the other predictors in the model. Any predictors that were no longer significant were removed from the multivariate model, resulting in a reduced list of predictors[6] (Austin et al., 2011). This final model is presented in Table 4. Cases involving violent charges had a lower probability of pretrial misconduct in comparison to other current charges (the reference category). Cases involving a charge listed under Florida Statute 907.014 had a significantly higher probability of pretrial misconduct than cases without a "dangerous" 907.014 charge. Cases involving unemployed individuals had a higher probability of pretrial misconduct than other employment status. Telephone or cell phone ownership was also found to be a significant predictor of pretrial misconduct, net of all other predictors included in the model. Cases in which individuals did not own either a telephone or cell phone had a higher probability of pretrial misconduct than cases with phone ownership. Cases involving one prior FTA and two or more prior FTAs had significantly higher probabilities of pretrial misconduct in comparison to cases with no prior FTA. Prior criminal history also significantly influenced the probability of pretrial misconduct. Cases involving suspects with one or more prior adult felonies had a higher probability of pretrial misconduct than cases with no prior adult felonies. Prior adult misdemeanors were also found to be a significant predictor of pretrial misconduct, net of all predictors included in the multivariate model.

Table 4. Predicting pretrial Misconduct[a].

	Revalidation of Florida Pretrial Risk Assessment Instrument			Examination of New or Amended Measures	
Case Characteristic	Odds Ratio	Std. Error		Odds Ratio	Std. Error
Constant	0.07**	(0.15)	Constant	0.06**	(0.15)
Current violent charge	0.22**	(0.26)	Current violent charge	0.22**	(0.26)
Current drug charge	0.73	(0.18)	Current drug charge	0.77	(0.19)
Current property charge	1.04	(0.22)	Current property charge	0.92	(0.24)
Florida Statute 907.014 Charge	1.55*	(0.21)	Florida Statute 907.014 Charge	1.90**	(0.22)
Unemployed	1.60**	(0.15)	Unemployed	1.64**	(0.15)
No telephone or cell phone	1.54*	(0.19)			
One FTA	1.86**	(0.22)	One FTA	2.13**	(0.22)
Two or more FTA	2.00*	(0.27)	Two or more FTA	2.54**	(0.27)
One or more previous adult felonies	2.29**	(0.17)	One or more previous adult felonies	2.54**	(0.17)
One or more adult misdemeanors	1.41*	(0.16)			
			Homeless	2.06**	(0.17)
$\chi 2$	160.17**		$\chi 2$	156.50**	

[a]Logistic regression model for binary outcome. $^{**}p < .01$; $^{*}p < .05$.

Examination of new or amended measures

Bivariate analyses

During data collection, pretrial services personnel were interested in investigating the association between the probability of pretrial misconduct and several additional measures, not originally included when the Florida Pretrial Risk Assessment Instrument was created and validated. These additional measures were recoded into dichotomous measures and examined *homelessness*, *reliable transportation*, and caring for small children (yes or no). Individuals were also asked if they were complying with mental health or substance use treatment (yes or no).

Following the statistical analysis plan outlined above, a series of cross-tabulations were calculated to investigate whether these additional measures were associated with pretrial misconduct. Table 3 presents these findings. While compliance with mental health services was not significantly associated with pretrial misconduct, compliance with substance use treatment was found to be significant ($\chi 2 = 9.86, p < .01$). Having reliable transportation was found to be significantly associated with pretrial misconduct ($\chi 2 = 25.69$, $p < .01$) as were cases involving homeless individuals ($\chi 2 = 35.91, p < .01$).

Using the multivariate analysis discussed above, these significant predictors were then added to the model to examine whether they had an independent impact on the probability of pretrial misconduct, net of all other predictors. This model is presented in Table 4. The predictors, telephone ownership and prior adult misdemeanors, were no longer significant and were subsequently removed from the multivariate model. Compliance with substance use treatment, while significant in the bivariate analysis, generated the highest VIF (5.06) and the lowest tolerance value (0.19), and therefore could not be included in the model due to issues surrounding multicollinearity (O'Brien, 2007). Once entered into the multivariate model, the predictor, having reliable transportation, was no longer significant, and was removed from the model. The only new measure that was added to the model and remained a significant predictor of pretrial misconduct was *homeless*. Cases involving individuals who reported to be homeless at the time of jail admission had a higher probability of pretrial misconduct than cases with individuals who were not homeless.

Discussion

The current study sought to revalidate the Florida Pretrial Risk Assessment Instrument. This risk assessment tool was originally validated ten years ago (Austin et al., 2011). The original validation of the instrument identified 11 factors that had an independent effect on the probability of pretrial misconduct (Austin et al., 2011). Six counties participated in the original study, and each county attempted to collect data for 250 cases. In comparison, the current study involved nine counties, representing urban, suburban, and rural counties, with a goal of 350 cases per county. While not all of the counties were successful in collecting data for 350 cases, this revalidation study included a total sample of 2,881 cases for suspects released before trial during the summer and fall of 2019.

Some interesting findings were noted through revalidating the Florida Pretrial Risk Assessment Instrument. The current study concluded that very few individuals committed a new criminal offense or failed to appear for future court hearings during the six months following pretrial release. In total, roughly five percent failed to appear for a court hearing and only four percent committed a new offense. While these results are similar to that of Austin et al. (2011), it is important to highlight that the majority of individuals on pretrial release did not engage in any type of misconduct across nine Florida counties. This supports the argument that many individuals can be safely placed on pretrial release while they await trial (Debora & Meils, 2019; Marlowe et al., 2020, Redefining the pretrial paradigm, 2022; VanNostrand & Keebler, 2009). Doing so allows these individuals to assist with their court cases, support their families, and avoid the many unintended consequences that they may experience if they remained in detention (Goulette & Wooldredge, 2018). Jurisdictions that support using pretrial release for low-risk individuals can also benefit as it can become very expensive to detain individuals for long periods of time (Goulette & Wooldredge, 2018; Henichson et al., 2015; Wiseman, 2014).

While many of the same predictors identified by Austin et al. (2011) were found to significantly influence the probability of pretrial misconduct in the current study, some differences were found that are worth noting. First, a history of substance use and/or mental health were not found to be significant predictors of pretrial misconduct in this item-based revalidation of the Florida Pretrial Risk Assessment Instrument. These issues are very personal, and can be difficult to admit to others. It could be that suspects were experiencing substance use or mental health issues, but these factors were not noted in their files, or they did not report these factors when interviewed by court personnel. It could also be that substance use and mental health issues were only collected for individuals who had received professional help in the past. Therefore, individuals who had not been diagnosed by a mental health professional or drug/alcohol counselor were not reported as having a history of these issues.

Another noteworthy difference involved Florida Statute 907.041 charges and their influence on the predicted probability of pretrial misconduct. Austin et al. (2011) concluded that cases *not* involving a Florida Statute 907.041 charge had a *higher* probability of pretrial misconduct. However, in revalidating the items included in the Florida Pretrial Risk Assessment Instrument, the current study found a positive relationship between cases involving a Florida Statute 907.041 charge and the probability of pretrial misconduct. While it might make intuitive sense that individuals who have been charged with a violent offense, or one characterized as "dangerous" within state statutes, would have a higher probability of committing a new offense or failing to appear for court, prior research has provided mixed results regarding the influence of offense severity and the probability of pretrial misconduct (Baglivio et al., 2020; Grattet et al., 2011). This is one reason why risk assessment tools can be used to guide decisions related to pretrial release and predicted risk to the community, but these instruments cannot be used in a vacuum. Decisions related to pretrial release and the probability of pretrial misconduct should involve multiple pieces of information (Desmarais & Lowder, 2019; Lowder & Foudray, 2021). Future research should continue to examine how current offense type is used within pretrial risk assessment instruments in predicting pretrial misconduct.

According to Austin et al. (2011), cases involving individuals who had spent less than 12 months at their current residence had a higher probability of pretrial misconduct. Debora and Meils (2019) also found that less than a year at the residence significantly predicted overall pretrial failure, the issuance of a warrant for FTA, re-arrest on a violent charge, and re-arrest for any new crime. Length at current residence was not found to be a significant predictor of pretrial misconduct in the current study. Conversely, the current study found that cases that involved individuals who reported being homeless at the time of jail admission had a higher probability of pretrial misconduct. It could be that the new predictor, homelessness, captured a lack of community ties more accurately than measuring an individual's time at their current residence in months. It could also be the case that reporting homelessness is easier for arrested individuals and court personnel to understand and identify than trying to calculate how long an individual has resided at any one place. This difference in findings between the original validation study and the current study reaffirms the argument that empirical evidence should be used to reevaluate the predictors included within these pretrial risk assessment instruments (T. P. Cadigan et al., 2012, NAPSA, 2020; VanNostrand & Keebler, 2009).

Finally, the current study highlights the complex association between community ties, their operationalization, and estimating pretrial risk. While marital status was not found to significantly influence the probability of pretrial misconduct, employment status did significantly impact the probability of an individual committing a new offense or failing to appear for a future court hearing. It could be that marital status is not a clear indicator of one's standing in the community, as it does not capture if the individual interacts with others or how the individual is perceived by others. Furthermore, a suspect's employment status may not be related to one's community ties at all, but just a sign that they can support themselves, making them more "dependable" (Goldkamp & Vilcica, 2009, p. 123). As discussed by T. P. Cadigan et al. (2012) and others (Goldkamp & Vilcica, 2009), predictors related to community ties are simply symbolic in nature, and often do not influence judicial decision-making related to bond and pretrial release, nor are they empirically supported. As a result of these mixed findings, it is suggested that future research continues to examine the use and operationalization of community ties within risk assessment tools to identify whether they should be used, and how much weight is given to these predictors.

Limitations

The current study provides an item-based revalidation of the Florida Pretrial Risk Assessment Instrument, however, it is not without several limitations to consider. First, court and jail personnel were tasked with collecting data for this revalidation study, and they may not have followed the sampling sequence they were given. In order to remedy this issue, the research team agreed to extend data collection into the month of November, asking six of nine participating counties to collect information for all cases processed during this time. These alterations may have impacted the data. Second, because pretrial service personnel thought their jobs may be at risk at the conclusion of data collection, the research team cannot be 100% confident that the outcome measure, pretrial misconduct, was coded accurately by all data collectors. While the research team and leadership of the APPF discussed this at length with staff members at the initial meeting, it could be that personnel gave individuals multiple chances before noting that they committed a new offense or failed to appear for a court hearing. If cases involved the commission of a new offense and FTA, it is unclear how court personnel coded these cases. Future revalidation efforts should attempt to collect data from police and court records directly to avoid these noted limitations.

Additionally, it should be noted that there is inherent bias in the analysis, as only cases involving "released" individuals were included in the current study. That is, cases in which individuals were not released prior to trial could not be included in this item-based revalidation study. A final limitation is the generalizability of the results reported here. Although the current study included nine counties, from across the state of Florida, representing urban, rural, and suburban counties, it is unclear whether the results reported here are unique to Florida or whether they are generalizable to other U.S. jurisdictions. Relatedly, between county variation was not accounted for in the analyses presented here. Future research should compare predictors within jurisdictions of differing sizes to further explore how they impact the probability of pretrial misconduct.

Conclusion

Despite these limitations, revalidating pretrial risk assessment tools is very important. As predictors, and their association with estimating pretrial risk, change over time, it is imperative jurisdictions use only the most relevant and timely factors when making decisions surrounding pretrial release (T. P. Cadigan et al., 2012; VanNostrand & Keebler, 2009). Risk assessment tools should be used to guide judicial decision-making to keep pretrial detention populations in check, saving money and space for higher-risk individuals. Doing so also allows lower-risk individuals to remain working and living in the community without jeopardizing community safety (Lowenkamp et al., 2008). Finally, the results of the current study have reinvigorated the conversation surrounding suspects' "community ties," how they are operationalized, and whether they should be included when assessing one's risk of engaging in pretrial misconduct (T. P. Cadigan et al., 2012; Goldkamp & Vilcica, 2009). Hopefully, scholars and practitioners will continue to evaluate the inclusion of these predictors so as to eliminate any implicit bias from pretrial risk assessment tools moving forward (Goldkamp & Vilcica, 2009; Terranova et al., 2020).

Notes

1. Prior to creation of the Florida Pretrial Risk Assessment Instrument, nine counties across the state of Florida used the VRAI-R for pretrial risk assessment. In 2020, 17 of 28 pretrial service programs across Florida reported using a pretrial risk assessment instrument, including the VRAI-R, the Florida Pretrial Risk Assessment Instrument, or another tool.
2. Austin et al. (2011) set a goal of 250 cases for each of the six counties that participated in the original validation project. Four of these counties exceeded this goal, collecting information for 391, 267, 305, and 300 cases, respectively. Two other counties collected information for 248 and 246 cases. Roughly 14% of cases involved pretrial misconduct.
3. A number of predictors were not found to significantly influence the probability of pretrial misconduct. These predictors included sex, race, posted bond before first appearance (yes or no), total number of charges at release (one, two, three or more), and type of bond release (cash, surety, release on own recognizance (ROR), or other).
4. Data collectors were instructed to skip any individuals who were already included in the data. A unique identifier was used to double-check that individuals only appeared in the data once.
5. Multicollinearity checks included examining the tolerance and variance inflation factors (VIFs) for each of the predictors included in the logistic regression models. The predictor, *current violent charge*, produced the highest VIF (2.18) and the lowest tolerance values (0.45), both of which are considered acceptable (O'Brien, 2007).
6. The predictors *substance use*, *single*, *bond types*, and *under 12 months at current residence* were no longer found to be significant predictors of pretrial misconduct when included in the multivariate model. Therefore, they are not included in Table 4. This follows the same statistical plan used by Austin et al. (2011).

Acknowledgments

The authors would like to thank Dr. Kimberly McCorkle and Dr. Richard Hough, East Tennessee State University, and members of the Association of Pretrial Professionals of Florida (APPF) for their assistance with the revalidation process.

Disclosure statement

No potential conflict of interest was reported by the author(s).

References

Austin, J., Bhati, A., Jones, M., & Ocker, R. (2011). Florida Pretrial Risk Assessment Instrument.

Austin, J., & Murray, T. (2009). *Re-validation of the actuarial risk assessment instrument for Harris County pretrial services*. The JFA Institute.

Baglivio, M. W., Jackowski, K., & Jackowski, K. (2020). The usefulness of a general risk assessment, the static risk assessment (SRA), in predicting pretrial failure: Examining predictive ability across gender and race. *Justice Evaluation Journal*, *3*(1), 1–26. https://doi.org/10.1080/24751979.2019.1668242

Barno, M., Martinez, D. N., & Williams, K. R. (2020). Exploring alternatives to cash bail: An evaluation of orange county's Pretrial Assessment and Release Supervision (PARS) program. *American Journal of Criminal Justice*, *45*(3), 363–378. https://doi.org/10.1007/s12103-019-09506-3

Bechtel, K., Holsinger, A. M., Lowenkamp, C. T., & Warren, M. J. (2017). A meta-analytic review of pretrial research: Risk assessment, bond type, and interventions. *American Journal of Criminal Justice*, *42*(2), 443–467. https://doi.org/10.1007/s12103-016-9367-1

Bechtel, K., Lowenkamp, C. T., & Holsinger, A. (2011). Identifying the predictors of pretrial failure: A meta-analysis. *Federal Probation*, *75*(2), 78–87.

Cadigan, T. P., Johnson, J. L., & Lowenkamp, C. T. (2012). Re-validation of the Federal Pretrial Services Assessment (PTRA). *Federal Probation*, *76*(2), 3–8.

Cadigan, T., & Lowenkamp, C. T. (2011). Implementing risk assessment in the federal pretrial services system. *Federal Probation*, *75*(2), 30–34.

Cohen, T. H., & Lowenkamp, C. T. (2018). Revalidation of the federal PTRA: Testing the PTRA for predictive biases. *Criminal Justice and Behavior*, *46*(2), 234–260. https://doi.org/10.1177/0093854818810315

Cohen, T. H., Lowenkamp, C. T., & Hicks, W. E. (2018). Revalidating the Federal Pretrial Assessment Instrument (PTRA): A research summary. *Federal Probation Journal*, *82*, 23–31. https://doi.org/10.2139/ssrn.3191533

Cohen, T. H., & Reaves, B. A. (2007). *Pretrial release of felony defendants in state courts*. Bureau of Justice Statistics. https://bjs.ojp.gov/content/pub/pdf/prfdsc.pdf

Debora, J. L., & Meils, J. (2019). Assessing risk among pretrial defendants in El Paso County: Validation of the El Paso pretrial risk assessment instrument and revision recommendations.

DeMichele, M., Baumgartner, P., Wenger, M., Barrick, K., Comfort, M., & Misra, S. (2018). The public safety assessment: A re-validation and assessment of predictive utility and differential prediction by race and gender in Kentucky. https://university.Pretrial.org/view-Document/the-Public-Safety-Assessment-A-Re

Desmarais, S. L., & Lowder, E. M. (2019). Pretrial risk assessment tools. Safety + justice challenge. https://www.safetyandjusticechallenge.org/wp-content/uploads/2019/02/Pretrial-Risk-Assessment-Primer-February-2019.pdf

Desmarais, S. L., Zottola, S. A., Duhart-Clarke, S. E., & Lowder, E. M. (2021). Predictive validity of pretrial risk assessments. *Criminal Justice and Behavior*, *48*(4), 398–420. https://doi.org/10.1177/0093854820932959

Dobbie, W., Goldin, J., & Yang, C. S. (2018). The effects of pretrial detention on conviction, future crime, and employment: Evidence from randomly assigned judges. *American Economic Review*, *108*(2), 201–240. https://doi.org/10.1257/aer.20161503

Duwe, G., & Rocque, M. (2019). The predictive performance of risk assessment in real life: An external validation of the MnSTARR. *Corrections: Policy, Practice and Research*, *6*(5), 1–18. https://doi.org/10.1080/23774657.2019.1682952

Goldkamp, J. S., & Vilcica, E. R. (2009). Judicial discretion and the unfinished agenda of American bail reform: Lessons from Philadelphia's evidence-based judicial strategy. In A. Sarat (Ed.), *Special issue new perspectives on crime and criminal justice (studies in law, politics, and society* (Vol. 47, pp. 115–157). Emerald Group Publishing Limited. https://doi.org/10.1108/S1059-4337(2009)0000047007

Goldkamp, J. S., & White, M. (2006). Restoring accountability in pretrial release: The Philadelphia pretrial release supervision experiments. *Journal of Experimental Criminology*, *2*(2), 142–181. https://doi.org/10.1007/s11292-006-9001-1

Goulette, N., Johnson, K., McCorkle, K., Hough, R., & Kilpatrick, J. H. (2021). *Revalidating the Florida pretrial risk assessment instrument*. The Association of Pretrial Professionals.

Goulette, N., & Wooldredge, J. (2018). Collateral consequences of pretrial detention. In B. Huebner & N. Frost (Eds.), *The consequences of sentencing and punishment decisions, handbook on corrections and sentencing* (Vol. 3, pp. 271–289). Routledge.

Grattet, R., Lin, J., & Petersilia, J. (2011). Supervision regimes, risk, and official reactions to parolee deviance. *Criminology*, *49*(2), 371–400. https://doi.org/10.1111/j.1745-9125.2011.00229.x

Heaton, P., Mayson, S., & Stevenson, M. (2017). The downstream consequences of misdemeanor pretrial detention. *Stanford Law Review*, *69*(3), 711–794. https://www.jstor.org/stable/26166245

Henichson, C., Rinaldi, J., & Delaney, R. (2015, May). *The price of jails: Measuring the taxpayer cost of local incarceration*. Vera Institute, Center on Sentencing and Corrections.

Kennedy, S., House, L., & Williams, M. (2013). Using research to improve pretrial justice and public safety: Results from PSA's risk assessment validation project. *Federal Probation*, *77*(1), 28–32.

Konig, P. D., & Krafft, T. D. (2021). Evaluating the evidence in algorithmic evidence-based decision-making: The case of US pretrial risk assessment tools. *Current Issues in Criminal Justice*, *33*(3), 359–381. https://doi.org/10.1080/10345329.2020.1849932

Latessa, E., Smith, P., Lemke, R., Makarios, M., & Lowenkamp, C. (2009). Creation and validation of the Ohio risk assessment system. Final report. University of Cincinnati School of Criminal Justice

Lawson, S. G., & Lowder, E. M. (2023). Differential prediction by race in IRAS-PAT assessments: An application of debiasing strategies. *Justice Quarterly*, *40*(4), 451–477. https://doi.org/10.1080/07418825.2022.2086481

Lowder, E. M., Diaz, C. L., Grommon, E., & Ray, B. R. (2020). Effects of pretrial risk assessments on release decision and misconduct outcomes relative to practice as usual. *Journal of Criminal Justice*, *73*, 101754. https://doi.org/10.1016/j.jcrimjus.2020.101754

Lowder, E. M., Diaz, C. L., Grommon, E., & Ray, B. R. (2022). Differential prediction and disparate impact of pretrial risk assessments in practice: A multi-site evaluation. *Journal of Experimental Criminology*, *19*(3), 561–594. https://doi.org/10.1007/s11292-021-09492-9

Lowder, E. M., & Foudray, C. M. A. (2021). Use of risk assessments in pretrial supervision decision-making and associated outcomes. *Crime & Delinquency*, *6*(11), 1765–1791. https://doi.org/10.1177/00111287211022642

Lowder, E. M., Lawson, S. G., Grommon, E., & Ray, B. R. (2020). Five-county validation of the Indiana risk assessment system – pretrial assessment tool (IRAS-PAT) using a local validation approach. *Justice Quarterly*, *37*(7), 1241–1260. https://doi.org/10.1080/07418825.2020.1829006

Lowenkamp, C. T., Lemke, R., & Latessa, E. (2008). The development and validation of a pretrial screening tool. *Federal Probation*, *72*(3), 2–9.

Marlowe, D. B., Ho, T., Carey, S. M., & Chadick, C. D. (2020). Employing standardized risk assessment in pretrial release decisions: Association with criminal justice outcomes and racial equality. *Law and Human Behavior*, *44*(5), 361–376. https://doi.org/10.1037/lhb0000413

National Association of Pretrial Services Agencies. (2020). Standards on pretrial release: Revised 2020. https://cdpsdocs.state.co.us/ccjj/committees/PRTF/Handout/2020_NAPSA_StandardsOnPretrialRelease.pdf

O'Brien, R. M. (2007). A caution regarding rules of thumb for variance inflation factors. *Quality & Quantity*, *41*(5), 673–690. https://doi.org/10.1007/s11135-006-9018-6

Office of Program Policy Analysis and Government Accountability. (2020). *County pretrial release programs: Calendar Year 2019.*

Picard, S., Watkins, M., Rempel, M., & Kerodal, A. (2019). Beyond the algorithm: Pretrial reform, risk assessment, and racial fairness. *Center for Court Innovation.* https://www.innovatingjustice.org/sites/default/files/media/documents/2019-06/beyond_the_algorithm.pdf

Redefining the pretrial paradigm. (2022 November 30). National Institute of Corrections, https://nicic.gov/resources/news-media/media-releases/redefining-pretrial-paradigm

Saks, M., & Ackerman, A. R. (2014). Bail and sentencing: Does pretrial detention lead to harsher punishment? *Criminal Justice Policy Review, 25*(1), 59–77. https://doi.org/10.1177/0887403412461501

Schmalleger, F., & Smykla, J. O. (2021). *Corrections in the 21st century* (9th ed.). McGraw-Hill.

Scurich, N., & Krauss, D. A. (2020). Public's views of risk assessment algorithms and pretrial decision making. *Psychology, Public Policy, and Law, 26*(1), 1–9. https://doi.org/10.1037/law0000219

Steffensmeier, D., Ulmer, J., & Kramer, J. (1998). The interaction of race, gender, and age in criminal sentencing: The punishment cost of being young, Black, and male. *Criminology, 36*(4), 763–797. https://doi.org/10.1111/j.1745-9125.1998.tb01265.x

Terranova, V. A., Ward, K., Slepicka, J., & Azari, A. M. (2020). Perceptions of pretrial risk assessment: An examination across role in the initial pretrial release decision. *Criminal Justice and Behavior, 47* (8), 927–942. https://doi.org/10.1177/0093854820932204

U.S. Census Bureau. (2023, May). Annual estimates of the resident population: April 1, 2020 to July 1, 2022. U.S. Census Bureau, Population Division. http://www.census.gov/

VanNostrand, M. (2003). Assessing risk among pretrial defendants in Virginia: The Virginia pretrial risk assessment instrument. Virginia Department of Criminal Justice Services. https://www.dcjs.virginia.gov/sites/dcjs.virginia.gov/files/publications/corrections/assessing-risk-among-pretrial-defendants-virginia-virginia-pretrial-risk-assessment-instrument.pdf

VanNostrand, M., & Keebler, G. (2009). Pretrial risk assessment in the federal court. *Federal Probation, 73*(2), 3–56.

Wiseman, S. R. (2014). Pretrial detention and the right to be monitored. *The Yale Law Journal, 123* (5), 1344–1404.

Wooldredge, J., Frank, J., & Goulette, N. (2017). Ecological contributors to disparities in bond amounts and pretrial detention. *Crime & Delinquency, 63*(13), 1682–1711. https://doi.org/10.1177/0011128716659636

Zeng, Z. (2018). *Jail inmates in 2016.* Bureau of Justice Statistics. https://bjs.ojp.gov/content/pub/pdf/ji16.pdf

Cyclical Pathways to Probation Violations: Housing, Financial Capabilities, and COVID-19

Andrea Giuffre, Kathryn Tapp, Beth M. Huebner, Kimberly R. Kras, and Lee Ann Slocum

ABSTRACT

Maintaining a stable residence is a primary requirement of probation compliance. Prior research has spoken to the increase in requirements for people on probation and how they are often tied to financial capability. Using data from in-depth interviews with people on probation and probation staff, our analysis extends extant research by highlighting the unique challenges of finding housing during a historic rise in housing and rental prices in the context of COVID-19. This work furthers research on the role that economic means play in the probation revocation process. Results from the research suggest that housing is a barrier to success on probation, which is further hampered by the lack of employment opportunities available to individuals with felony criminal records. Participants relayed that the lack of affordable housing led to heavy reliance on family members for assistance. Information from staff triangulated their concerns about how compliance was tied to poverty.

Introduction

Community supervision was originally developed to reduce the number of people incarcerated and to provide rehabilitative services to people in the community, but there is growing evidence that technical violations are a key driver of incarceration (Council of State Governments, 2019, Horowitz et al., 2018). There are many critical barriers to success on community supervision, including transportation, healthcare needs, and lack of financial independence. Unstable housing has been denoted as a key barrier (Bowman & Ely, 2020) and failure to maintain an approved residence can lead to a technical probation violation, prompting additional periods of incarceration (Brett et al., 2020). Stable housing serves as a foundation for employment, participation in treatment and support services, building social capital, and meeting conditions of community supervision (Remster, 2019, Steiner et al., 2015). However, locating a safe place to live is a significant challenge for people with criminal records (Evans & Porter, 2015, Middlemass, 2017), and maintaining housing is just as difficult (Harding et al., 2013, Herbert et al., 2015).

Housing insecurity is common among people on probation, with many reporting at least one period of being unhoused (Jacobs & Gottlieb, 2020). Many individuals on probation rely on family and friends for housing, but then must continue to navigate the process of securing longer-term solutions (Kras et al., 2016, Miller, 2021). This is a challenging prospect for many, due in part to limited financial resources for participating in the private housing market (Morenoff & Harding, 2014), reduced access to subsidized housing options due to restrictions on individuals with criminal records (Evans et al., 2019, Harding et al., 2013), and the unwillingness of landlords to rent to individuals with such histories (Evans & Porter, 2015, Miller, 2021).

The current study builds on extant work by considering the unique challenges that people on probation face in the housing market and its ties to financial insecurity, particularly during the COVID-19 pandemic when there was a dramatic increase in housing prices and a reorganization of the job market (Falk et al., 2021). Uniquely, we also draw upon narratives from individuals who work in the system to triangulate information about housing challenges. During the pandemic, housing became out of reach for many people, and these issues are exacerbated by a felony record and supervision conditions (e.g., time costs necessary to comply with treatment, meetings with probation officers), which can spur violations. Many people rely on family for help with housing, but for those who do not have readily available family support, housing can be a particularly difficult challenge. In the current study, we show how housing difficulties can be further amplified by individual characteristics, like the unique needs of women, which should continue to be explored in the post-COVID landscape.

Literature

Housing and probation outcomes

Securing stable housing is a critical challenge for people with a criminal record. Several factors act as barriers to housing. Individuals with a criminal record are often shut out financially in the market for safe and affordable homes, subject to foreclosures and evictions, and are ten times more likely to experience periods of being unhoused than the general public (Stanley-Becker, 2022). Housing discrimination perpetrated by the exclusionary policies of the public and private rental markets has been a critical factor in housing for individuals under community supervision, as having a criminal record is not a protected characteristic under the Fair Housing Act (FHA) (Evans et al., 2019, Petersilia, 2003). Formerly incarcerated persons are denied access to public housing due to "one strike" rules that require eviction when convicted of a crime, and those convicted of sexual offenses or drug crimes are denied Section 8 vouchers (Stanley-Becker, 2022, Tran-Leung, 2015).

Individuals who are barred from public housing programs and lack the funds to buy a home are forced to look to the private rental market, which is experiencing a shortage of affordable rental units for individuals who have incomes at or below the poverty line (Aurand et al., 2019, Desmond, 2018, Leasure, 2019). Nationally, the majority of rental properties are owned as private investments (Boeing et al., 2021). Most people living in rental communities are Black and are more likely to experience housing challenges (Reosti, 2020, Rosen et al., 2021). Black persons are disproportionately impacted by criminal justice records (Lageson, 2020), and the stigma of a criminal record likely restricts individuals even more from affordable housing. The rise of low–cost information technologies provided by criminal background check companies (Lageson, 2020, Rosen et al., 2021) made it easier for landlords to run criminal background checks and facilitated housing discrimination against people with criminal records (Thacher, 2008).

Although there is little specific information about the housing needs of people on probation, there is evidence that many people rely on family and friends to provide financial assistance (Condry & Minson, 2021, Giuffre, 2023) and housing for themselves and their families (Dong et al., 2018, Pleggenkuhle et al., 2016). However, some individuals may be estranged from family who would otherwise be relied on for assistance (Lutze et al., 2014). Further, supervision conditions may preclude association with other individuals with criminal records, preventing individuals from living with otherwise willing family and friends (Huebner et al., 2019).

Individuals on probation often experience housing instability. A recent study in San Francisco found that one quarter of the sample had unstable housing at the start of the probation term, and nearly half experienced at least one period of being unhoused (Jacobs & Gottlieb, 2020). Additionally, for people considered low-risk or with less severe offenses, the effect of housing instability on adverse outcomes, including technical violations and arrests for new crimes, was particularly strong. Housing instability and frequent moves have been associated with higher recidivism rates for people under correctional supervision (Clark, 2016, Jacobs & Gottlieb, 2020, Makarios et al., 2010, Steiner et al., 2015). Placements to nonresidential addresses (e.g., shelters, transitional housing) can also increase recidivism (McNeeley, 2018) and technical violations (Clark, 2016).

Economic security, financial sanctions, and revocation

Stable housing rests heavily on the economic security of family support, yet people under correctional supervision often face challenges sustaining economic support (Harris, 2016, Miller, 2021). As a condition of their probation, individuals must secure steady employment to be able to not only provide for basic necessities but also to meet the added task of paying any legal or probation-related fees (Brett et al., 2020, Huebner & Shannon, 2022, Link et al., 2020, Ruhland et al., 2020). Without steady employment or access to financial support, individuals often struggle to acquire the basic necessities, like housing, required for success in the community (Pattillo et al., 2022).

While difficulties securing housing have contributed to high rates of technical violations, other factors have also played a role. First, there is evidence that the use of supervision conditions (e.g., drug testing, electronic monitoring, treatment participation) has increased (Horowitz et al., 2018). Individuals on community supervision are often challenged by the compounded nature of conditions of compliance (Blomberg & Lucken, 1994, Uggen & Stewart, 2015). Probation conditions also often include unclear wording, which affords substantial discretion when system actors make decisions about technical violations (Doherty, 2016). Moreover, satisfying supervision conditions requires considerable time, as individuals must attend regular meetings with correctional staff, judges, and clerks (Doherty, 2016, Evans, 2014). In theory, many of these programs are mandated as a way to offer services to people on probation. In practice, however, even if there is some potential benefit from treatment, the programs are often coercive and come with financial and time costs (Phelps & Ruhland, 2021), further escalating incarceration risk.

Compounding these issues, most states levy costs for probation supervision (Brett et al., 2020). Failure to pay probation costs can lead to additional sanctions, the extension of supervision, and incarceration for noncompliance, among other outcomes (Ruhland, 2019, Shannon, 2020). The emerging research with individuals on probation suggests that many do not have the economic means to pay for monetary sanctions, and the costs associated with probation are stressful, as nonpayment can be used as a reason for noncompliance (Ruhland et al., 2020). In short, probation costs can exacerbate the harms of community supervision and are magnified for those without the financial means to comply (Brett et al., 2020).

COVID-19

The COVID–19 pandemic brought unforeseen challenges and consequences to the reentry process of formerly incarcerated persons. Individuals on probation at this time were met with a rapidly changing housing market, skyrocketing rents, and record unemployment numbers (Falk et al., 2021). In addition, many reentry programs had to, at least in part, suspend treatment programming or change the modality in which services were provided (Belisle et al., 2023, Martin & Zettler, 2022, Viglione et al., 2020). Social isolation and difficulties sustaining prosocial relationships within local communities were also exacerbated by the pandemic (LeMasters et al., 2023), leading to diminished mental health outcomes, increased substance use, and elevated suicidal ideation among the American population (Czeisler et al., 2021). The long-term effects of the COVID–19 public health crisis on probation outcomes remain undetermined, but it is clear that the pandemic resulted in an inherent increase in the challenges faced by people under correctional supervision (Abrams et al., 2023, LeMasters et al., 2023).

In this analysis, we explore how COVID-19 compounded the challenges of housing for a group of people on probation. Housing is an established challenge for people on probation who often also suffer from economic insecurity (e.g., Jacobs & Gottlieb, 2020), but how the pandemic shaped these barriers remains unexplored.

Method

Study site

Data for the current study come from in-depth interviews with probation officers and people on probation in the St. Louis, Missouri, metropolitan area, including St. Louis City and County. Many individuals in the St. Louis region struggle with economic and housing challenges (Johnson, 2020), which comports with broader U.S. trends (Stansfield & Semenza, 2022). St. Louis County is 67.4% white and 25.1% Black, while the City of St. Louis is 49.1% white and 44.3% Black.[1] This level of racial diversity makes it an appropriate site to examine the housing challenges of Black and white Americans. About 21.5% of St. Louis City and 10.5% of County residents live under the poverty line (United States Census Bureau, 2023a, 2023b). Data from the St. Louis region suggests that rental housing is not affordable for most people living below the poverty level. In the northernmost regions of the City and County, where residents are most likely to have household incomes under the poverty level, more than 50% of renters pay 30% or more of their monthly income on housing costs (Community Builders Network, 2022). Further, the minimum wage in Missouri ($12/hour) does not provide enough funds for an individual to be housing secure in the St. Louis Metropolitan region (National Low Income Housing Coalition, 2023). The National Low Income Housing Coalition (2023) estimates that a minimum wage worker in the state makes $624 monthly and a one-bedroom apartment costs $781 monthly. The median rent in the St. Louis area is higher at $1,195 per month (Zillow, 2023).

Data and recruitment

The research team conducted interviews with two groups of individuals – people on probation and probation staff.

People on probation

First, the team interviewed 56 people on felony probation.[2] We posted flyers at the four regional probation offices to recruit participants and asked probation officers to share copies of the flyer with clients. People on probation contacted a member of the research team to set up phone and Zoom interviews. We also waited at probation offices and interviewed people in person after their supervision appointments. At times, participants referred others to participate in Zoom and phone interviews (Biernacki & Waldorf, 1981).

The average age of participants was 33 years old (see Table 1). About 57.1% of the probation sample was white, and 30.4% was Black. Other racial groups comprised a little more than 10% of the people on probation. However, two participants (3.6%) identified as Hispanic. Further, 69.6% identified as men, and 30.4% identified as women. Approximately 82.1% identified as straight, while the remainder (17.9%) identified as queer. Half were unemployed, and 58.9% had prior probation violations. Moreover, around 30.4% of

Table 1. People on probation demographics ($n = 56$).

	% or Mean
Age	33.0
Race	
White	57.1%
Black	30.4%
Multiracial	7.1%
Native American	3.6%
Asian	1.8%
Ethnicity	
Hispanic	3.6%
Gender Identity	
Woman	69.6%
Man	30.4%
Sexuality	
Straight	82.1%
Queer	17.9%
Unemployed	50.0%
Past Violation	58.9%
Prior Conviction(s)	48.2%
Prison	30.4%
Supervision Location	
St. Louis County	73.2%
St. Louis City	26.8%

Table 2. Staff demographics ($n = 17$).

	% or Mean
Age	45.5
Race	
White	56.5%
Black	35.3%
Multiracial	5.9%
Asian	5.9%
Gender Identity	
Woman	52.9%
Man	47.1%
Role	
Probation Officer	52.9%
Probation Supervisor	23.5%
Jail Staff	23.5%

participants on probation had been incarcerated in prison. About three quarters (73.2%) of the participants were St. Louis County residents, and the remaining lived in the City of St. Louis.

Interviews with people on probation were semi-structured (Spradley, 2016) and took an hour on average. Participants were provided a $30 cash incentive. We audio recorded each interview and transcribed them verbatim using Zoom software or a third-party transcription service (Rev.com). To maintain participant anonymity, we assigned each participant a unique pseudonym, or they provided one. We also used the qualitative coding software NVivo to organize the two sets of interviews.

Probation staff

We interviewed 17 probation staff. To recruit these participants, the lead researcher for the project contacted the regional administrator for probation, who assisted in identifying potential staff participants, including (1) probation officers with a caseload, (2) supervisors who oversee other probation officers, and (3) jail staff who help supervise individuals who have been returned to jail for a probation violation. At the time of the interviews, there were 86 individuals employed as probation and parole officers in St. Louis County. The research team emailed and called potential participants to describe the study and invite individuals to participate. All of the staff interviews were conducted over Zoom.[3] These interviews also followed a semi-structured format (Spradley, 2016) and usually lasted one hour.

The average age of the probation staff was 45.5 years old. About half (56.5%) were white, and over one third (35.3%) were Black. The remainder of the staff were multiracial (5.9%) and Asian (5.9%). Additionally, about half of the staff were men, and half were women. The interviewed staff was mostly comprised of probation officers with their own caseloads (52.9%), while supervisors and jail staff each made up around one fourth (23.5%) of the sample (see Table 2).

Interview materials

Both interview guides were semi-structured, allowing researchers sufficient opportunity to probe and flexibility for participants to speak more about what was important to them. We asked participants on probation to provide information about their experiences and challenges with community supervision and the criminal legal system more broadly. We also queried these participants about any probation violations or revocations they had and their thoughts about the process. We asked the staff about the challenges individuals face on probation and to describe the violation and revocation processes.

Analysis

During the interviews with both samples, housing emerged as a central concern and challenge for the participants on community supervision, prompting us to consider the ways in which community supervision constrains and shapes housing, especially during the COVID-19 pandemic. Our themes emerged inductively, which means we did not structure our interviews around housing, but the participants' narratives pointed to the centrality of this issue and drove our theme development. We also collected and analyzed data concurrently. For example, when we noticed challenges with housing within and across interviews, we began to ask more specific questions about the supervised participants' living situations, their related perceptions, and what staff perceived as the factors behind housing issues. When no new information emerged from the interviews and the themes were sufficiently saturated, we stopped collecting data for each of our two participant groups (Charmaz, 2014).

We analyzed the interviews using Deterding and Waters's (2018) "flexible coding" approach. The authors met as a group to develop initial index codes centered around the interview questions and identified emergent themes. We created separate index codebooks for the people on community supervision and staff, though many codes overlapped, given the similarities in instruments. Next, we developed analytic codes which better captured the emergent themes. We coded one third of the interviews as a group to address discrepancies and then refined our coding scheme to capture any additional emergent codes. After this code refinement process, we each individually coded a group of interviews. We also queried our transcripts for "house," "housing," "live with," "apartment," "transitional housing," "transitional living," and "sober housing" to ensure we captured all relevant data (Maxwell, 1992). The first author compiled data in an analytic memo and the research team met to concept map variations and subthemes (Macia, 2015).

Findings

Financial challenges, pretrial detention, and supervision conditions

Like many states, Missouri community supervision policy mandates that individuals maintain a pre-approved place of residence throughout the term of their supervision. Any residency changes require the approval of their supervising officer, who has the right to deny potential home plans (Huebner et al., 2023). Individuals who do not meet this requirement can receive a violation of their supervision and potentially risk revocation and further incarceration. Although there is evidence that individuals are rarely returned to jail for initial residence violations, individuals on probation are regularly given technical violations, which can have collateral consequences (Shannon et al., 2020). Individuals who are deemed non-compliant with their probation cannot earn compliance credits, which have the potential to reduce the length of their sentence by 50%.[4] Therefore, failure to secure

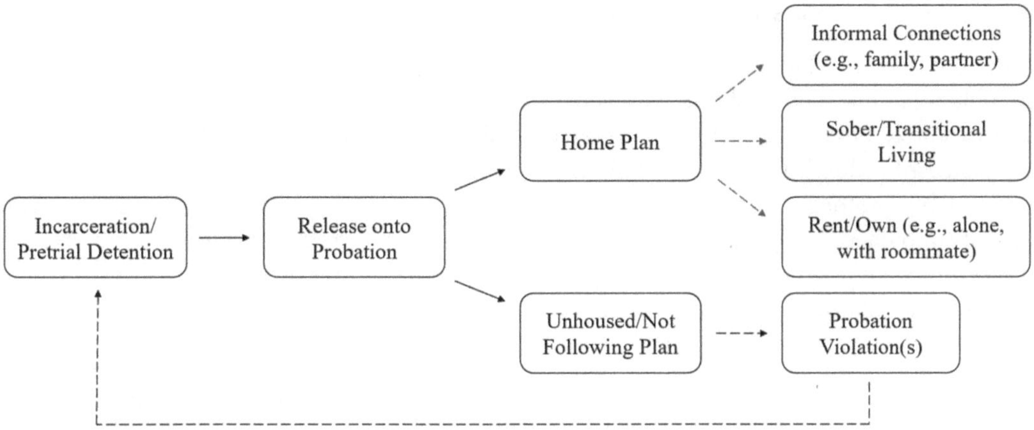

Figure 1. Paths from probation to housing. Note: Dashed lines indicate potential choices for housing and associated outcomes. The red lines indicate housing choices that require a person on probation or their informal connections have access to stable income.

an acceptable home plan can extend the term of probation and associated supervision costs. Figure 1 depicts the paths participants took from their probation sentence to housing.

Participants described how the process of being sentenced to probation, particularly when detained pretrial, left many with a dearth of economic resources, which increased the challenges associated with securing stable housing. Pretrial detention further damages employment opportunities, transportation, housing, and family relationships (Apel, 2016, Core Correctional Solutions, 2021, Loeffler & Nagin, 2022, Lowenkamp, 2022, Lowenkamp et al., 2013). For example, Staff member Saint John provided a hypothetical to illustrate the challenges when detained pretrial and then released on probation:

> Say if they have a pending case and they have to pay their rent on the first of the month, who knows when they're going to get out so they might not have the money to bond out, so then they're sitting here, month after month. So, who's paying their rent for them, you know, and then they're, you know, the job is going to only last for so long and then sometimes their employer doesn't even know that they're on supervision.

Therefore, some felt "behind the eight ball" the minute they began probation, referring to the notion they may be set up to fail. These participants explained they were already behind on housing payments and did not have strong linkages to employment.

Given these challenges, we highlight the ways that people on community supervision in the St. Louis region approach housing. We uncover the unique barriers to success on probation, particularly during the COVID-19 pandemic and the associated rise in housing prices and changes in the labor market. We also discuss the consequences of these housing difficulties for probation revocation and general long-term economic health. Four key themes emerged in this analysis. First, the stigma of the felony conviction amplified the housing challenges during COVID-19. Next, participants on probation relied heavily on informal sources of support to find and maintain housing. Further, violations featured prominently in the participants' discussions of lack of housing. Finally, inequalities were compounded for persons with marginalized identities.

Barriers to housing: Stigma and COVID-19

Individuals with felony records face challenges in terms of housing discrimination, and participants described probation officer approval of their home plan as an added burden. For instance, Frank asked to live in an extended stay hotel but was denied. Frank was convicted of a domestic violence offense involving a weapon and could not find housing without his mother's help. He felt hotels were a good option because they did not run background checks, "they just want that money." However, probation officers in the region did not classify hotels as a stable home plan. Frank, and many others, were critical of the resources probation officers provided to find help:

> I feel like they gave me some generic list of shelters and jobs. I asked the case worker, because that's who was supposed to do it, "Are these jobs for felons?" There needs to be [information for] violent felons, marijuana, drug related [crimes].

Frank alluded to the housing discrimination many faced and individuals with certain types of criminal records may be more susceptible to discrimination.

The COVID-19 pandemic, and associated changes in the housing market, further challenged participants and probation staff. Staff members had trouble keeping in contact with the people they supervised during the pandemic. Staff member Saint John detailed the issues with reporting to probation during the COVID-19 pandemic:

> I've been seeing a lot of people not having stable housing, so a lot of people will say that they're living on the streets and they couldn't get to the office, so you know there goes [violating condition] number three (residency), number eight (reporting), so and I'm like, you know, so a lot of issues with reporting.

Participants also shared their concerns about how issues with housing were exacerbated during the COVID-19 pandemic. Like others, Adam explained how housing was "a big problem that I've been dealing with. It's an ongoing thing" and attributed his ability to find an apartment to "luck" given his past drug convictions. He highlighted the housing discrimination he faced from prospective landlords when he said, "I mean, they see my background, they assume that I'm going to start selling drugs out of their unit or their house. So that turns them away." During the COVID-19 pandemic, Adam's housing issues compounded:

> It's a seller's market right now, and then [people selling their houses] have to find somewhere to live. So, then they're flooding the renter's market because they can't find anywhere to live because they don't want to overpay for a house. It's hard to compete with that when you have somebody that just sold their house.

He explained how the rental market became more competitive with individuals who could no longer afford to buy a house. Consequently, Adam could not "even compete with somebody who just sold their house." Adam explained he "probably paid close to $600 in application fees last year" to find a place to live. Adam had trouble with many of the rental companies and instead had "to find a private landlord that I can sit down, and I can talk with, and they can kind of see that's not who I am today." However, private individuals renting apartments or homes typically required more payment upfront. Adam described a situation with a potential landlord:

> I was going to have to pay over market value for the place. So basically, I needed $10,000 to move into the place for somewhere that wasn't even worth putting $5,000 up. It was in a horrible part of town. It was not a great house to move into in the first place. It was listed at $850. He wanted me to pay $1,300 and put all this money up upfront just because he has all these other people, supposedly, that I'm competing with that just sold their house or they make a combined income over $150,000. That's what he's telling me.

Housing options were often limited to private landlords because many rental companies legally discriminate against people with criminal records.[5] Individuals on probation were further pushed out of affordable housing options by individuals who had sold their homes to take advantage of the strong housing market. In light of probation restrictions, felony records, and the pandemic, most participants could not maintain independent housing or live with roommates. Consequently, they made alternative arrangements detailed in the following sections (see Table 3).

Housing patterns

Living with family and romantic partners

Without the ability to meet residence requirements on their own, most participants lived with family members and romantic partners who provided them with housing, paid their rent, or lived with them temporarily while they looked for more permanent housing. For instance, Tyler, who was convicted of a sexual offense, shared, "my mom pays my rent every month." Though Tyler lived alone in an apartment, he noted he was "afraid he [landlord] would just say, well, you can't live here anymore, and it was so hard to find a place to live" due to the nature of his conviction.

Occasionally, family members bartered with landlords to find their system-impacted loved ones' housing. Levi's mother was able to reason with a landlord to let him rent his current apartment despite his felony conviction. Levi explained he was working for a paint store and remodeled houses "on and off, but recently because I'm going to rehab, I got laid off." Levi further recounted how the conviction limited his housing options:

> Being on probation and being a felon is unreal. Nobody at all will rent to someone who's a felon, even if you have the letter that says that you're partly, you're SIS (suspended imposition of sentence), you're not a convicted felon yet, they still frown upon it and turned me down.

Even when participants received a suspended imposition of sentence (SIS), meaning the felony conviction would be removed from the record when probation is completed successfully, participants had difficulty securing housing. Those without access to housing support from others were at a considerable disadvantage to meet their supervision

Table 3. Living situations of participants on probation ($n = 54$).

Living Situation	%
With Family/Romantic Partner	64.3%
Alone	14.3%
Unhoused	10.7%
With Friend(s)/Roommate(s)	5.4%
Transitional/Sober Living	1.8%

Note: Two participants' living situations were unknown and are not represented in this table.

requirements. Isobel was one of the only participants who owned her own home, but discussed, "I know when I first started [probation], housing was a big thing. Find us somewhere to go. A lot of people don't have family." Isobel was working two jobs at the time of her interview and noted, "My family and my husband honestly helped me a lot with settling down." Family members had to be willing to help and provide significant financial assistance for people on community supervision to find housing. Marie was convicted of domestic abuse and was not working at the time of her interview. She described feeling guilty about asking her partner to support them financially while on supervision, "It was hard, because it's hard saying, 'Hey, I don't have a job right now. Can you pay for me to live here? Can you pay for me to stay out of jail? Can you pay for this?'"

Other family members were less amenable to helping system impacted persons in the transition, and even when family members were willing to help, there could be conflict within the family about shared living spaces. Ray was sporadically working construction and had been convicted of theft. He recounted the struggle of living at home with his mother and adult brother when he said, "Do I want to stay in the house and help my mom? And be miserable? Or just move out?" Ray's family had called the police during arguments when he noted, "my brother called the cops on me. Had them called on me twice" for having friends over to the house they shared with their mother. Therefore, Ray felt it was risky from a legal point of view to continue living with them. Staff member Edwards highlighted how an individual's victimization of others could break trust with a potentially supportive family:

> [Their family's] not too sure about whether or not you're going to be able to be on the straight and narrow this time, you know, coming out of prison and having a place to stay, you know, who – who's gonna trust you?

Often, family members were some of the only individuals the participants could turn to because they were barred from associating with other individuals with criminal records. However, when family members were unwilling or unable to help, the participants had to pay for alternative arrangements or be unhoused.

Sober and transitional living

One participant resided in a sober living house for women. Laura was on probation for felony drug convictions and was in drug court at the time of her interview. She described how she had received a warrant and went back to jail for failing to appear in court and not reporting where she was living to her probation officer. She described her current situation, "I'm in sober living, so I don't pay rent at the moment. And then I have food stamps, so that pays for my food." When she was released:

> The jail got me into sober living. They and then they had medically assisted treatment where, you know where, so that when you know, when I got back out that I was already stable on medicines that I wouldn't have those urges to go and get high and stuff like that. I think the jails really do offer a lot of resources, like with homelessness and... You just have to know who to talk to.

However, Laura's experience was unique compared to the other participants. Individuals on probation described how they had difficulties finding resources for affordable housing. Other participants noted how sober or transitional living spaces could cost money or come with additional employment requirements. Natalie was unhoused at the time of her interview and working, "side jobs," but because she did not have transportation, she had a difficult time maintaining regular employment. She explained some of the potential requirements to get into sober living:

> I got out of jail, I tried to get into sober living and I got denied because I didn't have a job right away. So, I literally try every day to look up resources and get help and it's not as easy as people make it seem. A lot of. . . And if you don't live at a place, [probation officers] send you back [to jail].

Natalie further explained how she was not sure how to access transitional living and compared the level of restriction to a prison:

> I know that there's transitional housing, which is just where you go straight out of prison. It's like a prison, they're a lot more strict. Sober living. But I don't know if they can get you in those. I don't really know how that works because none of them have ever really helped me with it.

Problematically, Natalie mentioned how other system-impacted people told her that transitional living is unsafe when she noted, "Yeah, they're not safe at all. There's a lot of drugs in there." Sober and transitional living arrangements were rarely accessed by the participants, given the additional requirements and safety concerns.

Being unhoused

More often, individuals who did not have family support were unhoused. Participants noted they were couch surfing and were reluctant to join transitional living because of potential adverse interactions with others. At the same time, unhoused participants typically described feeling hopeless about finding housing because locating important documents was difficult after incarceration and finding gainful employment even tougher.

Mark's experience exemplifies the experience of many in the sample. He described, "I'm going to be bouncing from couch to couch at the moment." Mark had been on probation four times in Missouri for drug charges and explained, "as of late, drug use has been my only hurdle that I've had problems with. I've always been employed my entire life." Mark attributed his recent struggles with drug use to the pandemic. He was able to obtain extended unemployment assistance during the early months of COVID, but this lack of structure was challenging and "gives me too much free time on my hands." When Mark was asked whether he worried about probation finding out he was unhoused, he discussed, "I worry about them finding out about that, because obviously, we're not allowed to do that. But I don't want to do the halfway house." Mark went on to explain how he perceived the halfway house would compromise his ability to remain sober, "I want to step away from drugs and not relive it every day of my life. And talk about it, and hang out with ex-drug addicts, and talk about drug use and alcohol abuse." Mark was hopeful about finding a new job at the time of his interview because he was able to find assistance securing identification documents.

Miranda also relayed how being unhoused could compromise one's ability to get a job. She was living in a shelter at the time of her interview and explained, "I currently don't have a job because I don't know, I just can't really necessarily be in the shower every day. I don't have any smart clothes, and if I do, they get stolen." Miranda was also waiting to hear back after applying to live in public housing. Miranda described that prior to living in the shelter,

> I was just living in a tent for weeks and before that I was like couch surfing or kind of just on the streets literally. Because I didn't know. . . I've been here a while, but I still don't know that many people out here.

Like Mark, Miranda noted, "I'm scared to tell [my probation officer] that I'm homeless because that could just be a violation." Participants were often not forthcoming about housing instability with probation officers because of the potential to receive violations, which made getting help more unlikely.

Consequences of housing instability

One of the primary consequences participants faced related to unstable housing during the COVID-19 pandemic were probation violations. Without a pre-approved place of residence, participants were at greater risk for these violations and other associated criminal legal consequences. At the same time, the pandemic exacerbated existing inequalities (see, for example, Perry et al., 2021) and compounded the challenges some participants faced. In this section we detail how violations were connected to supervision outcomes and the individual characteristics that made participants especially vulnerable to housing insecurity.

Violations

Given that individuals on probation can receive a violation when they do not inform their supervising officer about changes to their residence, housing instability was intimately connected to supervision outcomes. Participants reported that they worried their probation officer would find out they were unhoused or had moved somewhere they thought probation would not approve. At times, participants would opt to abscond or go "on the run" because they felt their probation officer would learn they were not in compliance with residence requirements. Lawrence lived with his wife and kids and owned his own business. He had received a probation violation for missing an appointment with his PO and highlighted, "a lot of people that come to see their probation officer, the moment that they missed their probation officer, they get scared. That's what makes them go on a run and makes it worse." Staff member Phillips described the typical process when someone fails to report and gets a residence violation:

> We'll declare them an absconder and have to issue a warrant if we cannot locate them and if they've missed an appointment, if they've lost their house and had to go move one county over and are scared that we're going to come, you know, try to arrest them or send them to prison, they don't want to contact us and let us know, that some of them will declare, declare them and issue a warrant, and they've dug themselves a deeper hole.

The staff members did not attribute absconding to personal failure, but instead that many individuals on probation lack access to a living wage. Staff member Grant highlighted the connection between finances and community supervision conditions:

> It's really overly simple but it's, it's having access to a livable income. You know if, if they can get by with whatever income is coming into their household regardless of what the source is,

> I'm not one to try to judge, you know, whether it should come from whatever source, but if, if they can get by and have their needs met with that I don't think we're going to see them with, with any sort of a significant violation, most of the time.

Though the staff members were aware of these issues, people on supervision were highly wary of reaching out for help with housing needs because they perceived they would receive a violation. Miranda explained how she felt she could not reach out to her probation officer because she feared the violation. Miranda described, "maybe she's not pushing [housing resources] because she doesn't know that I'm actually on the streets. Because that would be a violation." Olivia was also unhoused and piecing together income from informal work. She similarly mentioned, "me being homeless is also a violation and that's the hardest part" of being on probation. Participants on probation who were unhoused tended to remain unhoused given the lack of available, affordable options and because reaching out to a probation officer could induce violations.

Compounded inequalities. Inequality was layered for the participants and contributed to their housing difficulties. The staff members described poverty, substance use, and mental health issues as the most significant drivers of criminal behavior and housing issues. Staff member Grant explained:

> You know, substance use in the community drives a lot of the crime we see, but I think poverty is probably the bigger, the bigger driver there. If they weren't so poor, if, if they could get, you know, their, their needs met, with, with what's coming into their house, maybe they wouldn't be as deep into, into their drug use as they are, or you know, maybe their drug use wouldn't be a problem that rises to the criminal justice systems level.

Staff member Norris added, "it's hard for people with mental health issues to get housing. A lot of times it's because [of] their [criminal] history."

The requirements for probation compliance could interfere with an individual's ability to find employment and housing. Marie described how electronic monitoring and house arrest made it challenging for her to find a job. Marie recently attended "at least seven interviews" with no luck. She further expressed:

> Sometimes I hop from place to place. It's not good on anybody, but I would like to be at a job for a while and be financially stable to the point of where my car is taken care of, my house and my kids are taken care of.

However, the financial obligations of her house arrest made it difficult to pay rent. Consequently, she noted:

> We're looking at low-income housing. Of course, whenever they're like, "Hey, you're going to be on house arrest, but you have to pay this $300 to get on [house arrest], and then you have to pay $250 a month [to maintain house arrest]," that was just insane to me.

Rachel was on probation for a drug conviction and was unhoused. She denoted similar challenges:

> One challenge was finding a reliable place to go and home plan, too. Reporting so often was a big issue for me as well, because I didn't always have transportation to get down there every week. And besides that, they wanted me to do outpatient, of course, find a job, make all these payments for intervention fees. And it's kind of overwhelming, just all the stuff that they kind of put on you sometimes.

Often, participants discussed these mandates for treatment as detrimental to their ability to remain stable and locate housing. For instance, Cindy was on probation for theft and described how outpatient treatment requirements made it difficult to find a job and to obtain housing for her family. She noted she wished probation would, "help me get more stable housing for me and my family, not to have me in treatment so much of the day." Cindy perceived her supervision requirements were a hindrance, explaining, "I mean, I just needed to work, and I wasn't able to do that."

These compounding inequalities and requirements also affected participants' families. Staff member Carter described how incarceration could affect the financial situation of a hypothetical person on probation:

> I literally was arrested, and now I can't get a job. I literally was arrested, and the reason I lost my job, and the car was driving my family to the train station with is now impounded. I can't get that out because I don't have any income. My family has never had income so they can't borrow money. So, it's a generational thing, it affects the individual.

Families may be left without the support and income of their system-impacted relative and system-impacted persons may have little familial support (Condry & Minson, 2021).

Women in our sample appeared to be particularly affected by housing instability. At the same time, many had the added obligation of taking care of their children. Sara was on probation for a drug conviction and noted, "I have a son, and I have to take care of him first." Women with children had difficulty finding housing that would accept their children and work within their financial constraints. Childcare also posed a challenge given that many were unemployed. For instance, Sara stated, "I have a seven-month-old baby boy" and further explained, "I'm trying to figure out a job that works with very specific hours" so that her mother could watch her baby while she worked since Sara could not afford childcare. At the time of her interview Sara was doing "side work to help with rent I actually clean the condos in my complex . . . so that money directly goes toward rent."

Multiple participants described that transitional housing in the St. Louis area is limited for women. Lily described she was "kind of staying with friends" and unable to find work. She aspired to "start maybe like a sober living for girls . . . because I don't feel like there's a lot of resources or places for females." Similarly, Natalie relayed, "It's mainly for guys." As a result, the women were often unhoused and described their living situations as "couch surfing" or "staying with friends." Women explained that relying on individuals they did not know well for housing could be dangerous. Natalie alluded to these unsafe living arrangements:

> I guess it just depends on who the person is. Being a girl is a lot more difficult because alot of people are still willing to help you out, but they want something in return so it's not really helping you. And then, being in the situation, sometimes we feel like we have to do something in return just so we're not on the streets and not in certain situations.

Rachel further denoted the difficulty that couch surfing with unfamiliar people posed, "it also makes me feel like that if I didn't have [acquaintances] to help me, then I would be in a worse situation. So, it's kind of like, sometimes I feel like I don't have a choice." Though these women were able to sometimes find transportation and a place to temporarily stay, it came at a high cost. The participants who were unhoused had to risk receiving a violation if they reached out to their probation officer for help and disclosed their unhoused status, but they also incurred risk when living on the street or couch surfing.

Discussion

Housing provides a critical foundation for people on probation; however, recent changes in the rental and labor markets have made this resource inaccessible for many (Stanley-Becker, 2022, Stansfield & Semenza, 2022). Using data from samples of people on probation and probation staff, we found that participants described a combination of economic disadvantage, housing discrimination, and competing social obligations, like childcare, which created myriad barriers to secure housing. The unique timing of the data collection provides insight into how COVID-19 impacted participants' experiences with finding housing and employment, exacerbating existing challenges.

Overall, barriers to success were often not isolated but compounded to create a domino effect resulting in a cyclical pathway in and out of prison or jail through technical violations. The pandemic, a felony criminal record, and community supervision requirements left some participants unhoused, unemployed, and/or susceptible to further criminal legal sanctioning. The findings reaffirm the reciprocal relationship between housing instability and legal-financial obligations identified in prior research, which contributes to more financial strain and subsequent housing insecurity (Pattillo et al., 2022). In addition, housing discrimination based on a criminal record impacted the participants' ability to secure housing and diminished opportunities for gainful employment, further reducing options for compliant housing. Rent alone can consume most of one's income, and people on probation are still expected to pay court-mandated fines, supervision fees, and to fulfill their other basic needs (Ruhland, 2019, Ruhland et al., 2020). Individuals also were responsible for attending treatment and completing other requirements with related time costs, which complicated employment and, relatedly, their ability to secure funds for housing (Phelps & Ruhland, 2021). Together, this reveals how one barrier begets the next, and without stable housing, people on community supervision are left without a foundation for success. These findings reaffirm the need for actionable solutions to facilitate housing accessibility for system-impacted individuals.

Furthermore, the COVID-19 pandemic diminished some labor markets and simultaneously created an inaccessible housing market, even for those who are not system involved, amplifying the challenges system-impacted people face (Abrams et al., 2023). Many participants relied on familial or romantic support for housing to avoid further criminal legal sanctioning. Participants described that the housing options often readily available to them were temporary and not in compliance with the terms of probation, such as extended stay motel living. As a result, they avoided their probation officers and faced technical violations.

This work speaks to many opportunities for policy change. There is a particular need for additional, affordable housing that does not bar people with a criminal record. Most people on community supervision work with independent landlords who have little incentive to make their properties safe, clean, or affordable because system-impacted persons have very few housing options (Desmond, 2018, Miller, 2021). Despite policies enacted to reduce housing discrimination, system-impacted persons are left out of the legislation (Evans et al., 2019) and third-party entities control much of the housing market (Miller, 2021). Housing is a basic physiological need. The housing first model, for example, recognizes housing as an essential precursor to other life improvements and aspirations (Baxter et al., 2019, Padgett et al., 2006). However, public opportunities for housing for people with a criminal record remain few.

In addition, participants felt their community supervision officers provided little guidance regarding post-incarceration housing planning; likewise, staff members recognized access to housing as one of the most significant challenges people on community supervision face. As such, community supervision officers should work in tandem with their clients to identify accessible housing options through more extensive planning and the provision of targeted resources that specifically identify accessible, affordable, and compliant housing options before release and while under the supervision of the state. At the same time, this type of housing is likely to remain out of reach in many urban communities without substantial structural change in the housing market.

In congruence with prior research, characteristics such as gender further contribute to housing discrimination (Evans et al., 2019). Particularly related to housing, women report needing to find suitable housing for not only themselves but often their children as well. Many system-involved women are battling problem substance use and mental health problems and navigating motherhood while trying to remain in compliance with the conditions of their supervision (Cobbina et al., 2012, Huebner & Pleggenkuhle, 2015). Probation agencies should provide accommodations for parents with children and connect individuals with free or subsidized childcare, as research has shown that agency flexibility can reduce revocations and increase compliance (Stalans & Lurigio, 2015). Relatedly, system-impacted and staff participants mentioned that officers used their discretion to decide when to issue a technical violation. Therefore, in addition to being at the mercy of landlords in the private sector, people on probation are subjected to their probation officers' discretion concerning when and when not to issue a technical violation. Eliminating the use of technical violations for being unhoused may also reduce this burden. In turn, this could impact the rising revocation rates and interrupt the pipeline to reincarceration due to the inability to access secure housing.

Despite the strengths of this study in uncovering some of the compounding challenges associated with housing for individuals on probation, there are several areas we would recommend improvement upon in future studies. First, this study was conducted in a major metropolitan area in the Midwestern United States. Future research should explore whether the same themes hold true in other locales. At the same time, the cross-sectional nature of the data could also be improved upon. Future scholarship should address the long-term challenges of housing for this group given the deep and widespread impact of COVID-19. Relatedly, because the study was conducted during the COVID-19 pandemic, the nature of the themes and our access to participants may have been affected. Additional quantitative research may be able to uncover the impact of certain conditions of compliance related to financial capability on probation outcomes. For example, future studies might attempt to determine how insecure housing, ability to pay legal-financial obligations, and access to transportation are related to probation compliance.

Given the overlapping marginalization of people in the sample, future research should additionally center gender and race to identify the specific needs and challenges groups face with housing. Affordable housing in St. Louis, as it is in many communities, is a racial justice issue (Community Builders Network, 2022), as people of color are the most likely to have housing insecurity. Further, women described the lack of transitional housing, but these resources are rarely available for women and disproportionately affect families of color (Garcia-Hallett, 2019). Extant literature has demonstrated that women working to overcome problem drug use can be more successful when their children can live with them in their sober living environment (Stevens & Patton, 1998). Increasing housing options that accommodate women on community supervision could ameliorate some of the challenges system-impacted women face upon reentry and during their rehabilitation. Furthermore, due to the complex need for system involved women, prior research suggests that sober living housing should also cater to mental and physical health needs (Krentzman et al., 2022, Morash et al., 2019). More research on the housing first movement with diverse populations is needed (Woodhall-Melnik & Dunn, 2016).

Overall, this study shines a light on the compounded challenges that people on probation must navigate and furthers the already recognized bidirectional relationship between housing instability and legal, and financial obligations to include the interconnectedness of housing, financial capability, and compliance on community supervision. The housing market was fundamentally changed by COVID-19 which impacted the ability of system impacted people to find housing due to many supportive resources being restricted or further pushed out of reach. The cyclical pathway from housing instability to reincarceration through technical violations needs to be addressed through actionable solutions such as increased transitional housing, sober living environments, targeted resources for identifying housing opportunities, and increased flexibility within probation agencies to decrease the imposition of technical violations.

Notes

1. Other racial groups make up less than 10% of each county's population and both counties have less than 5% Hispanic or Latino identifying residents.
2. The majority of this group interviewed once, but one person interviewed twice. Each person on probation interviewed had a felony conviction given people with misdemeanor and ordinance convictions are supervised by private probation entities (Huebner & Shannon, 2022). The research team included the third author (the grant PI) and a graduate assistant (first author of the paper) and the fourth and fifth authors served as Co-PIs.
3. Like the group on community supervision, the staff interviews were audio recorded and transcribed verbatim and we gave participants pseudonyms to preserve their anonymity.
4. See RSMO 217.703.
5. See RSMO 213.040.

Disclosure statement

No potential conflict of interest was reported by the author(s).

Funding

This work was supported by a grant from the John D. and Catherine T. MacArthur Foundation [G-1705-151965].

References

Abrams, L. S., Reed, T. A., Bondoc, C., Acosta, D. R., Murillo, M., & Barnert, E. S. (2023). "It was there when I came home": Young adults and jail reentry in the context of COVID-19. *American Journal of Criminal Justice*, *48*(3), 767–785. https://doi.org/10.1007/s12103-022-09683-8

Apel, R. (2016). The effects of jail and prison confinement on cohabitation and marriage. *The Annals of the American Academy of Political and Social Science*, *665*(1), 103–126. https://doi.org/10.1177/0002716216629360

Aurand, A., Emmanuel, D., Threet, D., Rafi, I., & Yentel, D. (2019). The gap: A shortage of affordable rental homes. *National Low-Income Housing Coalition. tinyurl.com/rz2n2c2*

Baxter, A., Tweed, J., Srinivasa Vittal, K., & Hilary, T. (2019). Effects of housing first approaches on health and well-being of adults who are homeless or at risk of homelessness: Systematic review and meta-analysis of randomised controlled trials. *Journal of Epidemiology & Community Health*, *73* (5), 379. https://doi.org/10.1136/jech-2018-210981

Belisle, L. A., Salisbury, E. J., & Cowell Mercier, M. (2023). Gender-responsive probation during the COVID-19 pandemic: Learning from justice-involved women and their supervising officers. *Victims & Offenders*, *18*(8), 1498–1520. https://doi.org/10.1080/15564886.2023.2212254

Biernacki, P., & Waldorf, D. (1981). Snowball sampling: Problems and techniques of chain referral sampling. *Sociological Methods & Research*, *10*(2), 141–163. https://doi.org/10.1177/004912418101000205

Blomberg, T., & Lucken, K. (1994). Stacking the deck by piling up sanctions: Is intermediate punishment destined to fail?. *The Howard Journal of Criminal Justice*, *33*(1), 62–80. https://doi.org/10.1111/j.1468-2311.1994.tb00794.x

Boeing, G., Besbris, M., Schachter, A., & Kuk, J. (2021). Housing search in the age of big data: Smarter cities or the same old blind spots? *Housing Policy Debate*, *31*(1), 112–126. https://doi.org/10.1080/10511482.2019.1684336

Bowman, E. I., & Ely, K. (2020). Voices of returning citizens: A qualitative study of a supportive housing program for ex-offenders in a rural community. *The Prison Journal*, *100*(4), 423–446. https://doi.org/10.1177/0032885520939273

Brett, S., Khoshkhoo, N., & Nagrecha, M. (2020). *Paying on probation: How financial sanctions intersect with probation to target, trap, and punish people who cannot pay*. https://mcusercontent.com/f65678cd73457d0cbde864d05/files/f05e951e-60a9-404e-b5cc-13c065b2a630/Paying_on_Probation_report_FINAL.pdf

Charmaz, K. (2014). *Constructing grounded theory: A practical guide through qualitative research*. Sage.

Clark, V. A. (2016). Predicting two types of recidivism among newly released prisoners: First addresses as "launch pads" for recidivism or reentry success. *Crime & Delinquency*, *62*(10), 1364–1400. https://doi.org/10.1177/0011128714555760

Cobbina, J., Huebner, B. M., & Berg, M. T. (2012). Men, women, and postrelease offending: An examination of the nature of the link between relational ties and recidivism. *Crime & Delinquency*, *58*(3), 331–361. https://doi.org/10.1177/0011128710382348

Community Builders Network. (2022). *Saint Louis affordable housing report card*. https://www.affordablestl.com/

Condry, R., & Minson, S. (2021). Conceptualizing the effects of imprisonment on families: Collateral consequences, secondary punishment, or symbiotic harms? *Theoretical Criminology*, *25*(4), 540–558. https://doi.org/10.1177/1362480619897078

Core Correctional Solutions. (2021). *The hidden costs of pretrial detention revisited*. :https://craftmediabucket.s3.amazonaws.com/uploads/HiddenCosts.pdf

Council of State Governments. (2019). *Confined and costly: How supervision violations are filling prisons and burdening budgets*. Council of State Governments.https://csgjusticecenter.org/publications/confined-costly/.

Czeisler, M. É., Lane, R. I., Wiley, J. F., Czeisler, C. A., Howard, M. E., & Rajaratnam, S. M. W. (2021). Follow-up survey of US adult reports of mental health, substance use, and suicidal ideation during the COVID-19 pandemic, September 2020. *JAMA Network Open*, *4*(2), e2037665–e2037665. https://doi.org/10.1001/jamanetworkopen.2020.37665

Desmond, M. (2018). Heavy is the house: Rent burden among the American urban poor. *International Journal of Urban & Regional Research*, *42*(1), 160–170. https://doi.org/10.1111/1468-2427.12529

Deterding, N. M., & Waters, M. C. (2018). Flexible coding of in-depth interviews: A twenty-first-century approach. *Sociological Methods & Research*, *50*(2), 708–739. https://doi.org/10.1177/0049124118799377

Doherty, F. (2016). Obey all laws and be good: Probation and the meaning of recidivism. *The Georgetown Law Journal*, *104*, 291–354.

Dong, K. R., Must, A., Tang, A. M., Beckwith, C., & Stopka, T. J. (2018). Competing priorities that rival health in adults on probation in Rhode Island: Substance use recovery, employment, housing, and food intake. *BMC Public Health*, *18*(1), 289. https://doi.org/10.1186/s12889-018-5201-7

Evans, D. (2014). *The debt penalty—exposing the financial barriers to offender reintegration*. https://jjrec.files.wordpress.com/2014/08/debtpenalty.pdf

Evans, D. N., Blount-Hill, K.-L., & Cubellis, M. A. (2019). Examining housing discrimination across race, gender and felony history. *Housing Studies*, *34*(5), 761–778. https://doi.org/10.1080/02673037.2018.1478069

Evans, D. N., & Porter, J. R. (2015). Criminal history and landlord rental decisions: A New York quasi-experimental study. *Journal of Experimental Criminology*, *11*(1), 21–42. https://doi.org/10.1007/s11292-014-9217-4

Falk, G., Romero, P., Nicchitta, I., & Nyhof, E. (2021). Unemployment rates during the COVID-19 pandemic. Congressional Research Service. https://crsreports.congress.gov/product/pdf/R/R46554

Garcia-Hallett, J. (2019). "We're being released to a jungle": The state of prisoner reentry and the resilience of women of color. *The Prison Journal*, *99*(4), 459–483. https://doi.org/10.1177/0032885519852089

Giuffre, A. (2023). The impact of legal-financial obligations on relationships with family, friends, and acquaintances: A qualitative study of community supervised men with sexual and nonsexual offense convictions. *Criminal Justice & Behavior*, *50*(5), 747–765. https://doi.org/10.1177/00938548231162083

Harding, D. J., Morenoff, J. D., & Herbert, C. W. (2013). Home is hard to find: Neighborhoods, institutions, and the residential trajectories of returning prisoners. *The Annals of the American Academy of Political and Social Science*, *647*(1), 214–236. https://doi.org/10.1177/0002716213477070

Harris, A. (2016). *A pound of flesh: Monetary sanctions as punishment for the poor*. Russel Sage Foundation.

Herbert, C., Morenoff, W., & Harding, D. J. (2015). Homelessness and housing insecurity among former prisoners. *RSF: The Russell Sage Foundation Journal of the Social Sciences*, *1*(2), 44–79. https://doi.org/10.7758/rsf.2015.1.2.04

Horowitz, J., Utada, C., & Fuhrmann, M. (2018). *Probation and parole systems marked by high stakes, missed opportunities: 1 in 55 adults is under community supervision*. The Pew Charitable Trusts. https://www.pewtrusts.org/-/media/assets/2018/09/probation_and_parole_systems_marked_by_high_stakes_missed_opportunities_pew.pdf

Huebner, B. M., Kras, K. R., & Pleggenkuhle, B. (2019). Structural discrimination and social stigma among individuals incarcerated for sexual offenses: Reentry across the rural–urban continuum. *Criminology*, *57*(4), 715–738. https://doi.org/10.1111/1745-9125.12226

Huebner, B. M., & Pleggenkuhle, B. (2015). Residential location, household composition, and recidivism: An analysis by gender. *Justice Quarterly*, *32*(5), 818–844. https://doi.org/10.1080/07418825.2013.827231

Huebner, B. M., & Shannon, S. K. S. (2022). Private probation costs, compliance, and the proportionality of punishment: Evidence from Georgia and Missouri. *RSF: The Russell Sage Foundation Journal of the Social Sciences*, *8*(1), 179–199. https://doi.org/10.7758/rsf.2022.8.1.08

Huebner, B. M., Slocum, L. A., Giuffre, A., Kras, K., & Boxerman, B. (2023). Probation violations as drivers of jail incarceration in St. Louis County, Missouri. https://safetyandjusticechallenge.org/wp-content/uploads/2023/01/St.Louis_Probation_Final.pdf

Jacobs, L. A., & Gottlieb, A. (2020). The effect of housing circumstances on recidivism: Evidence from a sample of people on probation in San Francisco. *Criminal Justice & Behavior, 47*(9), 1097–1115. https://doi.org/10.1177/0093854820942285

Johnson, W. (2020). *The broken heart of America: St. Louis and the violent history of the United States.* Basic Books.

Kras, K. R., Pleggenkuhle, B., & Huebner, B. M. (2016). A new way of doing time on the outside: Sex offenders' pathways in and out of a transitional housing facility. *International Journal of Offender Therapy and Comparative Criminology, 60*(5), 512–534. https://doi.org/10.1177/0306624x14554194

Krentzman, A. R., Sharratt, M., Mannella, K. A., Foster, K. T., Yarosh, S., & Jester, J. M. (2022). Women in sober living: Baseline characteristics and their associations with reasons for leaving. *Journal of Social Work Practice in the Addictions, 22*(1), 21–39. https://doi.org/10.1080/1533256X.2021.1935156

Lageson, S. E. (2020). *Digital punishment: Privacy, stigma, and the harms of data-driven criminal justice.* Oxford University Press.

Leasure, P. (2019). Securing private housing with a criminal record. *Journal of Offender Rehabilitation, 58*(1), 30–49. https://doi.org/10.1080/10509674.2018.1549182

LeMasters, K., Benson, A., Corsi, C., Krajewski, T., Seide, K., Brinkley-Rubinstein, L., & Nowotny, K. (2023). Collateral consequences of COVID-19 for people on probation and parole. *Health & Justice, 11*(1), 1–7. https://doi.org/10.1186/s40352-023-00221-0

Link, N. W., Hyatt, J., & Ruhland, E. (2020). Monetary sanctions, legal and collateral consequences, and probation and parole: Where do we go from here? *UCLA Criminal Justice Law Review, 4*(1), 200–212.

Loeffler, C. E., & Nagin, D. (2022). The impact of incarceration on recidivism. *Annual Review of Criminology, 5*(1), 133–152. https://doi.org/10.1146/annurev-criminol-030920-112506

Lowenkamp, C. T. (2022). *The hidden costs of pretrial detention revisited.* Arnold Ventures. https://craftmediabucket.s3.amazonaws.com/uploads/HiddenCosts.pdf

Lowenkamp, C. T., VanNostrand, M., & Holsinger, A. (2013). The hidden costs of pretrial detention. Arnold Ventures. https://craftmediabucket.s3.amazonaws.com/uploads/PDFs/LJAF_Report_hidden-costs_FNL.pdf

Lutze, F. E., Rosky, J. W., & Hamilton, Z. K. (2014). Homelessness and reentry: A multisite outcome evaluation of Washington state's reentry housing program for high risk offenders. *Criminal Justice & Behavior, 41*(4), 471–491. https://doi.org/10.1177/0093854813510164

Macia, L. (2015). Using clustering as a tool: Mixed methods in qualitative data analysis. *The Qualitative Report, 20*(7), 1083–1094. https://doi.org/10.46743/2160-3715/2015.2201

Makarios, M., Steiner, B., & Travis, L. F. (2010). Examining the predictors of recidivism among men and women released from prison in Ohio. *Criminal Justice & Behavior, 37*(12), 1377–1391. https://doi.org/10.1177/0093854810382876

Martin, K. D., & Zettler, H. R. (2022). COVID-19's impact on probation professionals' views about their roles and the future of probation. *Criminal Justice Review, 47*(2), 167–184. https://doi.org/10.1177/07340168211052876

Maxwell, J. (1992). Understanding and validity in qualitative research. *Harvard Educational Review, 62*(3), 279–301. https://doi.org/10.17763/haer.62.3.8323320856251826

McNeeley, S. (2018). Do ecological effects on recidivism vary by gender, race, or housing type? *Crime & Delinquency, 64*(6), 782–806. https://doi.org/10.1177/0011128717714425

Middlemass, K. (2017). *Convicted and condemned: The politics and policies of prisoner reentry.* NYU Press.

Miller, R. J. (2021). *Halfway home: Race, punishment, and the afterlife of mass incarceration.* Little, Brown, and Company.

Morash, M., Kashy, D. A., Smith, S. W., & Cobbina, J. E. (2019). Technical violations, treatment and punishment responses, and recidivism of women on probation and parole. *Criminal Justice Policy Review*, *30*(5), 788–810. https://doi.org/10.1177/0887403417723425

Morenoff, J. D., & Harding, D. J. (2014). Incarceration, prisoner reentry, and communities. *Annual Review of Sociology*, *40*(1), 411–429. https://doi.org/10.1146/annurev-soc-071811-145511

National Low Income Housing Coalition. (2023). *Missouri State Facts*. https://nlihc.org/oor/state/mo

Padgett, D. K., Gulcur, L., & Tsemberis, S. (2006). Housing first services for people who are homeless with co-occurring serious mental illness and substance abuse. *Research on Social Work Practice*, *16* (1), 74–83. https://doi.org/10.1177/1049731505282593

Pattillo, M., Banks, E., Sargent, B., & Boches, D. J. (2022). Monetary sanctions and housing instability. *RSF: The Russell Sage Foundation Journal of the Social Sciences*, *8*(2), 57–75. https://doi.org/10.7758/RSF.2022.8.2.03

Perry, B. L., Aronson, B., & Pescosolido, B. A. (2021). Pandemic precarity: COVID-19 is exposing and exacerbating inequalities in the American heartland. *PNAS*, *118*(8), e2020685118. https://doi.org/10.1073/pnas.2020685118

Petersilia, J. (2003). When prisoners come home: Parole and prisoner reentry. Oxford University Press.

Phelps, M. S., & Ruhland, E. L. (2021). Governing marginality: Coercion and care in probation. *Social Problems*, *69*(3), 799–816. https://doi.org/10.1093/socpro/spaa060

Pleggenkuhle, B., Huebner, B. M., & Kras, K. R. (2016). Solid start: Supportive housing, social support, and reentry transitions. *Journal of Crime & Justice*, *39*(3), 380–397. https://doi.org/10.1080/0735648x.2015.1047465

Remster, B. (2019). A life course analysis of homeless shelter use among the formerly incarcerated. *Justice Quarterly*, *36*(3), 437–465. https://doi.org/10.1080/07418825.2017.1401653

Reosti, A. (2020). "We go totally subjective": Discretion, discrimination, and tenant screening in alandlord's market. *Law & Social Inquiry*, *45*(3), 618–657. https://doi.org/10.1017/lsi.2019.81

Rosen, E., Garboden, P. M., & Cossyleon, J. E. (2021). Racial discrimination in housing: How landlords use algorithms and home visits to screen tenants. *American Sociological Review*, *86*(5), 787–822. https://doi.org/10.1177/00031224211029618

Ruhland, E. (2019). It's all about the money: An exploration of probation fees. *Corrections*, *6*(1), 1–20. https://doi.org/10.1080/23774657.2018.1564635

Ruhland, E., Holmes, B., & Petkus, A. (2020). The role of fines and fees on probation outcomes. *Criminal Justice & Behavior*, *47*(10), 1244–1263. https://doi.org/10.1177/0093854820918877

Shannon, S. (2020). Probation and monetary sanctions in Georgia: Evidence from a multi-method study. *Georgia Law Review*, *54*(4), 1213–1234.

Shannon, S., Huebner, B. M., Harris, A., Martin, K. D., Pattillo, M., Pettit, B., Sykes, B. L., & Uggen, C. (2020). The broad scope and variation of monetary sanctions: Evidence from eight states. *UCLA Law Review*, *4*(1). https://doi.org/10.21428/cb6ab371.041cfb4e

Spradley, J. P. (2016). *The ethnographic interview*. Waveland Press.

Stalans, L. J., & Lurigio, A. J. (2015). Parenting and intimate relationship effects on women offenders' recidivism and noncompliance with probation. *Women & Criminal Justice*, *25*(3), 152–168. https://doi.org/10.1080/08974454.2014.909764

Stanley-Becker, T. (2022). Breaking the cycle of homelessness and incarceration: Prisoner reentry, racial justice, & fair chance housing policy. *University of Pennsylvania Journal of Law and Public Affairs*, *7*(2), 257–314.

Stansfield, R., & Semenza, D. (2022). Urban housing affordability, economic disadvantage and racial disparities in gun violence: A neighbourhood analysis in four US cities. *The British Journal of Criminology*, *63*(1), 59–77. https://doi.org/10.1093/bjc/azab119

Steiner, B., Makarios, M. D., & Travis, L. F. (2015). Examining the effects of residential situations and residential mobility on offender recidivism. *Crime & Delinquency*, *61*(3), 375–401. https://doi.org/10.1177/0011128711399409

Stevens, S. J., & Patton, T. (1998). Residential treatment for drug addicted women and their children: Effective treatment strategies. *Drugs & Society*, *13*(1–2), 235–249. https://doi.org/10.1300/J023v13n01_14

Thacher, D. (2008). The rise of criminal background screening in rental housing. *Law & Social Inquiry*, *33*(1), 5–30. https://doi.org/10.1111/j.1747-4469.2008.00092.x

Tran-Leung, M. C. (2015). *When discretion means denial. A national perspective on criminal records barriers to federally subsidized housing.* Sargent Shriver National Center on Poverty Law. https://www.nhlp.org/wp-content/uploads/Tran-Leung-When-Discretion-Means-Denial.pdf

Uggen, C., & Stewart, R. (2015). Piling on: Collateral consequences and community supervision. *Minnesota Law Review*, *271*, 1871–1910. https://scholarship.law.umn.edu/mlr/271

United States Census Bureau. (2023a). *Quick facts: St.* Louis city. https://www.census.gov/quickfacts/fact/table/stlouiscitymissouri,US/PST045222

United States Census Bureau. (2023b). *Quick facts: St.* Louis county. https://www.census.gov/quickfacts/fact/table/stlouiscountymissouri,US/PST045222

Viglione, J., Alward, L. M., Lockwood, A., & Bryson, S. (2020). Adaptations to COVID-19 in community corrections agencies across the United States. *Victims & Offenders*, *15*(7–8), 1277–1297. https://doi.org/10.1080/15564886.2020.1818153

Woodhall-Melnik, J. R., & Dunn, J. R. (2016). A systematic review of outcomes associated with participation in housing first programs. *Housing Studies*, *31*(3), 287–304. https://doi.org/10.1080/02673037.2015.1080816

Zillow. (2023). St. Louis, MO rental market. Retrieved from https://www.zillow.com/rental-manager/market-trends/saint-louis-mo/

Reducing Community Supervision Failure for People with Mental Illness: Strategies for Promoting Success

Sarah M. Manchak, Sarah Light, Alison J. Farringer, Francesco DiRienzo, Luis Guitierrez, and Jessica Warner

ABSTRACT

Justice-involved people with mental illness are at increased risk for failure while on community supervision. Probation and parole officers (POs) have significant influence on the outcomes of these individuals through various supervision tactics and approaches. Prior research on specialty mental health supervision has helped identify a number of specific tactics that are both necessary and effective for supervising people with mental illness. This study builds upon this evidence base to offer POs additional insight and guidance that can help them promote the success of people with mental illness on community supervision. Toward this purpose, this study centers the voices and lived experiences of both individuals with mental illness on probation and parole and the POs who supervise them. Using qualitative data collected from focus groups with specialized probation and parole officers and responses to semi-structured interviews conducted with people with mental illness on community supervision, this study describes the unique experiences and challenges faced by people with mental illness and identifies specific strategies POs can use to be more helpful, impactful, and effective in their supervision of people with mental illness.

Individuals with mental illness are at elevated risk for failure of community supervision (Baillargeon et al., 2009; Cloyes et al., 2010; Porporino & Motiuk, 1995; Solomon et al., 2002). While the reason for failure may hinge upon the person on supervision – that is, they are responsible for engaging in behavior that warrants punitive response – the decision to fail someone on supervision is made by a judge and is heavily influenced by a probation or parole officer's (PO) actions of filing a formal violation or initiating a revocation request. Thus, a significant amount of discretion resides with the PO. As they are often the sole person responsible for monitoring compliance with supervision conditions, POs have the opportunity throughout the course of supervision to go beyond merely preventing negative outcomes – they can also promote individuals' success. The behaviors and tactics used and the attitudes and values that influence them can have a profound impact.

Factors influencing PO discretion

How a PO handles violations or misconduct, particularly for people with mental illness, may be influenced by a couple of factors. First, a PO's internal protective instincts – paternalism or maternalism – may play a role in how they respond to noncompliance from those they supervise (see Skeem et al., 2011; Vandevelde et al., 2017). There is some evidence to suggest that this may be expressed in the form of more intensive monitoring and involvement (Eno Louden & Skeem, 2013; Eno Louden et al., 2008), perhaps to prevent worsening outcomes. However, increased monitoring can also increase detection of misconduct and, by default, the risk for violations and revocation (Matejkowski & Ostermann, 2015; Petersilia & Turner, 1990).

Additionally, a PO's orientation toward rehabilitation versus punishment may play a role in affecting outcomes for people on supervision. On one hand, POs may have a low tolerance for misconduct and adopt more controlling or punitive responses. On the other hand, a PO may support a therapeutic and rehabilitative approach that is more tolerant of missteps and noncompliant behavior, pursuing violations, jail, or revocation only when all other options have been exhausted (see Andretta et al., 2014). Somewhere in the middle is a delicate blend of care and control that is most effective for supervising people with and without mental illness (Paparozzi & Gendreau, 2005; Ricks & Eno Louden, 2015; Skeem & Manchak, 2008). This blend of a caring, trusting, and firm-but fair style has been referred to as the dual-role relationship (operationalized with the Dual-Role Relationship Inventory-Revised; DRI-R; Skeem et al., 2007). Dual-role relationships are the backdrop or foundation upon which PO-supervisee interactions and PO behavior is built, and they have been shown to relate to a variety of psychosocial and criminal-legal outcomes among general community correctional populations (Blasko et al., 2015; Kennealy et al., 2012; Mueller et al., 2022; Sloas et al., 2020) and among people with mental illness on community supervision (Epperson et al., 2017; Longmate et al., 2021; Manchak et al., 2014).

Effective practices in community supervision for people with mental illness

Beyond dual-role relationship quality, the research examining community supervision for people with mental illness has identified a number of useful and effective tactics that are particularly important for preventing supervision failure. Leveraging the expertise of POs, Eno Louden, Skeem, and colleagues conducted a series of studies that identified the importance of training POs in mental illness, supporting supervisees rather than confronting them, using problem-solving and positive pressures rather than threats or sanctions, and serving as part of the treatment team to facilitate better coordination of internal and external resources (Eno Louden et al., 2008, 2012; Skeem et al., 2006). This latter strategy is a hallmark skill of justice and mental health system boundary spanners – people who coordinate access to care, are able to break through the barriers of bureaucratic red tape, and advocate for the best interests of their clients (see Manchak et al., 2010, 2014; Munetz & Bonfine, 2015; Steadman, 1992). In a matched comparison study of people on traditional and specialty mental health probation, problem-solving, high-quality dual-role relationships, and boundary spanning (operationalized as knowledge, helpfulness or hands-on assistance, and general features like advocacy and care coordination) were associated with better supervision outcomes, including greater access to mental health and integrated dual diagnosis services, fewer formal violations despite more frequent incidents of violations (Manchak et al., 2014), and fewer arrests (Skeem et al., 2017).

Interestingly, the findings from studies of justice system-involved people with mental illness overlap quite a bit with the correctional rehabilitation literature (Bonta & Andrews, 2017) – more specifically, core correctional practices (Andrews & Carvell, 1998; Andrews & Kiessling, 1980; Dowden & Andrews, 2004). Although the research on core correctional practices may be more ubiquitous among criminal justice scholars, the two bodies of knowledge offer slightly different ways of thinking about supervision practices.

For example, both literatures identify problem-solving, relationship quality, and effective use of community resources. Whereas the CCP literature discusses effective use of authority as separate from relationship quality, the literature on justice-involved people with mental illness merges these concepts and operationalizes them together as firm-but-fair, caring, and trusting dual role relationships (Skeem et al., 2007) that avoid harsh, punitive, or otherwise authoritarian interaction styles. Similarly, whereas the CCP literature discusses the importance of effective use of community resources in a manner that emphasizes matching services to criminogenic needs and utilization of evidence-based practices, the specialty supervision literature uses the term "boundary spanning" to describe knowledge of mental illness and resources, coordination of internal and external resources, involvement in treatment, and advocacy (Manchak et al., 2014).

The current study builds upon these two branches of knowledge to provide POs with even more concrete guidance in implementing practices deemed helpful and effective for supervising people with mental illness. Specialty mental health caseloads are far more common today than they were when the research reviewed above was conducted, but very little new knowledge has been produced in this area relative to its growth. Although newer research that has been produced is consistent with prior findings (e.g., Van Deinse et al., 2021, 2021), the field can benefit from the expertise of individuals who have served in the role of a specialty mental health PO and a framing of best practice supervision strategies within the more widely known framework of Core Correctional Practices.

Furthermore, a recent trend in research advocates for the inclusion and value of lived experiences of people involved in the criminal-legal system and people with mental illness (Hawke et al., 2022; Tapsell et al., 2020; Visser et al., 2021). These experiences help researchers and practitioners humanize statistical findings and provide a more nuanced understanding of particular issues being studied. Consistent with this mentality, the present study leverages insights from those who know best about what specific actions, behaviors, and approaches support and promote the success of people with mental illness on community supervision. By centering the observations and experiences of specialty probation and parole officers and people with mental illness supervised on probation and parole, this study seeks to (1) describe the experiences of people with mental illness on community supervision, with a specific emphasis on their unique challenges and what they believe is needed for their supervision to be successful, and (2) identify prescriptive supervision behaviors and tactics that can help promote success for people with mental illness on supervision.

Method

This study utilized qualitative data collected from two unique independent projects, both of which were approved by [University of Cincinnati] Institutional Review Board. The first project, which took place in 2014, was a focus group study of probation and parole officers supervising mental health caseloads and treatment providers delivering court-ordered services to people on community supervision. This project's main focus was to understand how treatment and supervision professionals communicate and collaborate with one another, what challenges they face in doing so, and how improvements can be made to communication and collaboration to facilitate improved service delivery (and, ultimately, improved outcomes) for people with mental illness on community supervision. Although the primary results for this study are reported elsewhere (Manchak et al., 2023), many themes relevant to PO supervision practices emerged that have not yet been published until now.

The second project, which took place between 2018 and 2023, was a multi-site interview-based study of people on probation and parole that sought to better understand the differences in success – and reasons for these differences – between people with and without mental illness on community supervision. Individuals were recruited from community supervision agencies and correctional treatment facilities located in two states-one in the South and one in the Midwest.[1] Participant interviews were used to help contextualize the challenges that individuals with mental illness face when on community supervision and gauge their perceptions of what is helpful and harmful to their success.

Participants

POs

A total of 18 POs participated in one of four focus groups in the 2014 study. Each focus group was conducted with officers working in one of three different county agencies that neighbored one another within a large Midwest state. One county agency had two focus groups and was situated within a large urban area, whereas the other two focus groups were situated in areas that were a mix of suburban and rural locales. To be eligible to participate, all POs were required to supervise a specialized caseload of people with mental illness or co-occurring mental and substance use disorders. Although demographic information was not collected on the POs, they included both males and females with varying years of supervision experience.

People on probation

In total, 218 people on probation and parole participated in the interview-based study. Participants were categorized into two groups based on a conservative definition of mental illness, which was inferred from their answers to several interview questions. Those classified as having mental illness had a self-reported prior or current psychiatric diagnosis of schizophrenia or schizoaffective disorder, bipolar disorder, major depression, anxiety or panic disorder, or post-traumatic stress disorder *and* were either currently receiving treatment (medications or counseling) or experiencing symptoms. Using this criteria, 43% ($n = 93$) of the sample were identified as having mental illness, and only their responses were evaluated for this study. Their average age was 35.4 years old ($SD = 10.5$), and 34% ($n = 32$) were female. In terms of race, 82% ($n = 76$) identified as Caucasian, 5.4% ($n = 5$) as African American, 1% ($n = 1$) as American Indian or Alaskan Native, 1% ($n = 1$) as Asian or Pacific Islander, and 11% ($n = 10$) as biracial or multiracial. Additionally, 15% ($n = 14$) were of Hispanic or Latinx ethnicity. Among the 89 individuals who reported their diagnosis, the most commonly reported primary (i.e., most severe) diagnosis was major depressive disorder (48%; $n = 43$), followed by bipolar disorder (23.6%; $n = 21$), PTSD (12.4%; $n = 11$), anxiety or panic disorder (10%; $n = 9$), and schizophrenia or schizoaffective disorder (5.6%; $n = 5$). Many individuals self-reported multiple diagnoses, and almost all reported either problematic drinking or use of illicit drugs.

Measures

PO focus groups

All four focus groups with POs were conducted by a faculty member and doctoral student on-site in a conference room situated within each agency. As detailed by Manchak et al. (2023), the researchers met with POs who voluntarily agreed to participate on the day of the scheduled focus groups, went over the details of the study consent with all group members at once, and collected signed consent forms from each participant prior to beginning the focus groups. The focus groups were guided by an established set of questions (i.e., focus group guide) that were asked across all focus groups. As mentioned previously, the focus group prompts centered upon how community supervision officers communicate and collaborate with treatment providers who deliver services to individuals on probation or parole. During the course of these conversations, POs shared tactics and strategies that they have used to help various people with mental illness on their caseloads be successful. Their insights on these matters were centered in the current study. Each focus group lasted approximately two hours and was audio recorded for later transcription and analysis. Due to agency regulations, focus group participants could not be paid for their participation but were provided with refreshments during the focus group meeting. The results include quotes from POs across all four PO focus groups.

Participant interviews

The semi-structured interviews with people on community supervision focused on factors that contribute to challenges and successes individuals experience on parole and probation. During the course of an approximately 60- to 80-minute interview, individuals discussed family, work, mental health symptoms, substance use, and their experiences with supervision. The present study centers (a) the unique challenges experienced by people with mental illness on community supervision, and (b) their perceptions of what they need to be successful (and, conversely, what is harmful to their success).

Procedures

Because the data from focus groups and interviews were quite different with respect to the length of text and the narrowness (interviews) or breadth (focus groups) with which topics were discussed, and because the data from each group is meant to serve different purposes in the present study, the coding process was different for each data source. However, for both sets of data, at least two separate individuals with doctoral-level training were responsible for reviewing and coding the data into the categories described below. Further, both sets of data were coded using thematic analysis (TA; Braun & Clarke, 2006; Terry et al., 2017), which is flexible to a variety of qualitative data and qualitative coding goals.

PO focus groups

Processing and coding of the PO focus group data took place in two discrete phases. First, two independent researchers carefully reviewed all focus group transcriptions and listed to the audio-recordings for any mention of PO behaviors, attitudes, or actions that could be either helpful or harmful to the success of people with mental illness on community supervision. Any relevant quotes or information were then copied into an excel workbook and categorized into one of the four categories that were identified a priori to be typical ways a PO might engage with their clients (1) offering emotional/personal support (defined as demonstration of care, concern, connection, or show of emotion or empathy), (2) providing hands-on assistance (e.g., with applications, paperwork; defined as giving specific help in an active and engaged way), (3) setting and enforcing expectations and conditions (defined as what the PO holds people accountable for and why), and 4) day-to-day communication (defined as shared decision-making, information sharing, and general engagement) about general topics not covered in 1 through 3 above. Researchers were encouraged to note any additional possible ways by which POs might engage with their supervisees, but no new categories were identified.

Second, the two researchers met to review the qualitative data, iteratively develop and come to consensus on overarching themes that best reflected the context and content of the data, and identify exemplary quotations. PO behaviors and strategies were then categorized within a particular core correctional practice, retaining its prior designation in one of the four main mediums above, and corresponding exemplary quotes were selected to supplement these strategies.

Participant interviews

Because interviews were not coded or transcribed, coders reviewed the hand-written or typed responses and notes from the interviews originally administered and recorded by the study interviewers. Specifically, coders examined the answers to several questions about the interviewee's perceptions and experiences concerning their supervising officer: (1) Tell me a little bit about what an average probation appointment looks like. What happens? What do you talk about? (2) How does your PO usually treat you? (3) If you had to describe your PO what words would you use? (4) What happens when you slip up? Break the rules or misbehave? What does your PO typically do?[1]

Using Microsoft Excel to organize codes, answers to the questions above were first labeled as "helpful" or "harmful" based off of whether the actions promoted success, increased the risk of failure, or created more challenges or frustration for the person on probation. Determination of a tactic as harmful or helpful was informed by the connotation of the words used as well as any contextual information about the response that could be gleaned from the participant's answers to other related questions. Next, the behaviors were categorized into one of four domains defined above in which the PO might exert influence: (1) emotional/personal support (2) hands-on assistance, (3) expectations, and (4) communication. Finally, each behavior was earmarked as exemplifying one of three primary core correctional practices: dual role relationship quality (which blends effective use of authority and relationship quality), problem solving, and effective use of community resources.

---

[1] These questions were adapted from Skeem and colleagues' study of specialty mental health probation (Manchak et al., 2010, 2014; Skeem et al., 2017).

Finally, coders reviewed the full files for any supplemental notes elsewhere in the interview that were relevant to supervision and either reflected the challenges faced by those with mental illness or how POs managed these challenges or treated the individuals on supervision. All relevant information was coded and classified as above. The lead author reviewed the coding and categorization of all graduate-level coders and agreed with the designation of behaviors as harmful or helpful, which route of influence was being used, and which type of core correctional practice the behavior exemplified. Finally, the PI and one graduate student iteratively discussed all the responses and used TA to arrive at cohesive themes by which the results could be presented.

Results

As a reminder, our research aims for this study were to (1) describe the experiences of people with mental illness on community supervision, with a specific emphasis on their unique challenges and what they believe is needed for their supervision to be successful (predominantly informed by the participant interviews), and (2) provide prescriptive supervision behaviors and tactics that can help promote success for people with mental illness on supervision (predominantly informed by the PO focus groups).

Unique challenges facing people with mental illness on community supervision

The challenges faced by people with mental illness on community supervision were distilled across four primary themes.

First, ***they have complex needs that are not always due to mental illness but that may be made more challenging because of mental illness.*** Individuals on probation and parole discussed a wide variety of "normal" life challenges, such as the logistics of sharing custody of children, paying bills, and juggling work and home life. In addition to these everyday logistical responsibilities, many also encounter some of the collateral consequences of criminal legal system involvement, including transportation challenges due to loss of license or lack of vehicle, and inability to find adequate and stable employment. Such stressors are arguably challenging for any person, but these individuals also struggle with the symptoms of mental illness and, in some cases, addiction, which complicated matters substantially.

Day-to-day, the individuals interviewed had to manage or cope with their symptoms, which could make navigating other life stressors more difficult. Furthermore, and perhaps due to their psycho-emotional vulnerability, many individuals appeared to get overwhelmed by the combination of normal life stressors, expectations of supervision, and their mental state. One male with schizophrenia, for example, was distraught and frustrated because he lived 25 minutes from public transportation and over two-hour drive from the Veterans' Administration and kept incurring challenges with technology for virtual treatment appointments. This is just one example of many that demonstrates the variety of needs individuals with mental illness have. Indeed, one PO noted, "It is very difficult [group] to work with . . . these people are probably the most difficult people that we have all over the supervision."

Next, ***there is lack of knowledge about resources and skills to effectively navigate them.*** When discussing their experiences with the criminal-legal system and treatment, individuals with mental illness on supervision routinely identified personal challenges and frustration with accessing resources or engaging in activities that are required by supervision; at the same time, they demonstrated very little insight or awareness about what to do about these challenges. The lack of awareness of behavioral and logistical options was consistently evident across the interviews. One woman with depression and anxiety, for example, could not think of any way to pay for her fees except to continue in sex trade, as that was all she knew: "yeah- I don't have a job. I can't pay for everything . . . so I have to figure it out. So [I asked my PO] are you okay if I hook to pay for it?" In many cases, and as will be discussed below, individuals defer to and rely on their PO for exactly what to do or where to go, to handle the situation.

*Third, **individuals with mental illness on community supervision have little to no social support outside of their PO***. Both POs and those on supervision drew attention to the fact that the PO was often the only source of support in the individuals' lives. One PO noted, "These people have most of the time completely abandoned or been abandoned by their family because they've been nothing more than trouble their whole lives, constantly causing issues." Indeed, several people on supervision shared that they had no one to rely on for help with various life challenges and no one to turn to for the emotional and social support that many people typically get from family and friends. Another PO recounted, "Sometimes that's all they have for support . . . I have one client say, 'You're my only friend . . . you're my only support network. I don't have friends, I don't have family. You're it. If something in my life goes wrong, you're it.'"

Finally, ***community supervision makes everything that much harder***. When discussing what their average supervision appointment looks like, several participants shared how being on supervision only further complicates their already complicated and challenging lives. Beyond added expectations and requirements (testing, appointments, classes, treatment) that impact the lives of people on supervision, supervision appears to carry an emotional toll as well. Several individuals noted that they feel they are "under a microscope" and have little room to just be themselves, for fear of making some grave mistake. One woman with depression, anxiety, and PTSD said, "If you consider that there is 365 days a year . . . statistically, you might slip up . . . It's like a constant and you feel like you're being on the radar."

Factors supporting the success of people with mental illness on community supervision

Having described unique challenges facing people with mental illness on supervision, we next turn to insight from people on supervision about perceptions of what is needed to be successful on supervision – and, conversely, what is not helpful to success. Strategies and behaviors identified as helpful included being communicative, empathetic, firm-but fair, genuine, inspirational, nice, optimistic, polite, understanding, and reasonable, showing a rehabilitation focus, and demonstrating integrity. Unhelpful approaches are organized in Table 1 according to the domains by which POs can exert influence.

Apart from these descriptors, both POs and people on supervision discussed the need for supervision sessions that entail more than just a run-of-the-mill check in on supervision compliance. When describing the meetings with her PO, one woman with depression said, "They are kind of like a therapy session." Some POs did not view this type of time-intensive work as a positive and indicated concern that it would take too much out of their weekly

Table 1. Unhelpful PO supervision behaviors identified by people with mental illness on supervision.

	Descriptors	
Expectations	Hard-Headed	Out to Get Me
	Inconsistent	Straightforward*
	Matter-of-Fact*	Threatening
Emotional/Personal Support	Cold	Negative
	Demeaning	No Emotion
	Disrespectful	Preoccupied
	Distant	Rude
	Intimidating	Treats me Like a Number
	Lacks Empathy	
	Like a Robot	
Communication/Collaboration	Bitter	
	Bored	
	Busy	
	Just business/doing their job*	
Hands-On Assistance	Forgetful	
	Nonchalant	
	Unhelpful	
	Unthorough	

Note: Descriptors designated with an asterisk were discussed with a more neutral tone and emphasis than a negative one.

schedule. A PO in one focus group, for example, stated, "The needy factor is through the roof. You can sit with one or two people [and they] could take your entire week if you let them."

Several people on supervision discussed how helpful it is when a PO simply tries to get to know them. One male with depression, anxiety, and PTSD talked about how this took time but was well worth it: "At the beginning, my first PO treated me with a bit of a cold shoulder, but it's because she didn't know me. She had no reference of me. But she was gentle after that. Informative. She will definitely let me know about expectations she has for me." A woman with anxiety had a similar experience: "In the beginning she [PO] was a bit stand-offish. She treated me like someone on probation. After she saw that I was doing the right thing, like keeping my job, keeping my license current, following the rules, she kinda warmed up to me ... She treats me well." In contrast, lack of interest can be a particularly negative experience. One woman with depression on probation felt the impact of rejection: "She doesn't really want to deal with me. I can tell she has more important things to do."

Beyond building an acquaintance, the individuals on supervision drew attention to the importance of (1) investment in the relationship on the part of the PO: "He's really good. He sticks with me through the process. He just wants me to get better and succeed. He treats me good but is hard on me. He wants me to do better." (male with bipolar disorder); (2) attempts to better understand the experience of having mental illness and the challenges that accompany it: "I don't feel like she grasps the severity of my anxiety. She is supposed to be a mental health officer, but she doesn't seem to really care about my mental health ... I don't feel like she talks with me about problems" (female with major depressive disorder and anxiety); and (3) investment in helping the individual on supervision to be better and do better: "She [the PO] digs in a little about things. She has a list of things that can be improved. She shared it with me and asked what I would like to get out of probation (female with anxiety and opioid addiction) and "She is great; she makes sure she congratulates me on my sobriety milestone, talks about my treatment program and my upcoming move and upcoming new job." (male with bipolar disorder). In contrast one male with depression and anxiety demonstrated the downside to a lack of investment: "He talks to me like I am an idiot and a child. No respect whatsoever. Any question or concern I have for him, I am completely out of line for even asking him something."

Actions needed by POs to promote success of individuals with mental illness on community supervision

Consistent with the coding process, specific actions, behaviors, and approaches were classified across four domains: expectations, emotional and personal support, communication and collaboration, and hands-on assistance. Within each of these domains where POs can exert influence and support individuals' success, we identified specific strategies.

Expectations

Within the expectations domain, three primary themes emerged. First, it is important to ***set realistic expectations***. This theme came up across all four focus groups. POs talked about the importance of meeting people "where there are at" and avoiding imposing their own value system of right and wrong or notions of progress. When describing the importance of contextualizing probationers' success, one PO said, "they are doing better than they probably ever have," and another emphasized looking at more general indices of progress rather than some specific, finite goal: "Realize that there is a big picture there about how they haven't committed any offenses, how they haven't relapsed."

Across the focus group discussions, there was a theme of finding a balance between setting expectations that are too high for people to achieve and too low to promote successful outcomes. Several POs emphasized the importance of setting expectations that match the reality of what these individuals are experiencing and the complexity of problems that inhabit their lives. One PO stated, "by the time we get them, they usually have a pretty significant lifestyle behind them ... you can't expect those people to change in a couple weeks ... it's gonna take time ... they lived this way for 20 something years ... their old lifestyle is gonna come out for a while before they really start to change." Other POs discussed the value of seemingly simple accomplishments and incremental changes such as staying safe or reducing (but not necessarily stopping) drug use.

Second, POs need to ***be aware of and find a balance between enforcing rule adherence and meeting the individual's needs***. There are circumstances when an individual's needs may conflict with the expectation that they strictly abide by the rules of supervision. For example, one woman with schizoaffective disorder described how frustrating it was not to be able to see her sister and newborn baby niece who lived outside the county simply because she was not paying her fees. She felt like having this opportunity for personal connection and support would have otherwise been helpful to her, and her PO denied her this experience to instead enforce strict adherence to the rules. In contrast, a PO discussed the value of overlooking the fact that one woman on his caseload lived with her husband who used marijuana daily, because the woman was consistently testing clean and benefitted from the social support that her husband provided. Looking at these contrasting approaches, POs may wish to consider what is best for the individual for that particular moment in time.

Third, POs should ***empower individuals and foster their independence***. A final theme that emerged from coding of focus groups and interviews is the belief that POs need to set an expectation that the individuals they supervise be able to do things on their own. Acknowledging that individuals with mental illness rely on them in so many aspects of their lives, POs cautioned that this can lead to their failure if mechanisms are not in place to teach individuals to do things on their own and foster gradual independence. Indeed, one noted, "So it makes it harder for us to work with them and get them to continue on back to an independent life, because they have been so dependent, because they had this case manager right there by their side, in every step they were holding their hand." Similarly, another pointed out, "The problem is they [are] used to seeing the case manager every single day . . . being in groups four days a week . . . and they go from having this every day, all day to what they feel it's nothing. So it doesn't benefit them at all when you make them dependable on you." POs further suggested that it is important to teach individuals to advocate for themselves and their own care. One PO, for example, helped his supervisee recognize that he had the right to ask for a different treatment provider because the one he had was not "doing their job." Situations like this require POs not only to provide information but also to teach individuals how to do various tasks.

Emotional/Personal support

Across the focus groups, POs identified five specific strategies that fall within the realm of emotional and personal support that seem particularly helpful when supervising people with mental illness. First, ***offer encouragement and provide reinforcement***. "When they come into our offices, many times, nobody in their lives has told them that 'hey, I'm proud of you' or 'that's awesome, you doing great.'" Individuals with mental illness on community supervision have grown accustomed to people pointing out what they have done wrong, particularly when it comes to supervision. For many reasons, this is not only ineffective for shaping behavior, but it is also damaging to the relationship. Instead, encouragement and reinforcement for their efforts (even if they are not successful) can go a long way toward building the relationship and building the person's self-esteem. As one PO noted, "make sure that we give them enough incentives and praise rather than always try to knock them down."

Next, ***show genuine interest in their lives***. Showing a genuine interest in an individual's life makes them feel seen and heard. Routinely, POs already inquire about a whole host of factors at each appointment to monitor compliance and progress. Why not leverage these tactics to develop the relationship? Some strategies noted across interviews were remembering small details about their lives (i.e., asking about what their children are up to) and involving others in supporting the person on supervision. The key, however, is genuineness. This was a core theme that arose across the interviews with people on supervision.

Third, ***demonstrate grace***. Individuals with mental illness on supervision carry significant burdens and are often asked to do more with fewer resources. Several participants made clear during their interviews that they are well aware when they mess up and were disappointed in their own actions. As such, additional blaming or shaming from their PO was not viewed as necessary nor desired. Several participants expressed that they are trying their best, and POs can better support individuals with mental illness by showing patience, understanding, and providing them the room to make mistakes and learn from them.

Fourth, ***give the benefit of the doubt***. Several POs discussed examples of when they received conflicting information from the individual on supervision, his or her treatment providers or case managers, or when stories from their supervisees did not seem to add up. POs acknowledged that the default response is to distrust their supervisee and immediately react, typically with a punitive tone, but that this can be counterproductive. Indeed, one woman with depression, anxiety, and a history of prescription drug abuse described her interactions with her PO as "very uncomfortable [because] . . . I feel like everything I say he automatically assumes is a lie. I feel like I am having to prove myself." Instead, POs recognized the importance of trying to give the individual the benefit of the doubt and trust their story.

For example, one PO discussed a situation when a treatment agency was having difficulty with one of his male supervisees. The individual had also expressed to the PO that he was having frustrations with treatment. The PO's immediate response was to place blame on the individual until he visited the agency and observed their interactions for himself. He recounts, "I was just like 'ok maybe he is crazy' but then once they started calling me and I started seeing the dynamic of the relationship between him and them, I see why he complains all the time. So, I mean I kinda feel bad for him."

Finally, it is important for POs to ***set appropriate boundaries***. POs discussed how, perhaps because they are often their only source of support, individuals on probation require a lot from the PO, both logistically and emotionally. In fact, some POs discussed how individuals view them as friends but acknowledged that this was inappropriate. Just as it is beneficial to any relationship to have boundaries, it is important for POs to establish appropriate ones with those on their caseload as well to promote success during supervision. PO focus groups and participant interviews suggested that honesty and transparency about the limitations of both the relationship between officer and supervisee and the capacity of the PO to help with certain tasks or logistics can help to establish clear and healthy boundaries.

Communication

Two major themes arose from focus groups in the area of communication. First, it is important to ***provide information and resources to ensure success***. Both POs and those on supervision recognized the importance of communication in the form of having the PO provide the information and tools needed to be successful. Several POs shared the value of providing individuals on supervision with both verbal and written rules and regulations, so they know – and can reference on an ongoing basis – what is expected of them and precisely what will happen if they do not meet these expectations. Beyond this, however, people on supervision demonstrated a need to have their POs explain how things work – for example, what an assessment is and what treatment providers do with that information or how an individual can progress through phases of treatment. Participants also expressed a desire to have their POs provide information about options available to them for a wide variety of circumstances. For instance, one person on probation wanted to know if he could still get effective care without having to participate in a group treatment setting. Having his PO explain that there are other treatment approaches and options available to him gave him the tools to make an informed decision about his own care without having to compromise his mental health, as groups made him anxious.

The other major theme concerning communication is the importance ***of communicating concerns in a timely manner***. Several POs discussed the importance of communication between themselves, case managers, and treatment providers, particularly when it came to noticing concerning behavior or warning signs for negative outcomes like substance use, suicidality, and intentional noncompliance with the rules. POs recognized the value of this communication for early intervention and prevention of worsening outcomes. Some POs preferred a direct approach to communicating concerns about their supervisees. For example, one PO discussing communication with a case manager said, "I wanna know everything ... Tell me what is going on." Other POs get information from their supervisees more indirectly, vis-à-vis attending or observing treatment sessions. For example, one PO noted, "We will make additional visits there to talk to them face to face to get everything that's going on and then we can pull the probationer aside and talk to them face to face as well. See what kind of story they tell us based on what their case manager is telling us there. So we can address the issue as soon as possible." Similarly, another said, "Other weeks, I'm sitting in groups with them. It helps to see how they are responding to the stuff in group and then hear from their case manager or from the security guys. You get a whole picture to see how they are doing in there."

Hands-on assistance

In the domain of hands-on assistance, three primary themes emerged. First, it is important for POs to actively work to ***remove barriers to success***. Across participant interviews, people identified seemingly small challenges that get in the way of even their attempt to be successful. Some examples recounted by people on supervision included a bus that never arrived, leading the individual to miss her treatment assessment; not having minutes available on a cell phone, which meant the person was unable to check in with their PO; loss of insurance coverage, leading to the treatment agency declining services; and being mugged and losing an ID which was required for work. In another example, a PO recounted a situation where a supervisee struggled severely after being placed on psychiatric medication that caused them significant weight gain, which worsened their depression. Despite the person wanting to find a provider that would appropriately adjust their medication, they were unable to do so until their health insurance became active. As noted above, because people with mental illness often lack the knowledge and the tools to navigate these challenges, it would be beneficial for the PO to use these opportunities to develop problem-solving skills and teach the individual what they need to know to assist themselves in the future. In some cases, the PO may need to step in and remove the barriers themselves.

Tasks that lie outside the purview of the PO may require that the PO solicit the help of other professionals. To ensure that the person with mental illness is not only getting the services they need but also care that is effective, high quality and appropriate, POs must go beyond asking for outside help or securing a referral. They must ***advocate for the person on supervision***. This requires POs to be well-informed about what is happening with each person, as well as well-informed about what resources are available to best meet the needs of that person. One topic consistently discussed among the POs was making sure that people are stable on their psychiatric medications, particularly when going in and coming out of jail. POs discussed how they had to be aware of what changes in medications occurred while the individual was incarcerated, as well as be ready and proactive in making sure the individual was stabilized immediately upon release. This type of communication with other agencies, in which POs check in on a supervisee's progress or status, can promote their well-being and success during supervision.

Finally, it is important for POs to actively ***partner with treatment to provide continuity and consistency***. One supervision strategy that was discussed at length, in large part because it was the central topic of the focus groups, was the importance of developing a true partnership with other professionals involved in the care of the individuals with mental illness on supervision. If the partnership is not there, it can be detrimental to the success of the person on supervision. One PO pointedly identified the crux of the problem, "I mean if they are getting mixed signals from what we expect and what they expect, they're gonna get confused and give up. So it's important for all of us to be on the same page so they have a straight understanding."

POs emphasized the importance of several strategies to foster this partnership. First, shared decision-making and being on the same page with treatment providers is important. POs also identified the value of frequent communication, which allows for early identification of potential problems and proactive intervention before something more serious happens. One PO noted, "It helps when we have a better communication and when there is an issue or something going wrong we can deal with it a lot quicker than finding out a week or two later." Additionally, POs discuss the benefits of being in the same room together when engaging with people on supervision, as it shows a united front, provides consistency in messaging, and supports continuity of care.

Finally, having a good understanding of what is happening in treatment, what the treatment goals are, and what the "language" of treatment is can be incredibly helpful. One PO shared how being actively involved with treatment by observing groups helped him with one particular case. He said, "So you can go, 'I noticed you're in there and this is something that is going on with you, where are you at with that now? I think it really helps ... I'm like, "How's this going on?" and they are like, "How do you know that?" Because I've been watching you and keeping track of what's going on with you while you're there so we can just jump right into it. It helps to have that collaboration. You know what they are doing over there you can keep that going when they get out. It's a huge help." When POs take the initiative to learn about the treatment side of things, they have more tools in their toolkit to promote the success of people on supervision.

Discussion

Using rich narratives from focus groups of specialized mental health probation officers and, separately, elaborated responses from semi-structured interviews with people on community supervision who have mental illness, this study offers a detailed, nuanced, and personalized understanding of what it is like for individuals with mental illness on community supervision and how POs can best interact with them to promote their success.

In describing their experiences with POs and community supervision, the individuals interviewed discussed the challenges that they faced on a day-to-day basis that were compounded by their mental illness, a lack of knowledge about their supervision and how to navigate it, and many indicated that they had little or no social support outside of their supervision. At the same time, a common theme discussed was the toll that community supervision took on these individuals, requiring a great deal of time, effort, and organization to stay on top of conditions and a constant concern that they would "slip up." These findings speak to the logistical, emotional, and mental burden that community supervision can place on any person on community supervision and especially for those with mental illness. Participants also detailed the aspects of their supervision that were helpful or harmful to their success, indicating the importance of having a PO that is genuinely interested in their lives and their success, and willing to assist with problems that arise. Interestingly, having a PO that was willing to consider and learn about mental illness was also identified as valuable to their success.

Further, this study incorporated the experience and expertise of community supervision officers to inform effective practices and strategies. A number of specific behaviors and tactics are recommended across four domains with which POs can influence outcomes: through the expectations they set, how they provide personal and emotional support, how they communicate, and what they tangibly do to assist individuals on supervision in a hands-on manner. In organizing these behaviors and activities into the framework of core correctional practices (see Table 2), the study helps practitioners to see the varying ways they can exert influence within a framework with which they are likely familiar.

The study's main limitation is that it includes the experiences of POs and people on supervision in only two primary geographical jurisdictions and to a limited number of community supervision agencies within those jurisdictions. Probation and parole are organized and administered in different ways throughout the United States (and other countries). Thus, this study does not capture the diversity of experiences of either POs or people on community supervision with mental illness. Still, this study elevates the lived experience of the very groups who are likely to know most about the topics discussed, and it provides an impetus for other scholars to similarly investigate supervision strategies that can promote and hinder success of people with mental illness on community supervision.

The strategies and tactics identified in the present study complement and add to both the core correctional practices literature and the literature on specialized supervision for people

Table 2. Effective supervision strategies identified by POs across core correctional practices.

	Relationship Quality/Effective Use of Authority	Problem Solving	Effective Use of Community Resources
Expectations	X	X	
Set realistic expectations	X		
Balance individual needs and rules	X		
Empower/foster independence			
Emotional/Personal Support	X		
Encouragement/Reinforcement	X		
Show genuine interest	X		
Set appropriate boundaries	X		
Demonstrate grace	X		
Give benefit of the doubt			
Communication/Collaboration	X	X	
Provide information and resources	X	X	
Communicate concerns in a timely manner			
Hands-On Assistance	X	X	X
Remove barriers	X	X	X
Advocate		X	X
Collaborate/Team up			

with mental illness. Our findings underscore the importance of the core correctional practices of relationship quality and effective use of authority and reinforces the construct of high-quality dual role relationships (e.g., a firm-but fair interaction style and approach, genuine care and concern, and trust). Additionally, the findings also highlight the utility of effective use of community resources, but demonstrate that this is maximized when officers have specialized knowledge about mental illness, an ability to partner with mental health treatment providers, and a willingness to advocate for the person on supervision to ensure they receive the best care possible – akin to what has been discussed among mental health-justice system scholars as boundary spanning (Manchak et al., 2010, 2014; Munetz & Bonfine, 2015; Steadman, 1992). Finally, the findings demonstrate the unique domains in which people with mental illness require help and the unique problem-solving strategies that can be deployed to maximize their success and minimize their risk of failure.

The study findings offer more specific, concrete, behavioral tactics and strategies POs can use to engage with individuals who have mental illness, in order to promote their success. Additionally, the way with which the data were coded and the findings were organized also helps demonstrate that POs can exert their influence on their supervisees in different domains of interaction, and that these strategies can be adapted and combined across different types of interactions and situations. The findings in this study help to expand the operationalization of previously identified promising and evidence-based strategies for supervising people with mental illness. For example, POs wishing to build better dual role relationships with those they supervise now have some ideas about how to demonstrate care and concern while still being firm-but fair. Similarly, the study offers some ideas about what it takes and means to make effective use of community resources (a core correctional practice) when working with someone who has mental illness. In essence, the study offers POs more tools for their toolkit and demonstrates these tools can be used in different ways for different tasks, to best meet the needs at hand.

Together, the findings from these two studies help to shine a light on the unique and complex challenges that face people with mental illness face on community supervision, and they underscore the importance of centering the individual and their best interests to help promote their success. To help someone who has complex needs navigate one of the most difficult experiences of their lives is both a privilege and a challenge. The responsibility of supervising those with serious mental illness is challenging, and POs need to be supported through specialized training and access to resources necessary to achieve success in managing this population.

Note

1. Participants from the Midwest were on supervision in the same counties as where the PO sample was drawn for the focus group study. However, it is not likely the POs from that study were the same ones responsible for the supervision of those on probation or parole, given the different periods in which data were collected.

Acknowledgments

The authors would like to thank the many undergraduate and graduate student research assistants who helped with data collection and transcription on these two studies.

Disclosure statement

No potential conflict of interest was reported by the author(s).

Funding

The work was supported by the American Psychology-Law Society University of Cincinnati College of Education Criminal Justice and Human Services Faculty-Student Mentoring Grant; Early Career Professional Grant-in-Aid from the American Psychology-Law Society (Division 41 of APA).

ORCID

Sarah M. Manchak http://orcid.org/0000-0002-4703-4107
Jessica Warner http://orcid.org/0000-0001-9679-5239

References

Andretta, J. R., Odom, T., Barksdale, F., Barnes, M. E., Ramirez, A. M., & Woodland, M. H. (2014). An examination of management strategies and attitudes among probation officers. *Journal of Forensic Social Work*, *4*(2), 150–166. https://doi.org/10.1080/1936928X.2014.958644

Andrews, D. A., & Carvell, C. (1998). *Core correctional training–core correctional supervision and counseling: Theory, research, assessment and practice.* (Unpublished training manual). Carleton University,

Andrews, D. A., & Kiessling, J. J. (1980). Program structure and effective correctional practices: A summary of the CaVic research. In R. R. Ross & P. Gendreau (Eds.), *Effective correctional treatment* (pp. 441–463). Butterworths.

Baillargeon, J., Williams, B. A., Mellow, J., Harzke, A. J., Hoge, S. K., Baillargeon, G., & Greifinger, R. B. (2009). Parole revocation among prison inmates with psychiatric and substance use disorders. *Psychiatric Services*, *60*(11), 1516–1521. https://doi.org/10.1176/ps.2009.60.11.1516

Blasko, B. L., Friedmann, P. D., Rhodes, A. G., & Taxman, F. S. (2015). The parolee–parole officer relationship as a mediator of criminal justice outcomes. *Criminal Justice and Behavior*, *42*(7), 722–740. https://doi.org/10.1177/0093854814562642

Bonta, J., & Andrews, D. A. (2017). *The psychology of criminal conduct* (6th ed.). Routledge, Taylor & Francis Group.

Braun, V., & Clarke, V. (2006). Using thematic analysis in psychology. *Qualitative Research in Psychology*, *3*(2), 77. https://doi.org/10.1191/1478088706qp063oa

Cloyes, K. G., Wong, B., Latimer, S., & Abarca, J. (2010). Time to prison return for offenders with serious mental illness released from prison: A survival analysis. *Criminal Justice and Behavior*, *37* (2), 175–187. https://doi.org/10.1177/0093854809354370

Dowden, C., & Andrews, D. A. (2004). The importance of staff practice in delivering effective correctional treatment: A meta-analytic review of core correctional practice. *International Journal of Offender Therapy and Comparative Criminology*, *48*(2), 203–214. https://doi.org/10.1177/0306624X03257765

Eno Louden, J., & Skeem, J. L. (2013). How do probation officers assess and manage recidivism and violence risk for probationers with mental disorder? An experimental investigation. *Law and Human Behavior*, *37*(1), 22–34. https://doi.org/10.1037/h0093991

Eno Louden, J., Skeem, J. L., Camp, J., & Christensen, E. (2008). Supervising probationers with mental disorder: How do agencies respond to violations? *Criminal Justice and Behavior*, *35*(7), 832–847. https://doi.org/10.1177/0093854808319042

Eno Louden, J., Skeem, J. L., Camp, J., Vidal, S., & Peterson, J. (2012). Supervision practices in specialty mental health probation: What happens in officer–probationer meetings? *Law and Human Behavior*, *36*(2), 109–119. https://doi.org/10.1037/h0093961

Epperson, M. W., Thompson, J. G., Lurigio, A. J., & Kim, S. (2017). Unpacking the relationship between probationers with serious mental illnesses and probation officers: A mixed-methods examination. *Journal of Offender Rehabilitation, 56*(3), 188–216. https://doi.org/10.1080/10509674.2017.1290005

Hawke, L. D., Sheikhan, N. Y., Jones, N., Slade, M., Soklaridis, S., Wells, S., & Castle, D. (2022). Embedding lived experience into mental health academic research organizations: Critical reflections. *Health Expectations: An International Journal of Public Participation in Health Care & Health Policy, 25*(5), 2299–2305. https://doi.org/10.1111/hex.13586

Kennealy, P. J., Skeem, J. L., Manchak, S. M., & Eno Louden, J. (2012). Firm, fair, and caring officer-offender relationships protect against supervision failure. *Law and Human Behavior, 36* (6), 496–505. https://doi.org/10.1037/h0093935

Longmate, C., Lowder, E., Givens, A., Van Deinse, T. B., Ghezzi, M., Burgin, S., & Cuddeback, G. S. (2021). Social support among people with mental illnesses on probation. *Psychiatric Rehabilitation Journal, 44*(1), 70–76. https://doi.org/10.1037/prj0000428

Manchak, S. M., Skeem, J. L., Kennealy, P. J., & Eno Louden, J. (2014). High-fidelity specialty mental health probation improves officer practices, treatment access, and rule compliance. *Law and Human Behavior, 38*(5), 450–461. https://doi.org/10.1037/lhb0000076

Manchak, S. M., Skeem, J. L., & Vidal, S. (2010, March). *Boundary spanning: Assessing skills in bridging systems for offenders with mental disorder*. Paper presented at the American Psychology-Law Society (AP-LS) annual conference, Vancouver, British Columbia, Canada.

Manchak, S. M., Warner, J., Farringer, A. J., Pate, S., & Anderson, V. R. (2023). Building effective interpersonal collaborations between probation and behavioral health practitioners. *Psychological Services, Online First*. https://doi.org/10.1037/ser0000813

Matejkowski, J., & Ostermann, M. (2015). Serious mental illness, criminal risk, parole supervision, and recidivism: Testing of conditional effects. *Law and Human Behavior, 39*(1), 75–86. https://doi.org/10.1037/lhb0000094

Mueller, K. C., Noh, K., & Carey, M. T. (2022). The impact of fair relationships on rule compliance for women under community supervision. *Women and Criminal Justice, 32*(4), 342–358. https://doi.org/10.1080/08974454.2021.1900992

Munetz, M. R., & Bonfine, N. (2015). From boundary spanning to deep partnerships. *Psychiatric Services, 66*(9), 901–901. https://doi.org/10.1176/appi.ps.660902

Paparozzi, M. A., & Gendreau, P. (2005). An intensive supervision program that worked: Service delivery, professional orientation, and organizational supportiveness. *The Prison Journal, 85*(4), 445–466. https://doi.org/10.1177/0032885505281529

Petersilia, J., & Turner, S. (1990). Comparing intensive and regular supervision for high-risk probationers: Early results from an experiment in California. *Crime and Delinquency, 36*(1), 87–111. https://doi.org/10.1177/0011128790036001007

Porporino, F. J., & Motiuk, L. L. (1995). The prison careers of mentally disordered offenders. *International Journal of Law and Psychiatry, 18*(1), 29–44. https://doi.org/10.1016/0160-2527(94)00025-5

Ricks, E. P., & Eno Louden, J. (2015). The relationship between officer orientation and supervision strategies in community corrections. *Law and Human Behavior, 39*(2), 130–141. https://doi.org/10.1037/lhb0000098

Skeem, J. L., Emke-Francis, P., & Louden, J. E. (2006). Probation, mental health, and mandated treatment: A national survey. *Criminal Justice and Behavior, 33*(2), 158–184. https://doi.org/10.1177/0093854805284420

Skeem, J. L., Louden, J. E., Polaschek, D., & Camp, J. (2007). Assessing relationship quality in mandated community treatment: Blending care with control. *Psychological Assessment, 19*(4), 397–410. https://doi.org/10.1037/1040-3590.19.4.397

Skeem, J. L., & Manchak, S. (2008). Back to the future: From Klockars' model of effective supervision to evidence-based practice in probation. *Journal of Offender Rehabilitation, 47*(3), 220–247. https://doi.org/10.1080/10509670802134069

Skeem, J. L., Manchak, S., & Montoya, L. (2017). Comparing public safety outcomes for traditional probation vs specialty mental health probation. *JAMA Psychiatry, 74*(9), 942–948. https://doi.org/10.1001/jamapsychiatry.2017.1384

Skeem, J. L., Manchak, S., & Peterson, J. K. (2011). Correctional policy for offenders with mental illness: Creating a new paradigm for recidivism reduction. *Law and Human Behavior, 35*(2), 110–126. https://doi.org/10.1007/s10979-010-9223-7

Sloas, L., Lerch, J., Walters, S., & Taxman, F. S. (2020). Individual-level predictors of the working relationship between probation officers and probationers. *The Prison Journal, 100*(6), 709–725. https://doi.org/10.1177/0032885520968242

Solomon, P., Draine, J., & Marcus, S. C. (2002). Predicting incarceration of clients of a psychiatric probation and parole service. *Psychiatric Services, 53*(1), 50–56. https://doi.org/10.1176/appi.ps.53.1.50

Steadman, H. J. (1992). Boundary spanners: A key component for the effective interactions of the justice and mental health systems. *Law and Human Behavior, 16*(1), 75–87. https://doi.org/10.1007/BF02351050

Tapsell, A., Martin, K. M., Moxham, L., Burns, S., Perlman, D., & Patterson, C. (2020). Expert by experience involvement in mental health research: Developing a wellbeing brochure for people with lived experiences of mental illness. *Issues in Mental Health Nursing, 41*(3), 194–200. https://doi.org/10.1080/01612840.2019.1663566

Terry, G., Hayfield, N., Clarke, V., & Braun, V. (2017). Thematic analysis. In C. Willig & W. S. Rogers (Eds.), *The SAGE handbook of qualitative research in psychology* (pp. 17–36). Sage.

Van Deinse, T. B., Crable, E. L., Dunn, C., Weis, J., & Cuddeback, G. (2021). Probation officers' and supervisors' perspectives on critical resources for implementing specialty mental health probation. *Administration and Policy in Mental Health and Mental Health Services Research, 48*(3), 408–419. https://doi.org/10.1007/s10488-020-01081-8

Van Deinse, T. B., Givens, A., Cowell, M., Ghezzi, M., Murray-Lichtman, A., & Cuddeback, G. S. (2021). A randomized trial of specialty mental health probation: Measuring implementation and effectiveness outcomes. *Administration and Policy in Mental Health and Mental Health Services Research, 49*(3), 1–14. https://doi.org/10.1007/s10488-021-01172-0

Vandevelde, S., Vander Laenen, F., Van Damme, L., Vanderplasschen, W., Audenaert, K., Broekaert, E., & Vander Beken, T. (2017). Dilemmas in applying strengths-based approaches in working with offenders with mental illness: A critical multidisciplinary review. *Aggression and Violent Behavior, 32*, 71–79. https://doi.org/10.1016/j.avb.2016.11.008

Visser, R., Barber, A. X. A., Wheatcroft, S., Mullen, P., & Armes, J. (2021). Collaboration with people with lived experience of prison: Reflections on researching cancer care in custodial settings. *Research Involvement and Engagement, 7*(1), 1–48. https://doi.org/10.1186/s40900-021-00284-z

Improving Probation Outcomes for Emerging Adults: An Experiment Evaluating a Specialized Caseload in Texas

Kendra J. Clark, Jennifer Lerch, Faustino Lopez, and Faye S. Taxman

Abstract

Emerging adults present an array of developmental needs that community supervision agencies should address to improve outcomes including impulsivity, inability to regulate emotions, and being less likely to consider future consequences of their behavior. This study used a randomized controlled trial (RCT) to evaluate the Hidalgo County Emerging Adult Strategy (HCEAS)fja specialized caseload for emerging adults using principles of goal setting, incentives, and identity and relationship formation. This study examines how HCEAS influences progress on stability measures and probation outcomes, and how stability measure progress affects probation success. Analyses showed that HCEAS was effective in increasing either within- or between-group progress for every stability measure except education. HCEAS decreased outcomes such as arrests, motions to revoke, and failures to appear for probation office visits. These outcomes suggest that an age-specific focus on stability factors is feasible during supervision and likely to result in improved outcomes.

Emerging adults (EAs), or those ages 18 to 24, are a unique subpopulation that present specific challenges for corrections and community supervision. Not only is this age group one of the highest risks for undesired behavioral and legal system outcomes (Baltodano et al., 2005; Hartwell et al., 2010; Sweeten et al., 2013), they also have specific developmental and social needs that are different from other age groups (Arnett, 2000; Bernard et al., 2020; The Council of State Governments Justice Center, 2015; National Registry of Evidence-Based Programs and Practices NREPP, 2016; Zajac et al., 2013). Emerging adults have higher levels of instability and impulsivity, as well as poorer rationalization and moral judgments due to their developing brains (Berlin et al., 2010; Nader, 2019). This stage of brain development positions this subpopulation to be at a disadvantage for a "supervision as usual" (SAU) probation program. In traditional supervision, individuals typically meet with officers monthly where they check in and occasionally get referred to services. Programming is less cohesive and consistent making it more difficult for individuals to work toward long-term goals, gain structure in their lives, and be held accountable and motivated for their path forward. Satisfying these conditions may be challenging for the emerging adult age group that is characterized for their high impulsivity, underdeveloped decision-making skills, and instability in adult roles. Therefore, this population may benefit from probation practices that assist in identifying future goals, viewing their prospects in a positive light, and receiving reinforcement for achieving positive goals. One challenge is to determine what supervision strategies can improve outcomes for unique populations, such as EA.

The current study used a randomized controlled trial (RCT) design to test the efficacy of the Hidalgo County Emerging Adult Strategy (HCEAS) which was exclusively implemented among the EA aged individuals on probation. By comparing individuals who participated in the HCEAS and those who did not on a series of stability measures and probation outcomes, this study seeks to examine an EA program in terms of its impact on addressing the unique needs of the EA population to improve probation outcomes compared to SAU.

Probation in the United States

In 2020, nearly 3.9 million individuals in the United States were under community supervision with roughly 79% on probation (Kaeble, 2021). Of the 1.4 million people who exited probation in 2020, over 53% did not successfully complete their sentence and nearly 10% of their probation periods ended with incarceration (Kaeble, 2021). Although probation intends to increase public safety while optimizing the return on investment (i.e., divert people from incarceration), the size of the supervision population has undermined agencies abilities to effectively work toward these goals (Horowitz et al., 2018).

Emerging adults—developmental and social needs

The criminal legal system implemented juvenile courts over a 100 years ago due to the consensus that young people were fundamentally different than adults in terms of neurological and social development. Historically, 18 years has been used as the cut-off age for who is considered a juvenile; however, this relatively arbitrary cutoff age is old and outdated (Schiraldi et al., 2015). Recent studies have discovered that brain development in the areas that influence social skills is not complete until well into the 20s (Howell et al., 2013; Konrad et al., 2013), despite the social expectations to take on adult roles and responsibilities at age 18. EA brains have mature limbic and rewards systems, but not fully developed prefrontal control systems. This combination makes this age group highly emotionally reactive, sensitive to rewards and punishments, and inclined to risky behaviors (Konrad et al., 2013).

Individuals ages 18 to 24 present an array of developmental needs that community supervision agencies should be aware of and address including impulsivity, the inability to regulate emotions, and being less likely to consider future consequences of their behavior (Carson & Golinelli, 2013; Schiraldi et al., 2015). These unique needs make this population especially vulnerable to legal system involvement and recidivism and should be intentionally considered in the way the legal system responds to EA on supervision as suggested by the responsivity principle of the Risk-Need-Responsivity model (Andrews & Bonta, 2010). In 2005, nearly 18% of those released from prison were aged 18 to 24, of which 78% were reported having been rearrested within 3 years (Durose et al., 2014). SAU may be particularly poorly suited to address the needs of this population.

Emerging adulthood is considered a distinct stage that occurs between adolescence and adulthood and is characterized as having a high degree of instability (Arnett, 2000). Cognitive and social development theories for the 18 to 28-year-old individual recognize that the brain is not fully developed until close to 30 years old for males, which means adulthood cognitive skills such as thinking, reasoning, and moral judgment are lacking (Steinberg, 2007). Besides neurobiological hinderances, this developmental period of adulthood has social deficits. The changing context of young adults' lives means they tend to be less involved in normative social institutions (Berlin et al., 2010) and may lack preparation to be independent. Gaining and maintaining stability is areas of housing, employment, education, and pro-social relationships and leisure time activities can be particularly challenging for this population. These areas of stability are not only expected of individuals at this stage of the lifecourse, but they are essential for avoiding involvement in the legal system. Lack of stability in these areas also increases the chances of recidivism for those who have already encountered the sytem. For persons involved in the legal system, the emerging adult period may exacerbate the causes and consequences of offending behavior through anxieties and frustrations with life events and choices (Mulvey et al., 2004; Schiraldi et al., 2015; Sheidow et al., 2016; Steinberg, 2007).

Probation services should address the developmental and age-related processes that may influence one's success or failure on supervision (Schiraldi et al., 2015). At every stage of intervention, the focus should be placed on keeping EA in the community. The impulsivity and inability to anticipate consequences of risky behaviors that characterize this population makes them especially vulnerable to being derailed on their path toward a prosocial lifestyle. Any removal from the community undermines their development and impedes their ability to maintain and gain prosocial relationships and involvement in social institutions necessary for stability during the transition to adulthood (e.g., education, housing, employment (Schiraldi et al., 2015);). Placing stringent demands on a subpopulation that is developmentally unequipped to be independent and often lack stability may not be the most effective use of time and resources. Instead, addressing the unique needs of EA in a way that accounts for their developmental stages, such as increasing their stability in key areas of life such as employment, housing, and relationships, may improve outcomes and cost efficiency of probation. This age group struggles with impulse control, emotional self-regulation, interpreting the intentions of others which are all qualities that will hinder the successful transition into adult roles and responsibilities. To successfully prepare EA for adulthood – especially those who have become involved in the legal system – correctional programming should focus on increasing programming targeting social and technical skills that will increase the stability in this populations lives and improve their ability to sustain life independent of the legal system (Byrne, 2020; Chung et al., 2005).

Hidalgo County Emerging Adult Strategy (HCEAS) program overview

Hidalgo County Community Supervision and Corrections Department (CSCD) is the sixth largest probation agency in Texas with roughly 11,000 individuals supervised under community supervision for misdemeanor and felony offenses (F. Lopez, personal communication, May 5, 2022). Failure in probation is often gauged by revocation rates, meaning the rate at which people on probation violate conditions of probation and acquire a new case.[1] In 2015, 21% of all individuals and 46% of 18–25 years old on probation in Hidalgo County were revoked according to the data Faustino Lopez, the then Assistant Director (now Director), communicated to us during the conception of this study (F. Lopez, personal communication, 2016). Other outcomes that are used to signal progress on probation include failure to appear, motions to revoke, arrests, and absconding as each may provide insight into whether or not an individual is desisting (National Academies of Sciences, Engineering, 2022; Rocque, 2021). With a focus on desistance rather than recidivism alone, improvements in each of these outcomes would indicate a positive program effect. The Hidalgo County Emerging Adult Strategy (HCEAS) program was implemented to improve probation outcomes of EA.

Adopting principles from the Risk-Need-Responsivity (RNR) model, the HCEAS targets the unique needs of EA with an emphasis on helping the EA to identify future goals, view their prospects in a positive light, and be reinforced for achieving positive goals. After assessing the needs of the EA population, Hidalgo County created the HCEAS program as a responsive approach to address these unique needs as empirically supported by the RNR framework (Andrews & Bonta, 2010). The program began in April 2017 in Hidalgo County, Texas and aims to help EA probationers see themselves as an asset to their community by increasing their stability in adult roles and responsibilities and recognizing opportunities for change. To accomplish these goals, the project involved creating an infrastructure to support EA and to target key issues such as impulsivity, reduced emotional control, and difficulties in assessing consequences of one's behavior. To improve these developmental challenges, individuals will be better able to see the value in goal setting and goal-based activities, imagine themselves successfully filling stable adult roles, and understand the association between their own behaviors and outcomes. Individuals under supervision should be better equipped to achieve and maintain stability in key areas of adulthood such as employment, housing, educaitons, and relationships.

Program components

The case management and supervision plans focused on stages emphasized in the theory of emerging adulthood (Arnett, 2000, 2014), specifically: 1) identity exploration, 2) becoming self-focus, 3) addressing instability, 4) identifying future possibilities, 5) feeling in-between adolescence and adulthood (Arnett, 2000), and 6) incentivizing positive behavior (Sheidow et al., 2016). Issues related to *instability* were addressed by stabilizing the individual needs pertaining to any Texas Risk Assessment System (TRAS) identified as high risk/high need areas such as housing, employment, or substance abuse. Officers worked to establish a stable and prosocial residence for the individual on supervision, and address plans and goals for financial stability and independence. Second, issues surrounding *self-focus* were addressed through the use of cognitive behavioral therapy (CBT) programming, especially related to criminal thinking, criminogenic peer associations, and substance abuse disorders. The third component, *feeling in-between*, focused on the EA establishing independence and autonomy. While independence might be challenging since the EA are under the authority of the Hidalgo County Adult Probation (HCAP), the case management process is for the officer, social support actor, and other resource partners to be involved in helping the individual transition. Fourth, the officer assisted with identifying and facilitating *possibilities* for the EA's future. This case management element was linked with resource brokering to education and employment services, while overcoming obstacles such as criminal peer associations and substance use. The last element of EA principles is *identity exploration*. Identity exploration occurs simultaneously with addressing feeling in-between adolescence and adulthood and developing possibilities. To address this, the officer assisted the participant in realizing and actualizing the varied adult roles he or she might assume. For EAs, it is common to float between phases three and four, and officers were trained to recognize relapse events and address these struggles with reassessment, goal setting, and incentives.

Important to all of these program components was the relationship that the officers were able to build with the individual on probation. Research suggests that building a positive working relationship between the probation officer and the individual under supervision can lead to more successful probation outcomes (Blasko et al., 2015; Cherkos et al., 2008; Morash et al., 2015). For instance, Morash et al. (2015) found that supportive probation officers promoted more positive self-efficacy to avoid future crime and lower anxiety, while punitive officers had the opposite effect on women during supervision. This demonstrates the potential importance of the HCEAS officers' ability to support these EAs and be responsive to their specific needs.

Incentives and sanctions

The program uses graduated incentives and sanctions to emerging adults on probation as an alternative to using revocations. Study participants in the treatment arm received incentives for progressing through the HCEAS program and the conditions of their probation. Incentives were given to participants for completing required outpatient treatment, cognitive behavioral therapy programs, recovery support services, and journal entries. Incentives included reduction in probation fees, gift cards for restaurants and Lyft, and GED testing reimbursement. Sanctions were applied for positive or missed urine analyses (UA), failing to appear for court, treatment, or office visits, getting arrested, or violating curfew. Sanctions included verbal admonishments, small amounts of jail time, house arrest/curfews, and removal from the program.[2]

Recruitment and eligibility

Individuals sentenced to Hidalgo County CSCD are assessed using the Texas Risk Assessment System (TRAS (Lovins et al., 2018);). Their TRAS score is evaluated by the intake unit to determine if the individual meets eligibility criteria for the HCEAS program. Eligibility criteria include: 1) moderate to high risk on the TRAS score, 2) 18–25 years of age; 3) probation sentence of 12+ months, 4) not on a mental health caseload, and 5) no sex-related offenses.[3] HCEAS treats moderate and high-risk individuals with the same programming dose, just as SAU in Hidalgo County. More aligned with the RNR principles, the low-risk individuals receive lower dosing of programming and requirements (Andrews & Bonta, 2010). If an individual is eligible, they are introduced to the program and given the opportunity to voluntarily participate or not. Should they decide to participate, the program is added as a condition of supervision.

Officer training

HCEAS included an EA case management curriculum for supervising and training officers in this strategy to ensure the treatment was delivered consistently. Two officers were selected to take on the caseload of the HCEAS participants. These officers demonstrated capacity for rapport building and interpersonal relationships, as well as a commitment to working with the EA subpopulation – all important characteristics to support successful outcomes among these EAs (Blasko et al., 2015; Cherkos et al., 2008; Morash et al., 2015). They were trained on 1) developmentally appropriate risk communication strategies, 2) offering timely and dependable rewards and reinforcement, and 3) creating an environment with fair and just processes (Tyler, 2003). This training was provided internally from the Hidalgo County CSCD Training Department. This ensured these practices were consistent with existing policies, while still promoting a new approach for this age group. Additionally, officers received training deliver evidence-based CBT curriculum Decision Points from Decision Points Authors LLC and work with the individuals on journaling activities. The officer's were trained on techniques to ensure the programming was delivered consistently and with fidelity to participants throughout the duration of the program. To protect the integrity of the experiment, none of these trainings were provided to officers outside of the two selected to administer the HCEAS program.

Program structure

The HCEAS program lasts 12 to 18 months and consists of four potential phases. Phase I includes intensive substance abuse outpatient treatment for those in need of treatment. If an individual is not assessed with a need for substance use treatment, they automatically begin in Phase II. Phase II includes participation in the CBT program Decision Points (http://www.decisionpointsprogram.com/) and using journals such as the Change Company "What Got Me Here?" journal.[4] Decision Points focuses on cognitive restructuring and gives individuals the tools needed to examine their thinking patterns and related actions and identify alternative thinking patterns for potentially problem causing behaviors. Phase III includes participation in peer support experiences through education and vocational services. Phase IV includes continued court appearances and meeting with probation officers at each individuals' predetermined frequency. This phase is also when participants may be considered for early termination or transfer of their sentence.

On standard supervision, individuals meet with their officer monthly and only appear in court upon receiving a motion to revoke supervision and drug tests are only administered three to nine times a year depending on the individual's substance use risk level. The HCEAS program keeps individuals much more involved than SAU. At the start of the program, participants meet with their probation officers weekly and appear in court biweekly. Future frequency of court appearances and probation officer meetings are based on participants' progression through the program and the incentives they have received, and drug tests are administered biweekly. This is a developmentally appropriate approach for the EA age group who are less skilled at assessing the consequences of their actions and more impulsive. This approach is designed to motivate compliance with supervision requirements when they occur more frequently and reflect an individual's own behaviors and incentives. While increased contacts and stricter focus on compliance (i.e., intensive supervision programs (ISP)) has largely been found ineffective at reducing recidivism (Bouchard & Wong, 2018, Taxman, Smith, & Rudes, 2020; Hyatt & Barnes, 2017; Petersilia, 1997; Turner et al., 1992), similar increased contacts but with a focus on intensive treatment and the quality of interactions has produced more positive outcomes (Bonta, 2023; Petersilia, 1997). The increased contacts with treatment models tend to align with the RNR principles by varying the intensity of treatment and control with the individual's risk level (Andrews & Bonta, 2010; Bonta, 2023). The HCEAS program does increase the intensity of supervision, with a focus on programming (e.g., journaling, Decision Points) and a supportive relationship between the officer and the individual under supervision..

Judicial supervision

The HCEAS team, including the Court Judge, assistant district attorney, defense attorney, program coordinator, caseworkers, and treatment providers, meets prior to regularly scheduled status hearings to review and discuss the progress of the program participants. During the meeting, all current and new cases scheduled for the HCEAS Court session are reviewed. This conference provides a scheduled time for the team to discuss each participant's progress and to make recommendations concerning incentives, sanctions, or any additional services that the participant may need.

Current study

The purpose of this study is to assess the effectiveness of the HCEAS ability to be successful on supervision. HCEAS is a novel program that combines multiple evidence-based practices into one program focused on improving outcomes for EA. HCEAS has never been evaluated. If found to be successful, HCEAS could serve as a model program for other jurisdictions across the country who are struggling to effectively assist EA toward desistance. This study was approved by the Institutional Review Board of George Mason University under IRB number 1,222,855 and used a random controlled trial (RCT) with individuals assigned to HCEAS or SAU. Specifically, this study will examine whether the HCEAS program affects 1) progress on key stability measures (e.g., education, employment, housing), and 2) outcomes of supervisions (i.e., arrests, failure to appear in office visits and treatment, motions to revoke, revocations, and absconding). Next, this study will assess how progress in stability factors influences success in probation. Specifically, this study will address three research questions:

(1) How does HCEAS influence progress in key stability measures for individuals on supervision – overall progress, employment, education, housing, associations with criminal peers, attitudes toward officers, social networks, and prosocial leisure time?
(2) How does HCEAS influence probation outcomes – arrests, failure to appear at office visits or treatment (FTA), motions to revoke (MTR), revocations, and absconding?
(3) What role does progress in key stability measures have for probation outcomes in the HCEAS group?

Program enrollment and study randomization

On-site research assistant recruited participants for the study and obtained consent from participants. Figure 1 shows the study flow and design of this program evaluation including the randomization, consent, and data collection process and timing. Both the treatment and control groups included 65 participants each.

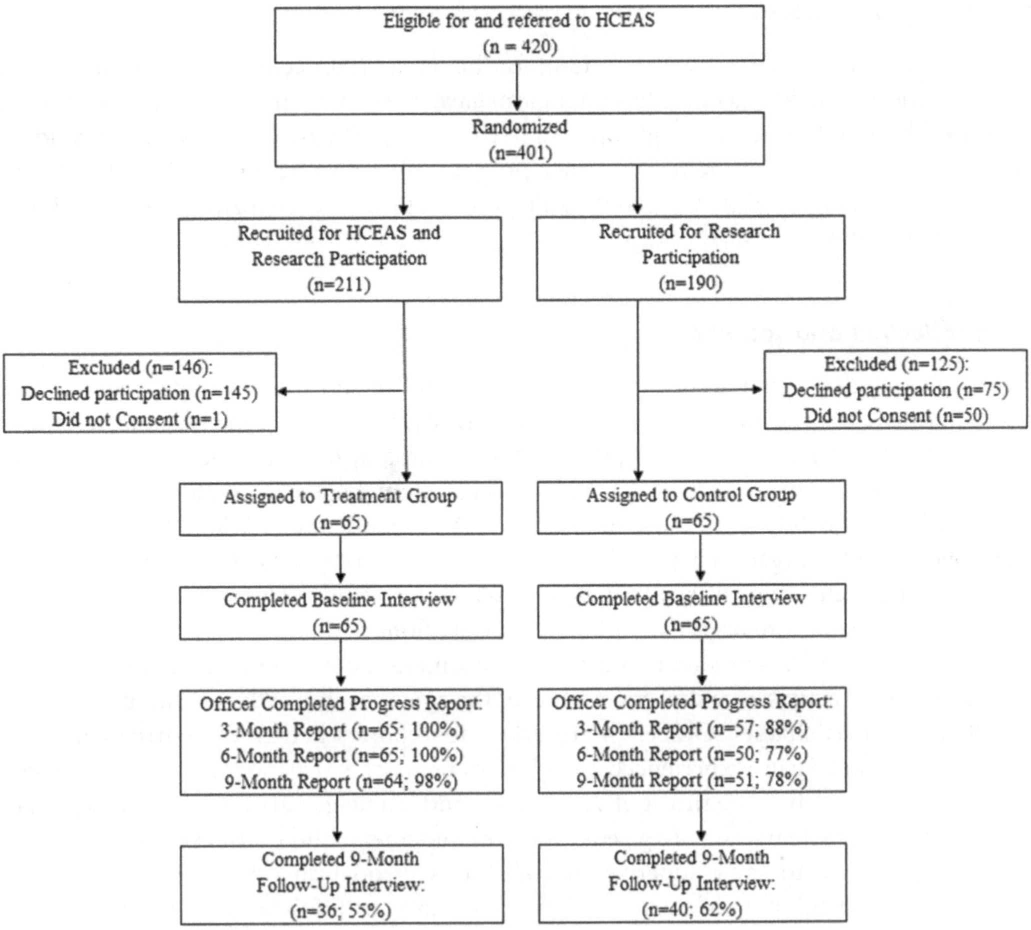

Figure 1. CONSORT Diagram. NOTES: Data collection for the 9-month follow-up interview was interrupted by COVID-19 restrictions and could not be completed by all who were eligible. Declined participation indicated the respondent did not want to participate in the research portion of the study – those in the treatment group still may have participated in the HCEAS programming.

Randomization

Random assignment was conducted in blocks where a random date was selected for each month of data collection. Starting on the randomized date each month, a target number of eligible participants were recruited for the treatment arm. For the first 4 months of recruitment, seven participants were targeted for recruitment into the treatment arm each month, for the following four months 12 individuals were targeted for recruitment into the treatment arm, and for the final 3 months eight individuals were targeted for recruitment into the treatment arm. At the start of each month, recruitment resets for a new block even if a targeted number of individuals have not been recruited for the treatment arm. Up to 10 individuals that met the eligibility requirements for HCEAS were recruited for the control arm each month. Once 10 participants were recruited into the control arm, all other eligible individuals were sent to regular probation and not included in the study.

Consenting procedures

Individuals in both study arms gave consent for the research procedures prior to the start of data collection. Individuals in the treatment arm gave consent separately for participation in HCEAS. Those in the treatment group who declined to participate in the research study – often due to over commitment with other programming and hesitancy of adding to the required probation conditions – could still participate in the HCEAS program without study participation.

Data collection and sources

The study included 3 sources of data: 1) survey data collected from respondents at baseline and 9-months after study enrollment, 2) survey-style progress reports collected from probation officers for each study participant at months 3, 6, and 9) administrative data collected from the probation office. Study recruitment began in September 2018 and continued through July 2019. Due to the COVID-19 pandemic restrictions of in-person data collection that began in March 2020, the follow-up survey data could not be collected from all participants, which is why it is not used in this study. The progress reports and administrative data were used to conduct this evaluation.

Progress Reports. Progress reports gathered information concerning treatment and control participants' activities and progress during the previous 3 months and at months 3, 6, and 9 for all participants. Officers were asked to report whether the participants had reported for office visits, experienced road blocks of success (e.g., arrests, injuries, illness, cultural barriers, such as the threat of deportation and language barriers), made progress in various areas of stable building (e.g., education, employment, and housing), and if they had any changes made to their supervision conditions. Probation officers received e-mail reminders at the beginning of each month from research staff if they have a progress report due. Fifty-four (54) probation officers consented to participate in the study and 38 submitted progress reports.[5] A total of 352 (90%) of the 390 total reports (3 for each of the 130 participants) were completed. Overall, 96% of the respondents had at least one progress report completed on their behalf (for more details about the progress report completion rates see Figure 1).[6]

Administrative Data. Administrative data were acquired from the probation office to examine outcome measures and probation progress. These data include TRAS risk/need assessment information, interactions with the criminal legal system (i.e., arrests, revocations, etc.), key sentence dates, and records of condition violations.

Measures

Dependent Variables. The dependent variables used to assess progress in key stability measures were *overall* progress, *employment* progress, *education* progress, *housing* progress, progress with disassociating with *criminal peers*, progress with *attitudes toward officers, social networks* progress, and *prosocial leisure time* progress. Each variable measures the officer's perceptions of the amount of progress participants made in each area during the preceding 3 months.[7] For example, "[s]elect the number representing your view of the defendant's overall progress on supervision during the past 3 months" or "[s]elect the number representing your view of the defendant's progress on his/her housing during the past 3 months." These measures were collected as part of the progress reports completed by each participant's probation officer. These questions were answered using a 10-point-Likert -scale where 1 indicated negative progress and 10 indicated positive progress.

Arrest, motion to revoke (*MTR*), and failure to appear (*FTA*) to a meeting with the officer or to treatment, *absconding, revocation*, and *cumulative negative outcome* were the outcome variables used to measure probation outcomes. Each is a dichotomous variable where any participant that had any events in the first 12 months of the program was coded as a 1. These measures were obtained from administrative data and are not mutually exclusive (i.e., one participant could experience multiple negative outcomes in the 12-month period). Cumulative negative outcome is a dichotomous indicator that is coded as a 1 if a participant experienced any of the negative outcomes in the first 12 months of the program. Observing each outcome independently provides a more nuanced insight into areas where HCEAS may have an effect, while the cumulative measure provides a broader understanding of how HCEAS may influence positive and negative outcomes and behaviors among individuals on community supervision as a whole.

Control Variables. Age, gender, Hispanic ethnic identity, TRAS risk level, and treatment assignment were included as control variables in the models assessing the stability measures effect on probation outcomes. *Age* is a continuous variable measuring participants age at the time of enrollment. *Male* is a dichotomous indicator coded as 1 for participants who self-identified as male.[8] *Hispanic ethnicity* is a dichotomous indicator coded as 1 for participants who identify as Hispanic. *TRAS Risk Level* is a categorical variable indicating whether a participant scored at low, moderate, or high risk. *HCEAS (treatment)* is a dichotomous indicator coded at 1 for participants assigned to the treatment group. Each measure of stability was aggregated across the three waves to create a 9-month average progress score for each of the measures. These variables were only calculated for participants that had at least two out of the three waves of progress reports. These 9-month averages were used as covariates for determining the influence of stability measures on negative probation outcomes.

Sample Characteristic Variables. Number of criminal friends, attitudes toward violence and associates (Mills et al., 2002), anti-social intent (Mills et al., 2002), sensation seeking (Lynam et al., 2006), self-control (Tangney et al., 2004), self-efficacy (Schwarzer & Jerusalem, 1995), prior community supervision, capacity to contribute to supervision plan (Matejkowski et al., 2018), and working alliance (Horvath & Greenberg, 1989; Matejkowski et al., 2018) were used to describe the characteristics of the sample and verify randomization was successful. Each of these measures personality traits that may be underdeveloped for EA and other variables that may have influenced participants probation outcomes and receptivity to the treatment.

Analysis

To test the proposed research questions, descriptive statistics that were gathered in the baseline survey data were compared between the treatment and control arms to ensure the treatment groups were equivalent to several observable baseline characteristics. Repeated measures ANOVAs were used to analyze within- and between-group differences for the eight stability measures in the first research question. Treatment-by-wave interactions were assessed. To address research questions two, independent sample t-tests were used to test for significant differences between the two groups' means for each of the probation outcomes. A logistic regression was used to determine the influence the stability measures had on negative probation outcomes. Results that are marginally significant ($p < 0.1$) and significant ($p < 0.05$) are discussed.

This study used an intent-to-treat (ITT) study design to preserve the prognostic balance acquired through randomization. ITT designs keep participants in their assigned study arm for analyses whether the participant completed the program or not. This means that even if a participant did not complete the entire program or was removed from community supervision early, they remained in the analysis in their original study arm.

Results

Characteristics of the sample

Table 1 shows descriptive statistics collected from the baseline survey data. There were no observable differences between the treatment and control groups after randomization was complete. This indicates randomization was successful in eliminating observable differences between the treatment and control groups.

Stability factors

Table 2 and Figure 2 show the results of the repeated measures ANOVA analyses for stability measures. Within-group main effects for all eight ANOVAs were significant suggesting that there were significant differences in the average amount of progress reported for each stability measure across waves. Significant differences were detected in

Table 1. Descriptive statistics by study arm.

	Overall ($N = 130$)	HCEAS ($N = 65$)	SAU ($N = 65$)	Comparison
Variable	Mean/% (n)	Mean/% (n)	Mean/% (n)	T-score
Age	21.59	21.88	21.31	$t = 1.45, p = 0.15$
Male	81.5% (106)	76.9% (50)	86.2% (56)	$t = -1.36, p = 0.18$
White	100% (123)			
Hispanic Ethnicity	95.9% (118)	93.2% (55)	98.4% (63)	$t = 1.46, p = 0.15$
TRAS Risk Level				
Low	3.1% (4)	4.6% (3)	1.5% (1)	$t = 1.01, p = 0.31$
Moderate	75.4% (98)	78.5% (51)	72.3% (47)	$t = -0.81, p = 0.42$
High	21.5% (28)	20.0% (13)	23.1% (15)	$t = 0.42, p = 0.67$
# of Criminal Friends	1.05	1.05	1.06	$t = -0.08, p = 0.94$
Attitudes Toward Violence	4.46	4.03	4.89	$t = -1.40, p = 0.16$
Attitudes Toward Associates	5.16	4.75	5.57	$t = -1.86, p = 0.07$
Anti-Social Intent	3.05	2.62	3.48	$t = -1.64, p = 0.10$
Sensation Seeking	2.85	2.82	2.87	$t = -0.74, p = 0.46$
Self-Control	48.24	48.58	47.89	$t = 0.43, p = 0.67$
Self-Efficacy	32.01	32.09	31.92	$t = 0.20, p = 0.84$
Prior Community Supervision	36.9% (48)	38.5% (25)	35.4% (23)	$t = -0.36, p = 0.72$
Capacity to contribute to supervision plan	10.02	10.14	9.89	$t = 0.85, p = 0.40$
Working alliance	14.06	14.20	13.92	$t = 0.81, p = 0.42$

NOTES: T-tests compare treatment and control group means. Capacity to contribute to supervision plan ($N = 129$), working alliance ($N = 129$), race ($N = 123$), and Hispanic ($N = 123$) statistics are reported based on reduced sample sizes due to missing data in the baseline survey and administrative data.

ABBREVIATIONS: N = sample size; n = subsample size; SAU = supervision as usual (control group); HCEAS = Hidalgo County Emerging Adult Strategy (treatment group); TRAS = Texas Risk Assessment System.

Table 2. Repeated measures ANOVAs analyzing changes within-group, between-group, and within-between interaction differences.

	Within-Between Interaction (Treatment * Wave)												Within-Group Comparison		Between-Group Comparison	
	WAVE 1		WAVE 2		WAVE 3		W1 v. W2 Sig.		W2 v. W3 Sig.		W1 v. W3 Sig.					
Stability Factor *(control n; treatment n)*	Month 1–3 Progress SAU ($\bar{x}$)	HCEAS ($\bar{x}$)	Month 3–6 Progress SAU ($\bar{x}$)	HCEAS ($\bar{x}$)	Month 6–9 Progress SAU ($\bar{x}$)	HCEAS ($\bar{x}$)	C	T	C	T	C	T	*F*	Par. η2	*F*	Par. η2
Overall *(n = 31; n = 53)*	5.84	6.72*	6.19	7.08*	6.55	7.13	-	-	-	-	-	-	4.23*	0.05	7.54*	0.08
Employment *(n = 27; n = 51)*	4.96	6.43*	6.11	6.61	6.63	7.10	*	-	-	-	*	-	8.34*	0.10	7.56*	0.09
Education *(n = 12; n = 21)*	4.75	4.95	6.92	5.48*	6.00	5.38	*	-	-	-	†	-	7.15*	0.19	1.51	0.05
Housing *(n = 31; n = 54)*	5.97	6.09	6.48	6.74	6.71	6.87	-	*	-	-	-	*	7.68*	0.09	0.68	0.01
Attitude toward Officer *(n = 31; n = 54)[a]*	6.58	7.11†	7.19	7.52	7.26	7.72	†	-	-	-	-	*	7.23*	0.08	3.61†	0.04
Social Network *(n = 31; n = 54)*	5.68	5.56	6.06	6.35	6.52	6.63	-	*	-	-	*	*	13.9*	0.14	0.15	0.00
Criminal Peers *(n = 24; n = 52)[a]*	5.38	5.40	6.42	5.98	6.75	6.62	-	-	-	*	*	*	12.6*	0.15	0.40	0.01
Prosocial Leisure Time *(n = 29; n = 52)*	5.72	5.35	6.03	6.00	6.41	6.56	-	*	-	*	-	*	16.8*	0.12	0.12	0.00

NOTES: Sample sizes for education are substantially smaller because officers only reported on this measure for participants who had education related conditions of supervision. [a]Violate sphericity assumption and report within-group comparison significance based on the Greenhouse-Geisser corrected p-value.

ABBREVIATIONS: SAU = supervision as usual (control group); HCEAS = Hidalgo County Emerging Adult Strategy (treatment group); C = control group; *T* = treatment group; W1 = Wave 1; W2 = Wave 2; W3 = Wave 3; Sig. = significant difference; Par. η2 = Partial eta-squared; *n* = subsample size; $\bar{x}$ = sample mean.

† $p < 0.1$; * $p < 0.05$.

between-group effects for the treatment and control group means for overall progress and employment progress (($F = 7.54$; $p = 0.007$); ($F = 7.56$; $p = 0.007$), respectively), and moderately significant differences were detected for attitudes toward officers ($F = 3.61$; $p = 0.061$).

Post hoc analyses examine the interaction terms in each repeated measure ANOVA, which reveals simple effects comparing between-group differences on stability factors reported by probation officers during the 3-, 6-, and 9-month progress reports. Post hoc analyses were conducted to disaggregate the interaction effects into simple effects comparing within-group differences across wave. The results to the post hoc analyses help answer the first research question concerning the effect of HCEAS on key measures of stability (see Table 2 and Figure 2).[9] The results to the post hoc analyses are discussed below.

Overall Progress. After disaggregating the interaction effect from the repeated measures ANOVA for overall progress reported by probation officers, results show that there are no significant changes across waves for either the treatment or control group. Although the group means increase for both groups across time, these increases were not substantial enough to be deemed significant. The post-hoc analyses for between-group differences at each time point suggest the treatment group made significantly more progress at wave 1 and

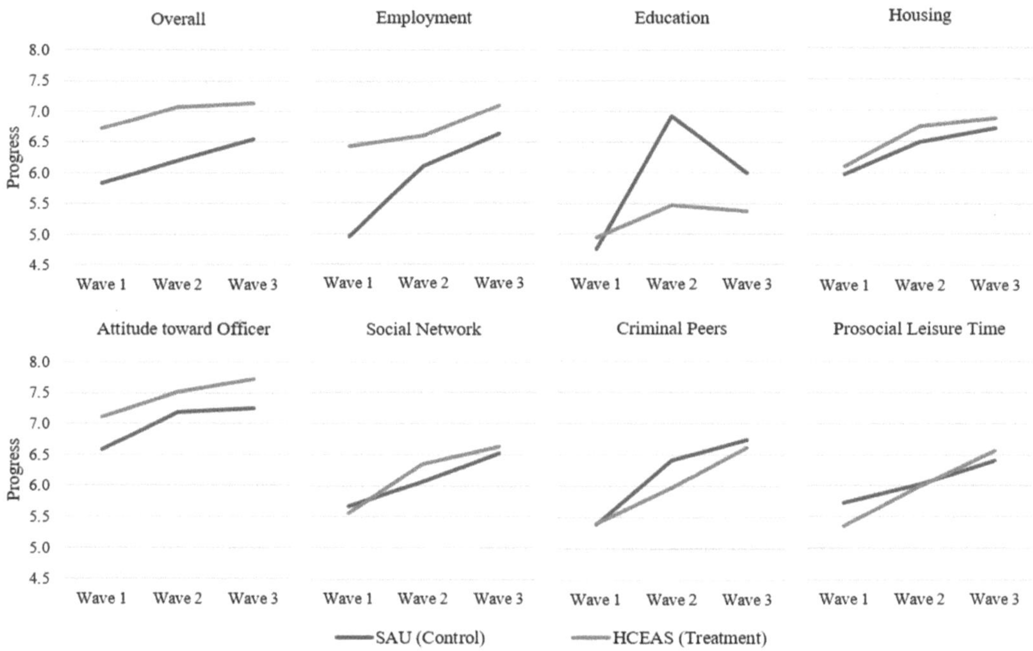

Figure 2. Treatment-by-wave interaction in repeated measure ANOVAs for stability measures. ABBREVIATIONS: SAU = supervision as usual (control group); HCEAS = Hidalgo County Emerging Adult Strategy (treatment group)

wave 2 than the control group. In summary, the treatment group made significantly more overall progress at each wave than the control group, while the level of progress reported at each wave remained relatively constant for both groups.

Employment. Between-group differences were observed at wave 1 with the treatment group showing significantly higher levels of progress. However, these differences were eliminated by the latter two waves. Post hoc analyses for within-group employment progress reported by probation officers show the control group made significant increases in progress between wave 1 and 2 and wave 1 and 3, whereas the treatment groups progress remained relatively constant across waves.

Education. Post hoc analyses for educational progress revealed a marginally significant quadratic effect ($F = 3.65$; $p = 0.065$). Temporal trends for both treatment and control groups demonstrated increased levels of progress in wave 2 (6 months), but decreases in progress by wave 3 (9 months). Although not statistically significant, this temporal trend is unique to education. The between-group differences for educational progress were significant at wave 2 where the control group made a higher level of progress than the treatment group. This is the only stability factor that demonstrated significantly higher progress for the control group than the treatment group.

The sample size for educational progress was substantially smaller than the sample for the other stability factors because fewer individuals had educational supervision conditions. In addition, the average age of participants in the education sample was significantly lower ($t = -2.35$; $p = 0.03$) than the other groups. Either factor could have played a role in inconsistent outcomes for educational progress compared to the other stability factors.

Housing. Post hoc analyses for housing progress showed no between-group differences at any of the three waves. This was expected based on the insignificant between-group main effect. The treatment group made significantly more progress in wave 2 compared to wave 1 and in wave 3 compared to wave 1. The control group made statistically consistent progress across the three waves. In summary, the treatment and control groups were indistinguishable in their housing progress; however, the treatment group did make more significant progress over time.

Attitudes toward officers. The between-group difference in attitude progress was a marginally higher level of progress for the treatment group at wave 1 than the control group. This difference was eliminated at wave 2 because the control group had a significantly higher level of progress at wave 2 compared to wave 1. The treatment group has significantly higher progress at wave 3 than at wave 1. In summary, the treatment group was consistently higher than the control group, but this difference is only significant at wave 1.

Social networks. Social network progress was not statistically distinguishable between-groups in post hoc analysis at any of the waves. However, the treatment group did make more progress at wave 2 than wave 1 and wave 3 than wave 1. The control group also improved their social network progress by wave 3 when compared to wave 1. In summary, both treatment and control groups improved their social network progress across waves; however, the control group improvement occurred slower than the treatment group.

Criminal peers. Progress with separating from criminal peers was indistinguishable in between-group post hoc analyses in all three waves. Although the treatment and control group means remained relatively similar to each other at each wave, the treatment group made significantly more progress at wave 3 when compared to wave 1 and wave 2. The control group made significantly more progress at wave 3 when compared to wave 1. In summary, both treatment and control groups improve their progress toward separating from criminal peers across the 9-month period; however, the treatment group made a large portion of their progress during wave 2 (months 3–6), whereas the control group made more gradual and consistent progress across each wave.

Prosocial leisure time. Much like the last two stability factors, there were no observable differences between the treatment and control groups in leisure time progress in any of the three waves. Within-group analyses show the treatment group made significant progress across every time point in how they spent their leisure time, whereas the control groups progress in prosocial leisure time did not appear to change across time.

Probation-related outcomes

Table 3 presents probation outcomes obtained from administrative data. For arrest rates, 41.5% of those in the control group were arrested within 12-month of study enrollment compared to 20% of those in the treatment groups ($t = 2.71$; $p = 0.008$). Similarly, 30.8% of the control group participants had motions to revoke as compared to 6.2% of the treatment group participants ($t = 3.78$; $p < 0.001$). Next, 26.2% of those in the control group failed to appear for office visits with their probation officers, compared to 7.7% in the treatment group ($t = 2.87$; $p = 0.003$). Both groups had low rates of failing to appear for treatment, absconding, and revocations and none of these rates were statistically difference (treatment FTA ($t = -0.73$; $p = 0.469$); absconding ($t = 0.00$; $p = 1.000$); revocation ($t = -0.39$; $p = 0.700$)). Overall, 50.8%

Table 3. Independent sample T-tests comparing treatment and control group means for 12-month probation outcomes.

	SAU ($n = 65$)	HCEAS ($n = 65$)
Arrest	41.5%	20.0%*
Motion to Revoke	30.8%	6.2%*
Failure to Appear to Office Visit	26.2%	7.7%*
Failure to Appear to Treatment	4.6%	7.7%
Absconded	3.1%	3.1%
Revoked	4.6%	6.2%
Cumulative Negative Outcome	50.8%	30.8%*

NOTES: Symbols of significance indicate treatment group means are significantly different than control group means.
ABBREVIATIONS: SAU = supervision as usual (control group); HCEAS = Hidalgo County Emerging Adult Strategy (treatment group); n = sub-sample size.
† $p < 0.1$; * $p < 0.05$.

of the control group experienced a negative outcome in the 12 months following enrollment compared to 30.8% of the treatment group ($t = 2.35$; $p = 0.020$). HCEAS program was found to make significant improvements in three out of six probation outcomes—arrests, motions to revoke, and failure to appear to office visits – and the aggregate negative outcome measure.

Stability and probation outcomes

Table 4 presents the logistic regression models examining the influence of 9-month averages for stability measures on negative probation outcomes at 12-months. The bivariate analysis suggested a marginally significant protective effect of HCEAS for negative probation outcomes at 12 months post-enrollment ($OR = 0.34$; $p = 0.02$). This effect remains significant ($OR = 0.35$; $p = 0.03$) after adding in demographic controls for age, gender, Hispanic ethnic identity, and TRAS risk level indicated the treatment was successful in decreasing negative probation outcomes for individuals regardless of their demographic statuses for these variables.[10] After including seven covariates for the 9-month average progress in key stability measures, the treatment effect is continued to be significant ($OR = 0.28$; $p = 0.04$).[11] This suggests that progress in stability measures does not account for the difference between the HCEAS and SAU groups. The treatment provided a protective effect beyond the benefit individuals gained through progress on stability measures. Progress separating from criminal peers had a marginally significant protective effect ($OR = 0.57$; $p = 0.098$) against negative probation outcomes when controlling for treatment assignment and all other covariates. This suggests disassociating with criminal peers was important for avoiding negative probation outcomes for individuals in both study arms. Progress in employment ($OR = 1.62$; $p = 0.061$) and housing ($OR = 1.99$; $p = 0.048$) appear to have increased the odds of negative probation outcomes after controlling for other covariates. Model fit was improved with the addition of each set of covariates as shown by the increasing pseudo R^2 and the decreasing x^2 for the Hosmer–Lemeshow tests in Table 4.

Discussion

HCEAS is a probation program designed for EA with a focus on improving developmental and social factors unique to this age group. The case management and supervision plans focused on stages emphasized in the theory of emerging adulthood, such as: 1) identity

Table 4. Logistic regression model examining predictors of negative probation outcomes at 12-months post-enrollment ($N = 90$).

	Negative 12-Month Outcome					
	Bivariate		Demographics		Stability Measures	
	Odds Ratio	SE	Odds Ratio	SE	Odds Ratio	SE
HCEAS (treatment)	0.34*	0.15	0.35*	0.16	0.28*	0.17
Demographics						
Age			0.92	0.10	0.86	0.11
Male			1.50	0.91	1.13	0.78
Hispanic Ethnicity			0.40	0.44	0.29	0.34
TRAS Risk Level			1.31	0.82	1.00	0.76
Stability Measures (9-month averages)						
Overall Progress					0.53	0.23
Employment Progress					1.62†	0.41
Housing Progress					1.99*	0.69
Attitude toward Officer Progress					1.33	0.67
Social Network Progress					0.50	0.22
Criminal Peers Progress					0.57†	0.19
Prosocial Leisure Time Progress					1.09	0.40
Constant	1.06	0.35	8.29	23.46	469.45	1674.67
Pseudo R^2	0.07		0.08		0.16	
Hosmer-Lemeshow Test x^2	–.–		92.54		84.93	

NOTES: Education progress was omitted from this analysis to avoid substantially reducing the sample size. Negative probation outcomes include arrest, MTR, FTA (office visit), FTA (treatment), absconding, and revocation. Sample size is reduced to those with at least 2 progress report waves completed in order to calculate 9-month average progress variables. Race was excluded from these models since there is not variation in this sample.
ABBREVIATIONS: N = sample size; HCEAS = Hidalgo County Emerging Adult Strategy (treatment); SE = Standard Error; TRAS = Texas Risk Assessment System.
† $p < 0.1$; * $p < 0.05$.

exploration, 2) becoming self-focus, 3) addressing instability, 4) identifying future possibilities, 5) feeling in-between adolescence and adulthood, and 6) incentivizing positive behavior. This study served as an evaluation of the HCEAS where there were mixed results.

First, when examining key measures of stability (e.g., housing, employment, education) the HCEAS group made statistically significant progress in terms of overall and specifically employment progress. Individuals in the HCEAS group made marginally significantly more progress in their attitudes toward their probation officers when compared to the control group meaning that HCEAS participants were perceived to have more positive thoughts and actions toward officers. HCEAS officers were trained to understand this developmental stage and think critically about the approaches used to address issues with the EA they supervised. Officers were trained to cultivate a just, and fair environment with these individuals and these results suggest this may have been effective. Increasing positive attitudes toward officers and improving individuals' perceptions of the legitimacy of legal system could have significant implications as perceived legitimacy is one of the leading predictors of compliance with the law (Jackson et al., 2012; Papachristos et al., 2012; Tyler, 1990). Progress in the other factors were not different between the two groups. The HCEAS group's growth in progress across waves (over 9 months) often surpassed the control groups growth. The HCEAS within-group progress levels grew significantly between wave 1 and wave 3 in five (i.e. housing, attitudes toward officers, social network, criminal peers, and prosocial leisure time) out of the eight stability factors.

This raises some conversations of how success is measured. Desistance is a process wherein criminal conduct and criminality declines over time until cessation. When measuring desistance from crime, it is necessary to measure change over time to observe the growth and progress one has made in terms of criminal attitudes and behaviors (Rocque, 2021). This study followed the National Academy of Science (National Academies of Sciences, Engineering, 2022) recommendations to use measures of well-being along with or instead of recidivism. In this study, we measured progress in terms of key stability measures longitudinally. If success were to be based only on absolute levels of progress at a single point in time, the HCEAS program had limited success. If success is based on absolute levels of progress *or* growth in progress over time, the HCEAS program was largely successful in improving all areas of stability except education.

The results for the stability measure assessing overall progress on probation revealed an interesting pattern – or lack thereof. Although overall progress had the most substantial differences between groups at each wave, these differences did not translate into differences between the more specific stability measures. It was as though the probation officers' global assessment of those in the treatment group was scored less harshly than specific assessments. This may suggest that probation officers conceptualize "overall" progress to be scoring something other than simply a summative measure of the individual factors. Similar to the Global Assessment of Functioning (GAF) scale that is used by mental health providers to assess individuals' functioning from a broad perspective rather than focusing on specific symptoms and diagnoses, probation officers may have used overall progress scores to assess the general, day-to-day functioning of the participant (Aas, 2011). Perhaps overall progress was thought of as personality characteristics or other unobserved factors that individuals in the treatment group, who spent substantially more time with their officers than members of the control group, showed unique progress in that did not translate into progress in the other individual factors. When probation officers are fixated on the specific factors it may have been easier to scrutinize and find faults; whereas when thinking about the participant more generally they may not have been as particular in their assessment.

Another interesting finding regarding stability factors was the seemingly lower levels of progress among the treatment group for separating from criminal peers and prosocial leisure time at waves 2 and/or 3. Although the treatment group made significant gains in progress over time in each of these factors, they were still reported to have lower progress than the control group in multiple waves. This is the Achilles heel of supervision. More frequent contact often results in officers learning more about an individual, which can translate to a negative assessment or revelation of behaviors that are in violation of supervision. But in this case, HCEAS provided officers with the tools to help individuals that were still involved with criminal peers and who lacked prosocial leisure time activities through more journaling and CBT. Contrary to SAU, HCEAS prepares officers to identify and respond to gaps in community supervision to ensure participants did not fall through the cracks.

Probation outcomes examined in research question two measure participants' behaviors (i.e. MTR, FTA, absconding) *and* the criminal legal system's responses to participant's behaviors (i.e. arrests and revocations). The HCEAS group proved to be significantly more successful in select behavior- and response-based outcomes. Taken in part with the fact that HCEAS participants progressed more than the control group in key stability factors, it may be reasonable to conclude that the HCEAS had a largely positive effect on EA's experiences during their probation sentences. However, since the HCEAS participants were not more successful in avoiding revocations – the primary measure of success in probation – the question of whether HCEAS is effective in improving probation outcomes for EA remains. Although the treatment group had significantly fewer MTRs than the control group, the treatment group obtained more revocation than the control group overall (see Table 3). This could be because the HCEAS program uses a specialty court and therefore, processes cases and MTRs more quickly than the standard court. With additional follow-up time, the difference in revocation rates could diminish or disappear entirely.

Part of this is a challenge of how success is measured in corrections. If a dichotomous measure of recidivism (i.e., arrest, revocation) is the only outcome used to assess success in probation, any progress toward desistance and a conventional lifestyle are undermined. Desistance is a process that anticipates a certain amount of "failure" along the way to complete cessation of criminality and criminal conduct (Rocque, 2021). If only revocations were examined, it would look as if the HCEAS was entirely ineffective. But if measures of stability and other outcomes (e.g., arrests, MTR, FTA) are included in what is deemed successful, the HCEAS was at least partially effective. Future research should continue parsing out how recidivism and success are defined in corrections, as well as considering how we can more effectively translate intermediate progress into sustained success in probation outcomes. The results from this study raise the concern that there is a disconnect between participants behaviors and participants outcomes. Future research should further explore the source of this disconnect – whether it be that POs are misjudging progress, inappropriately applied arrests and revocations, or some other cause.

Overall, HCEAS was designed to focus on developmental and social factors that limit individual's success on probation and the stability measures indicate that the program was influential in these areas. HCEAS targets the unique needs of this subpopulation with an emphasis on helping the EA to identify future goals, view their prospects in a positive light, and be reinforced for achieving positive goals. In order to accomplish these goals, the project used principles from the RNR model creating an infrastructure to support EA and to target key issues such as impulsivity, reduced control over emotions, and difficulties in assessing consequences of one's behavior. The focused curriculum and specialized training for participating officers show promise as being successful means of improving outcomes of EA on probation, even in the early years of implementation.

Limitations

As with all data collection and research efforts that were underway during the onset of the COVID-19 pandemic, this study faced challenges related to agency closures. Due to COVID-19, survey data collection procedures were interrupted during the follow-up period, which limited the opportunity to examine treatment effects on participants attitudes and beliefs such as those reported in Table 1 (e.g., attitudes toward violence, sensation seeking, self-control). This would have added to our understanding of how the HCEAS affected the EAs in the more subjective, difficult to observe, aspects of life that may contribute to probation outcomes.

A second limitation of the study is that probation officers were not blinded to the treatment assignment of participants. Blinding probation officers may have further decreased bias in how the officers interacted with participants during supervision but this would have been difficult to accomplish because the individual was directed to the HCEAS program. While this could not be avoided, future studies may want to consider larger samples where officers are not aware of the subjects' study condition.

A third limitation of the study is the portion of participants who were randomized into the treatment group, but who chose not to participate in the research part of the study ($n = 146$; ~69%). Although we do not have any data to compare those who declined to participate in the survey, those who completed our exit interview overwhelmingly reported their hesitancy to participate was based on not wanting to add another requirement to their probation terms. We do not anticipate that this presents any internal validity issues since the rate of declining to participate in control group was comparable ($n = 125$; ~66%). While it is possible that this rate of decline influenced the generalizability of our results to the applicable EA on probation, but it also indicates individuals did not feel coerced or obligated to participate in order to improve their supervision outcomes.

A fourth limitation of the study is that there is no way to account for variation in the probation officers supervision style in either the treatment or control groups. Given that the officers in the treatment group were selected based on their capacity for building rapport with the EA population, it is possible their supervision styles varied from those in the control group. Like other experimental studies, decisions were made to maximize the internal validity of the study including selecting the officers that were best suited for HCEAS. Further testing is needed to determine if the officer training for HCEAS is adequate to address variation in supervision styles among the general officer pool.

A larger sample size and a longer follow-up period would be desirable but could not be obtained due to COVID-19 and the available funding. Although the current study is sufficiently powered by the primary outcomes, a large sample size would allow for subgroup analyses among specific populations and allow smaller treatment effects to be detectable. While a 12-month follow-up period is common and acceptable for studies looking at post-release outcomes, a longer follow-up period would allow for more detailed understanding of the long-term influence HCEAS has on EA success post-release.

Conclusion

This study evaluated the effectiveness of the HCEAS's ability to improve probation outcomes for emerging adults using an RCT. Analyses showed that the HCEAS was effective in increasing progress across time for five stability measures and improving absolute levels of progress for two other stability measures when compared to the control group. The HCEAS was effective in decreasing outcomes such as arrests, motions to revoke, and failures to appear for probation office visits. With the HCEAS, Hidalgo County has implemented a specialized caseload designed for emerging adults that is at least partially successful during the period of early implementation. Emerging adults' developmental stage requires specific and intentionally designed approach to community supervision. From this, we learned that age-specific focus on stability factors is feasible during supervision and that it is also likely to result in helping young adults identify future goals. Research should continue honing in on ways to isolate and address the needs of this population, as well as investigating ways to sustain the intermediate success into long-term success of probation.

Notes

1. In Hidalgo County, arrests do not indicate a guaranteed revocation.
2. Removal from the program does not indicate revocation, just removal form the HCEAS program.
3. Mental health caseloads and those with sex-related offenses were excluded from the study because they already have specialized caseload and service provisions tailored to their specific needs which were deemed necessary to address instead of the needs in the HCEAS program.
4. In piloting the project, the probation officers found that using the adolescent version of the Change Company journals was more effective with this age group than the adult ones.
5. In most cases, the consenting officers that did not complete progress reports because they were not supervising a participant in the study. In a few cases, consenting officers failed to submit progress reports when they were asked.
6. The 4% of missing progress reports were missing randomly across age, gender, ethnicity, TRAS risk level, 12 and 18 month outcome, and treatment group so it is not assumed that this missingness influences the analysis.
7. Each timepoint was considered one wave of data and each one covers a 3-month recall period. Therefore, wave 1 measures progress made between months 0 and 3, wave 2 measures progress made between months 3 and 6, and wave 3 measures progress made between months 6 and 9.
8. This variable was collected as nominal measure including categories for transgender man and transgender female. Since all respondents identified as cisgender male or female, it was entered as a dichotomous variable in the models.
9. This analysis was replicated with a sample restricted to those who were successful on probation (i.e. did not experience any of the negative probation outcomes). The results remained relatively consistent and are not included in the text.
10. TRAS is the standardize risk-need assessment tool. The risk level was a significant predictor of negative outcomes in a bivariate model; however, with each additional covariate was added to the model, that relationship was suppressed and ultimately was null. This suggests that risk level does not matter as much as other stability and demographic factors when it came to the outcomes of this study.
11. Education progress was excluded from this model to avoid listwise deletion of an additional 36 respondents who did not have educational supervision requirements.

Abbreviations

HCEAS Hidalgo County Emerging Adult Strategy

Disclosure statement

No potential conflict of interest was reported by the author(s).

Funding

The work was supported by the Bureau of Justice Assistance [2016-HO-BX-K005]

ORCID

Kendra J. Clark http://orcid.org/0000-0001-5450-072X

References

Aas, I. M. (2011). Guidelines for rating Global Assessment of Functioning (GAF). *Annals of General Psychiatry, 10*(1), 11. https://doi.org/10.1016/s0924-9338(12)74747-8

Andrews, D. A., & Bonta, J. (2010). *The psychology of criminal conduct.* Routledge.

Arnett, J. J. (2000). Emerging adulthood: A theory of development from the late teens through the twenties. *American Psychologist, 55*(5), 469–480. https://doi.org/10.1037/0003-066X.55.5.469

Arnett, J. J. (2014). A longer road to adulthood. *Etica e Politica,* 15(1), 1–29. Oxford University Press. https://doi.org/10.1093/acprof.

Baltodano, H. M., Mathur, S. R., & Rutherford, R. B. (2005). Transition of incarcerated youth with disabilities across systems and into adulthood. *Exceptionality, 13*(2), 103–124. https://doi.org/10.1207/s15327035ex1302_4

Berlin, G., Furstenberg, F. F., Waters, M. C., & Donahuefragile, E. (2010). Transition to adulthood: Introducing the Issue. *The Future of Children, 20*(2), 3–16. https://doi.org/10.1353/foc.2010.0005

Bernard, K., Schwager, D., & Sitney, M. (2020). Reimagining probation and parole for young adults in the United States. *European Journal of Probation, 12*(3), 200–218. https://doi.org/10.1177/2066220320981180

Blasko, B. L., Friedmann, P. D., Rhodes, A. G., & Taxman, F. S. (2015). The paroleeparole officer relationship as a mediator of criminal justice outcomes. *Criminal Justice and Behavior, 42*(7), 722–740. https://doi.org/10.1177/0093854814562642

Bonta, J. (2023). Training community supervision officers in the risk-need-responsivity model of offender rehabilitation: A review and implications. *Journal of Offender Rehabilitation, 62*(1), 39–58. https://doi.org/10.1080/10509674.2022.2158986

Bouchard, J., & Wong, J. S. (2018). Examining the effects of intensive supervision and aftercare programs for at-risk youth: A systematic review and meta-analysis. *International Journal of Offender Therapy and Comparative Criminology, 62*(6), 1509–1534. https://doi.org/10.1177/0306624X17690449

Byrne, J. M. (2020). The effectiveness of prison programming: a review of the research literature examining the impact of federal, state, and local inmate programming on post-release recidivism. *Federal Probation, 84*(1), 3–20.

Carson, E. A., & Golinelli, D. (2013). *Prisoners in 2012: Trends in Admissions and Releases, 1991-2012* (Report No. NCJ 243920). Washington, DC: Bureau of Justice Statistics.

Cherkos, R., Ferguson, J., & Cook, A. (2008). Do we care what offenders think? *Perspectives, Summer, 32*(3), 53–58.

Chung, H. L., Little, M., Steinberg, L., & Altschuler, D. Network on Transitions to Adulthood, Policy Brief. (2005). *Juvenile Justice and the Transition to Adulthood.*

The Council of State Governments Justice Center. (2015). *Reducing recidivism and improving other outcomes for young adults in the juvenile and adult criminal justice systems.* The Council of State Governments Justice Center.

Durose, M. R., Cooper, A. D., & Snyder, H. (2014). *Recidivism of prisoners released in 30 states in 2005: Patterns from 2005 to 2010* (Report No. 28). Washington, DC: US Department of Justice, Office of Justice Programs, Bureau of Justice Statistics.

Hartwell, S. W., Fisher, W. H., & Davis, M. (2010). Emerging adults with psychiatric disabilities involved with the criminal justice system. *International Journal of Offender Therapy and Comparative Criminology, 54*(5), 756–768. https://doi.org/10.1177/0306624X09338018

Horowitz, J., Utada, C., & Fuhrmann, M. (2018). *Probation and Parole Systems Marked by High Stakes, Missed Opportunities.* The Pew Charitable Trusts. https://www.pewtrusts.org/-/media/assets/2018/09/probation_and_parole_systems_marked_by_high_stakes_missed_opportunities_pew.pdf

Horvath, A. O., & Greenberg, L. S. (1989). Development and validation of the working alliance inventory. *Journal of Counseling Psychology, 36*(2), 223–233. https://doi.org/10.1037/0022-0167.36.2.223

Howell, J. C., Feld, B. C., Mears, D. P., Farrington, D. P., Loeber, R., & Petechuk, D. (2013). *Bulletin 5: Young Offenders and an Effective Response in the Juvenile and Adult Justice Systems: What Happens,*

What Should Happen, and What We Need to Know (Study Group on the Transitions Between Juvenile Delinquency and Adult Crime) (Report No. 242935). U.S. Department of Justice, Office of Justice Programs.

Hyatt, J. M., & Barnes, G. C. (2017). An experimental evaluation of the impact of intensive supervision on the recidivism of high-risk probationers. *Crime & Delinquency*, *63*(1), 3–38. https://doi.org/10.1177/0011128714555757

Jackson, J., Bradford, B., Hough, M., Myhill, A., Quinton, P., & Tyler, T. R. (2012). Why do people comply with the law?: Legitimacy and the influence of legal institutions. *British Journal of Criminology*, *52*(6), 1051–1071. https://doi.org/10.1093/bjc/azs032

Kaeble, D. (2021). *Probation and parole in the United States, 2020*. US Department of Justice, Office of Justice Programs, Bureau of Justice Statistics.

Konrad, K., Firk, C., & Uhlhaas, P. J. (2013). Brain development during adolescence. *Deutsches Ärzteblatt international*, *110*(25), 425–432. https://doi.org/10.3238/arztebl.2013.0425

Lovins, B. K., Latessa, E. J., May, T., & Lux, J. (2018). Validating the ohio risk assessment system community supervision tool with a diverse sample from Texas. *Corrections*, *3*(3), 186–202. https://doi.org/10.1080/23774657.2017.1361798

Lynam, D. R., Whiteside, S. P., Smith, G. T., & Cyders, M. A. (2006). *The UPPS-P: Assessing five personality pathways to impulsive behavior*. West Lafayette, IN: Purdue University.

Matejkowski, J., Lee, S., & Severson, M. E. (2018). Validation of a tool to measure attitudes among community corrections officers toward shared decision making with formerly incarcerated persons with mental illness. *Criminal Justice and Behavior*, *45*(5), 612–627. https://doi.org/10.1177/0093854818761991

Mills, J. F., Kroner, D. G., & Forth, A. E. (2002). Measures of Criminal Attitudes and Associates (MCAA): Development, factor structure, reliability, and validity. *Assessment*, *9*(3), 240–253. https://doi.org/10.1177/1073191102009003003

Morash, M., Kashy, D. A., Smith, S. W., & Cobbina, J. E. (2015). The effects of probation or parole agent relationship style and women offenders' criminogenic needs on offenders' responses to supervision interactions. *Criminal Justice and Behavior*, *42*(4), 412–434. https://doi.org/10.1177/0093854814551602

Mulvey, E. P., Steinberg, L., Fagan, J., Cauffman, E., Piquero, A. R., Chassin, L., Knight, G. P., Brame, R., Schubert, C. A., Hecker, T., & Losoya, S. H. (2004). Theory and research on desistance from antisocial activity among serious adolescent offenders. *Youth Violence and Juvenile Justice*, *2* (3), 213–236. https://doi.org/10.1177/1541204004265864

Nader, E. S. (2019). *Desistance among emerging adults: a mixed methods approach to understanding identity formation, community, and relationships* (August). University of Massachusetts Lowell.

National Academies of Sciences, Engineering and M. (2022). *The limits of recidivism: measuring success after prison*. The National Academies Press. https://doi.org/10.17226/26459

National Registry of Evidence-Based Programs and Practices (NREPP). (2016).

Papachristos, A. V., Meares, T. L., & Fagan, J. (2012). Why do criminals obey the law? The influence of legitimacy and social networks on active gun offenders. *Journal of Criminal Law and Criminology*, *102*(2), 397–440. https://doi.org/10.0914/169/12/10202/0397

Petersilia, J. (1997). A decade of experimenting with intermediate sanctions: What have we learned. *Perspectives on Crime and Justice: Lecture Series 2*.

Rocque, M. (2021). *But what does it mean? Defining, measuring, and analyzing desistance from crime in criminal justice (October)*. US Department of Justice, Office of Justice Programs, National INstitute of Justice.

Schiraldi, V., Western, B., Bradner, K., & Mason, K. V. (2015). *New Thinking in Community Corrections: Community-Based Responses to Justice-Involved Young Adults* (Report No. 1). National Institute of Justice. https://www.hks.harvard.edu/sites/default/files/centers/wiener/programs/pcj/files/ESCC-CommunityBasedResponsesJusticeInvolvedYA.pdf

Schwarzer, R., & Jerusalem, M. (1995). The General Self-Efficacy scale *(GSE). J. Weinman, S. Wright, & M. Johnston, Measures in health psychology: A user's portfolio. Causal and control beliefs, 35*, 37.

Sheidow, A. J., McCart, M. R., & Davis, M. (2016). Multisystemic therapy for emerging adults with serious mental illness and justice involvement. *Cognitive and Behavioral Practice, 23*(3), 356–367. https://doi.org/10.1016/j.cbpra.2015.09.003.Multisystemic

Steinberg, L. (2007). Risk taking in adolescence: New perspectives from brain and behavioral science. *Current Directions in Psychological Science, 16*(2), 55–59. https://doi.org/10.1111/j.1467-8721.2007.00475.x

Sweeten, G., Piquero, A. R., & Steinberg, L. (2013). Age and the explanation of crime, revisited. *Journal of Youth and Adolescence, 42*(6), 921–938. https://doi.org/10.1007/s10964-013-9926-4

Tangney, J. P., Baumeister, R. F., & Boone, A. L. (2004). High self-control predicts good adjustment, less pathology, better grades, and interpersonal success. *Journal of Personality, 72*(2), 271–324. https://doi.org/10.1111/j.0022-3506.2004.00263.x

Taxman, F. S., Smith, L., & Rudes, D. S. (2020). From Mean to Meaningful Probation: The Legacy of Intensive Supervision Programs. In *Handbook on Moving Corrections and Sentencing Forward* (pp. 61–78). Routledge.

Turner, S., Petersilia, J., & Deschenes, E. P. (1992). Evaluating intensive supervision probation/parole (ISP) for drug offenders. *Crime & Delinquency, 38*(4), 539–556. https://doi.org/10.1177/0011128792038004009

Tyler, T. R. (1990). *Why people obey the law*. Yale University Press.

Tyler, T. R. (2003). Procedural justice, legitimacy, and the effective rule of law. *Crime and Justice, 30*, 283–357. https://doi.org/10.1086/652233

Zajac, K., Sheidow, A. J., & Davis, M. (2013). *Transition age youth with mental health challenges in the juvenile justice system*. Washington, DC: Technical Assistance Partnership for Child and Family Mental Health.

A Rapid Review of Literature on Factors Associated with Adult Probation Revocations

Carmen L. Diaz, Staci Rising, Eric Grommon, Miriam Northcutt Bohmert, and Evan Marie Lowder

ABSTRACT
Criminal justice stakeholders have increasingly relied on probation supervision as an alternative to incarceration and yet, probation revocations often result in incarceration. As such, increased understanding of the mechanisms behind revocations and strategies to reduce them is critical. We conduct a rapid review of the literature on factors associated with probation revocations. Specifically, we review 50 articles on how probation officer behavior, officer-client relationships, caseload size, supervision intensity, monetary sanctions, probation client characteristics, or programming and services are associated with probation revocations. Though the literature is limited, and findings are mixed, the most consistent findings indicate that officer-client relationships involving trust, support, respect, and empathy as well as reduced caseload sizes and cognitive behavioral therapy programs are associated with probation success while intensive supervision programs; greater monetary sanctions and nonpayment of those sanctions; and being Black and less educated are associated with poorer supervision outcomes. Implications for future research, policy, and practice are discussed.

Introduction

In an era of decarceration in the United States (Bureau of Justice Statistics, 2019; Petersilia & Cullen, 2014), strategies to divert offenders away from prison and into the community are being utilized more frequently than in prior years (Glaze & Bonczar, 2009). One of the most common strategies to divert individuals away from prison is probation (American Correctional Association, 2006). Most criminal justice stakeholders assert that the purpose of modern probation is to rehabilitate justice-involved individuals in their communities by encouraging prosocial behavior; yet, some subscribe to a more punitive philosophy emphasizing deterrence over rehabilitation (Brilliant, 1989; Skeem & Manchak, 2008).

Despite the fact that probation is increasingly relied upon as a strategy for diverting justice-involved individuals away from more punitive prison sanctions, individuals under supervision still often end up experiencing incarceration. When probation clients violate

This article has been republished with minor changes. These changes do not impact the academic content of the article.

supervision conditions, such as attending meetings with a probation officer and not being rearrested, the term of supervision can be revoked and may result in incarceration. Prior research indicates that approximately two-thirds of probation clients are arrested for a new charge during or after their term of probation, often resulting in revocation even if the charges are later dropped (Jalbert et al., 2010; Petersilia et al., 1986). Yet, probation serves both rehabilitative as well as supervisory functions. Understanding the mechanisms driving probation revocations may help inform strategies to reduce them and better fulfill the goals of the probationary period.

There is a critical need for timely information on the factors associated with probation revocations that extends beyond the goals for rehabilitation. Such knowledge can inform national initiatives that are currently examining probation revocations, such as the Arnold Ventures Reducing Revocations Challenge (CUNY, n.d.). Knowledge on factors associated with revocations is also relevant to current conversations on reducing racial and ethnic disparities in criminal-legal processing (e.g., see, Crutchfield et al., 2010), longstanding concerns regarding recidivism, and recent growing concern over the impacts of monetary sanctions (Harris, 2016). Moreover, there is a lack of synthesis of probation revocation literature beyond highly specific systematic reviews and meta-analytic investigations (e.g., Sirdifield et al., 2020).

Thus, this paper provides a rapid review of the literature on factors associated with probation revocations. The goals of this review are to inform stakeholders about how probation revocation has been studied, highlight the most consistent research findings, and provide new insights about how to build on existing knowledge to further improve probation outcomes.

Methods

The rapid review is a common method in the healthcare field; its main purpose is to review a particular body of literature in a reduced timeframe when compared with a systematic review method (Ganann et al., 2010). Previous research on the rapid review method has found that while systematic reviews delivered more detailed information, the central conclusions of rapid reviews were largely consistent with those resulting from systematic reviews (Watt et al., 2008). Thus, this approach allows practitioners and policy makers to make informed decisions about factors related to probation revocations in a context where time and resources are limited. Given the current sociopolitical climate (e.g., concerns over racial disparities in criminal legal processing) and calls for criminal legal reform, information on probation revocations is urgently needed.

For the current review, three reviewers independently searched for peer-reviewed journal articles. Articles were selected for full review if they related to the influence of probation officers, caseload size, supervision intensity, legal financial obligations, probation client characteristics, or programming and services on probation revocations. Search engines included Google Scholar, ProQuest Sociological abstracts, EBSCO Criminal Justice Abstracts, EBSCO Academic Search, ProQuest Social Sciences, Indiana University-Purdue University Indianapolis Library, and Indiana University-Bloomington Library. The reviewers also relied on reference lists in articles to identify other works of interest. Search terms used included "probation" and "revocation" or "recidivism"; in addition to one of the following terms: "officer probationer relationship," "probationer demographics," "programming," "caseload size," "intensive supervision program," "monetary sanctions," "criminal justice debt," "legal financial obligations," "fines and fees," "probationer characteristics," "age," "gender," "race," "education," "employment," "programs," "drug treatment," or "cognitive behavioral therapy."

The reviewers conducted a full-text review of an estimated 68 articles; a total of 50 articles were selected for final inclusion and are detailed in Table 1. Articles were excluded if they were published prior to 1990, published in a language other than English, focused on juvenile rather than adult probation clients, or if the topic focused on parole or another form of community corrections (e.g., home detention) rather than probation. Additionally, for articles related to programming and services, articles were excluded when program outcomes were not reported. Qualitative and quantitative studies were both included. After each article was reviewed, one reviewer independently assessed each section of the review, noting what she believed to be the most relevant findings and gaps in the research. The other two reviewers then examined these findings and noted any suggested additions or revisions, which were resolved in collaboration.

Results

Effects of probation officer behaviors and officer-client relationships on revocations

Probation officers' supervision strategies have often been considered secondary to the specific probation programming their clients are regularly ordered to complete (e.g., cognitive behavioral therapy). Therefore, relatively few studies have focused on the effect officers have on probation outcomes. However, studies that do exist suggest probation officers may have more substantial impacts on client outcomes than initially thought.

Some research suggests that PO behavior influences probation outcomes. For example, a 2007 study examined the effects of decisions by the courtroom workgroup members (i.e., judges, prosecutors, and probation officers) on probation violations, revocations, and incarcerations. Using data on 2,840 Arizona probation clients, researchers found that, in the courtroom workgroup, probation officers had the largest impact on probation revocation cases (Rodriguez & Webb, 2007). Given that the most common cause of revocation is technical violations and not new arrests, power lies with probation officers who have the ultimate responsibility of deciding whether to address a client's behavior with an informal reprimand or a formal violation.

Another more recent study examined one type of probation officer behavior that may impact client behavior: the use of rewards and sanctions. Using administrative data on 283 participants from the Wyoming Department of Corrections, analyses found that the utilization of both rewards and sanctions increased successful program outcomes for probation clients and decreased revocation rates. The effect was particularly strong when rewards and sanctions were applied with a 4 (or more) rewards to 1 sanction ratio (Wodahl et al., 2011).

However, other research suggests PO behavior may not influence probation outcomes. A study on officers' responses to client activities suggested that PO behavior had no significant effect on either client criminal or violation behaviors (MacKenzie et al., 1999). Another more recent study examined the impact of PO actions on recidivism of female clients and found that, although anxiety caused by punitive officer-client relationships may

Table 1. Literature on factors associated with adult probation revocations.

	Sample size/population	Method	Findings
Probation Officer Behaviors & Officer-Client Relationships			
MacKenzie et al., 1999	126 clients from three Virginia probation departments	Regression analyses & Linear Structural Relationships analysis	• There was no evidence that responses by officers within a month of a violation have any impact on probation outcomes in terms of crime or violation behaviors.
Morash et al., 2016	226 female clients and 73 officers from Michigan probation departments	Path analysis	• Officer actions measured had no measurable effect on probationer recidivism. • Probationer anxiety caused by punitive officer-client relationships may have had negative effects on probationer recidivism.
Morash et al., 2014	330 female clients from Michigan probation and parole departments	Regression analyses	• Probation and parole clients with officers who utilized supportive (rather than punitive) behaviors had less anxiety and less tendency toward reactive behaviors. • Punitive supervision style was most related to reactance and anxiety for female clients at lowest risk for recidivism, while supportiveness was most related to positive outcomes for highest risk female clients.
Okonofua et al., 2021	216 officers from California probation and parole departments	Akaike information criterion (AIC) model	• Compared to the control group, probation and parole clients receiving "empathetic supervision" experienced a 13% reduction in violations and recidivism. • Training effects on officer "collective blame" remained for as long as ten months post-training.
Rodriguez & Webb, 2007	2,840 clients from Arizona probation departments	Regression analyses	• Within the courtroom workgroup, probation officers had the largest impact on probation revocation cases.
Skeem et al., 2003	32 officers and 20 clients from several major cities' probation departments	Qualitative analysis of focus group data	• Specialty probation agencies emphasized offender rehabilitation, while traditional probation agencies emphasized community safety. • Clients experienced better mental health treatment outcomes when supervised by specialty probation agencies rather than traditional agencies.

(Continued)

Table 1. (Continued).

	Sample size/population	Method	Findings
Smith et al., 2020	69 Michigan probation and parole officers and 353 probation and parole clients of these officers	Regression analyses	• Clients supervised by officers with procedurally fair approaches were more likely to be rearrested within 24 months of beginning probation. • Clients supervised by officers with authoritarian approaches were less likely to be rearrested within 24 months of beginning probation.
Sturm et al., 2021	199 clients from Netherlands probation departments	Regression analyses	• Clients who reported greater trust in their probation officers were less likely to recidivate within a four-year follow up period.
Wodahl et al., 2011	283 clients from Wyoming probation departments	Regression analyses	• Utilization of both rewards and sanctions increased successful program outcomes for clients and decreased revocation rates. • Most effective ratio for applying rewards and sanctions was 4:1.
Supervision Intensity & Specialized Caseloads			
Barnes et al., 2010	1,559 low-risk probation and parole cases that began between 2002 and 2004	Randomized controlled trial & random forests model	• There were not significant differences in arrests in the follow-up period between the cases receiving standard intensity supervision and those receiving low-intensity supervision.
Buttars et al., 2016	885 sex offenders from a Midwestern state department of corrections	Analysis of covariance, survival analysis & logistic regression	• Intensive supervision community corrections clients were more likely to be revoked from placement than clients receiving standard community corrections supervision. • No differences in recidivism or severity of recidivated offenses were found between groups.
Duru et al., 2020	2,999 low-risk clients from one of the largest probation departments in the U.S.	Regression analyses	• Clients on the low-risk caseloads were significantly less likely to be revoked than clients on high-risk, intensive supervision caseloads. • Rates of rearrest were similar across both groups, suggesting that the reduced supervision intensity did not negatively influence criminal behavior.

(*Continued*)

Table 1. (Continued).

	Sample size/population	Method	Findings
Fox et al., 2022	Review of five studies on impact of probation caseload sizes on client outcomes	Rapid evidence assessment	• Studies reviewed suggested smaller caseload sizes do not result in more intensive supervision or more probation violations.
Frailing et al., 2020	Program evaluation of the Swift and Certain (SAC) Probation Program in Jefferson Parish, Louisiana	Program evaluation	• The majority of the SAC program's goals were being met, including measurable reductions in new crime, substance use, and jail overcrowding.
Hyatt & Barnes, 2017	832 clients from a Philadelphia, Pennsylvania probation department	Randomized controlled trial & program evaluation	• No differences in recidivism were found between probation clients who received ISP and those who received traditional supervision. • ISP clients had significantly more violations, incarcerations, and abscondments.
Jalbert et al., 2010	8,878 clients from an Iowa department of corrections	Regression discontinuity design & survival analysis	• ISP reduced the likelihood of recidivism by 25.5% in the first six months after release. • Effects lasted beyond 18 months for some types of arrest (property and violent). • ISP had no significant effect on revocations for non-arrest related violations (e.g., positive drug screens).
Jalbert et al., 2011	39,295 cases from probation departments in Oklahoma, Iowa, and Colorado	Randomized controlled trial, difference in differences design, focus groups, & interviews	• Clients on smaller caseloads had fewer arrests for new crimes and were more likely to receive correctional interventions. • Technical violations were slightly higher for clients on smaller caseloads compared to clients on larger caseloads. • Positive effects were only found in cases where evidence-based practices were utilized by officers.
Manchak et al., 2014	359 cases from two undisclosed probation agencies in the U.S.	Longitudinal multimethod multi-measure matched design & regression analyses	• Smaller, specialty caseloads yielded significantly more effective officer practices (problem solving vs. sanction threats), greater treatment engagement, and fewer rates of violation reports than traditional caseloads.
Taxman, 2002	Review of 15 studies on ISPs from 1960 to 1998	Literature review	• Studies reviewed suggested ISPs elicit either no difference in recidivism or higher incidence of recidivism compared to traditional probation.

(Continued)

Table 1. (Continued).

	Sample size/population	Method	Findings
Van Deinse et al., 2022	100 clients with serious mental illness from probation departments in two southeastern U.S. counties	Randomized controlled trial	• Clients on specialty mental health probation caseloads had higher rates of mental health treatment engagement, as well as higher rates of new crime violations.
Monetary Sanctions			
Brett et al., 2020	Review of statutes and policies in all 50 U.S. states & Interviews with over 100 justice system stakeholders (e.g., defense attorneys, probation officers, judges)	Policy analyses & qualitative analyses of interviews with criminal justice stakeholders	• Statutes in 8 states allow revocation due to nonpayment without referencing ability to pay & those in 23 states outline ability to pay requirements. • Statutes in 3 states prohibit revocation due to nonpayment alone. • Remaining states do not have statutes on revocation for nonpayment, but several allow revocation for violation of any probation condition (such as nonpayment). • Revocations based on nonpayment alone are rare, but probation officers may accumulate violations including nonpayment which increase revocation odds.
Cadigan & Kirk, 2020	126 interviews of Illinois and Washington State residents sentenced to pay monetary sanctions & Courtroom observations totaling 300 hours	Qualitative analyses of interviews & ethnographic observations	• Court processes associated with LFO collection complicate maintenance of employment and housing which in turn complicates compliance with probation requirements.
Gordon & Glaser, 1991	824 cases sentenced to probation in Los Angeles County municipal courts between 1981 and 1984	Regression analyses	• Clients assigned probation, jail, and financial penalty had higher odds of revocation compared to those who were only assigned financial penalties. • Greater financial penalties appeared to be linked with revocation.
Harris, 2016	Observations of 85 sentencing hearings & 50 violation hearings; Interviews with 102 court stakeholders (e.g., judges, attorneys)	Policy analyses, qualitative analyses of court observations, & interviews of court officials	• 44 U.S. states and Washington D.C. have statutes allowing imprisonment for nonpayment. • Court officials in different jurisdictions had varied interpretations of legal concepts (e.g., willfulness).
Iratzoqui & Metcalfe, 2017	358 indigent adult felony cases in a Florida public defender's office	Regression analyses	• Monetary sanctions were not significantly associated with probation violations, though effects were in the expected direction.
Minor et al., 2003	200 federal probation clients supervised in Kentucky, 1996–1999	Chi-square tests & Regression analysis	• There was not a significant association between fines, restitution, and violations.

(*Continued*)

Table 1. (Continued).

	Sample size/population	Method	Findings
Ruhland et al., 2020	1,257 clients from one Texas probation department	Regression analyses	• Compared to fines, fees had a larger influence on revocations. • Clients with larger fee assessment amounts, but not fine assessment amounts, had a significantly greater likelihood of revocation. • Clients with a greater percentage of unpaid fines and fees were more likely to be revoked.
Shannon, 2020	11 probation officers and 60 clients from three judicial circuits in Georgia	Qualitative analysis of interview data	• Probation officers reported clients were never revoked due solely to nonpayment but could be revoked due to nonpayment in combination with other kinds of noncompliance. • Clients reported threats by officers and fear of incarceration for nonpayment.
Client Characteristics			
Albonetti & Hepburn, 1997	617 clients in Phoenix, Arizona	Survival analysis & Cox regression	• Among the most disadvantaged group of clients – those with less than a high school education who also had a prior arrest record – men and younger clients were significantly more likely to be revoked. • For clients with higher levels of education and/or no arrest record, age and sex did not significantly predict revocation.
Dagenhardt, 2021	347 cases in domestic violence courts in one urban Midwestern county in 2016 & 100 cases selected for qualitative analysis	Regression analyses & Critical discourse analysis	• Likelihood of noncompliance sanctioning did not vary by race or ethnicity. • Hispanic and Black clients had shorter jail stays for noncompliance. • Judges tended to sanction Black and Hispanic clients for minor drug use violations with a short jail stay but White clients tended to be punished with longer jail stays only when they committed more serious violations.
Gordon & Glaser, 1991	824 probation cases sentenced in Los Angeles municipal courts in from 1981–1984	Regression analyses	• Black and younger clients were more likely to be revoked. • Revocation odds for Hispanic clients were not significantly different from those of White clients.

(Continued)

Table 1. (Continued).

	Sample size/population	Method	Findings
Gray et al., 2001	1,574 clients committed to probation in Michigan in 1996	Survival analysis & Cox regression	• Sex was not significantly associated with technical violations or new crimes. • Nonwhite clients were more likely to commit technical violations but were no more likely to commit new crimes.
Jannetta et al., 2014	105,200 clients from four probation departments in Texas, Iowa, Oregon, and New York and 50 probation staff and judges	Regression analyses & qualitative analysis of interviews	• Age was not significantly associated with success, but the relationship was in the anticipated direction. • Black clients were more likely revoked compared to White and Hispanic clients across all sites. • Compared to White clients, in one location, Hispanic clients had higher rates of revocation, in two other locations the rate was lower, and in one final location there was no discernable difference. • Probation staff and judges suggested racial minorities were more likely have justice system contact and revocations due to increased police presence in minority neighborhoods.
Morgan, 1994	266 Tennessee felony clients with cases that ended from 1980–1989	Regression analyses	• Male clients and those with lower education levels were more likely to be unsuccessful. • Race and age were not significantly associated with probation outcomes, but the associations were in the expected direction.
Olson & Lurigio, 2000	2,400 Illinois clients that were discharged in 1997	Regression analyses	• Sex was not significantly associated with revocation. • Younger clients were more likely to be revoked.
Ruhland et al., 2020	1,257 clients from one Texas probation department	Regression analyses	• Men were more likely than women to be revoked for new offenses but not for technical violations. • Age, race, and ethnicity were not significantly associated with revocation. • White compared to non-white clients experienced revocation more quickly.
Sims & Jones, 1997	2,850 felony clients that exited probation in North Carolina in 1993	Regression analyses	• Younger, African American, and male clients were significantly more likely to experience probation failure.

(Continued)

Table 1. (Continued).

	Sample size/population	Method	Findings
Steinmetz & Henderson, 2016	115,384 clients that exited probation between 2000–2010 in two of the largest counties in a large southwestern state	Regression analyses	• Clients who were Black, Hispanic, and male were more likely to be revoked. • The interaction of being Black and male was a strong predictor of revocation. • Age was a poor predictor for revocation.
Tapia & Harris, 2006	1,514 felony clients in a large southern state who started probation in 1993	Regression analyses	• For male, female, White, and Hispanic clients, unemployment was associated with higher odds of revocation. • Unemployed Black clients did not have a significantly higher likelihood of revocation compared to employed Black clients. • Black men aged 17–29 had the greatest chances of revocation regardless of employment. • Revocation odds for Hispanic clients were similar to those of White clients.
Turner et al., 2022	6,600 misdemeanor cases from one county in Georgia in which clients began probation between 2016–2018	Regression analyses	• Younger and male clients were more likely to be unsuccessful. • Hispanic clients were more likely to be successful compared to White clients.
Zettler & Martin, 2020	123 clients who were felony drug court participants between 2015 and 2017 in a southwestern urban county	Regression analyses	• Clients with higher levels of education had reduced odds of revocation.
Programming and Services			
Barnes et al., 2017	904 high-risk probation and parole clients assigned to a standard intensive supervision or a CBT treatment condition in Philadelphia, Pennsylvania	Randomized field trial & Intention-to-treat analyses	• Clients who received CBT treatment had a significantly reduced likelihood of being charged for a new crime in the one-year follow-up period.
Golden, 2002	142 clients from a Texas probation department	Quasi-experimental design & regression analyses	• New criminal offense rates for probation clients who completed Thinking for a Change were 33% lower than that for comparison groups. • There were no differences in technical violation filings between Thinking for a Change completers and comparison groups. • Being a Thinking for a Change dropout, being classified as "high risk" on risk assessments, and having poor problem-solving skills were all predictors of technical violations.

(*Continued*)

Table 1. (Continued).

	Sample size/population	Method	Findings
Goodson et al., 2020	200 female clients from several Michigan probation departments	Regression analyses	• Peer support was positively related to violations and arrests when a client's treatment engagement was low, contraindicating group treatment for some individuals.
Hatcher et al., 2012	Experimental group: 173 male clients sentenced to probation in 2002 in England and Wales who were referred to a cognitive skills program. Comparison group: 173 male clients matched one-to-one based on criminogenic variables	Quasi-experimental design, intention to treat & treatment received analyses	• Intention to treat analysis revealed no difference in reconviction across different groups. • Treatment received analysis showed moderate completion effects. For every three clients that completed the program, five clients in the matched comparison group were reconvicted. • Treatment received analysis also showed a noncompletion effect in that clients who did not complete the program were two times more likely to be reconvicted compared to the matched comparison group.
Hollin et al., 2008	4,935 male clients sentenced to probation in 2002 in England and Wales who: (1) completed a structured cognitive-behavioral treatment program, (2) began but did not complete a program, (3) were assigned to a program but failed to start the program, or (4) had not been assigned to a program	Quasi-experimental design & regression analyses	• Clients that completed a program showed reduced reconviction rates relative to all other groups.
Jacobs et al., 2022	772 clients with either mental health, substance use, or co-occurring disorders from a San Francisco probation department	Cox proportional hazards models	• Use of mental health services significantly predicted decreased recidivism for individuals diagnosed with a mental disorder. • There was no significant relationship between services and recidivism for those with substance use and co-occurring disorders.
Jalbert et al., 2011	39,295 cases from probation departments in Oklahoma, Iowa, and Colorado	Randomized controlled trial (OK) or a regression discontinuity design (IA & CO), & survival analysis	• Clients on smaller caseloads had fewer arrests for new crimes and were more likely to receive correctional interventions. • Technical violations were slightly higher for clients on smaller caseloads compared to clients on larger caseloads. • Positive effects were only found in cases where evidence-based practices were utilized by officers.

(*Continued*)

Table 1. (Continued).

	Sample size/population	Method	Findings
Kosson et al., 2019	287 clients from an Illinois probation department	Survival analyses	• Treatment group clients (those who attended *Thinking for a Change)* were more likely to complete probation successfully and survive longer before rearrest. • Treatment was predictive of lower recidivism among certain ethnicities, including European Americans and African Americans, but not Latino Americans.
Longshore et al., 2004	35,947 cases from California probation departments	Program evaluation & regression analyses	• Only one in five clients who participated in treatment under Proposition 36 were revoked from probation, a rate lower than traditional probation.
Lowenkamp et al., 2009	217 felony clients in Tippecanoe County, Indiana. 121 clients were referred to a CBT program, 96 clients were not referred to the program.	Regression analyses	• Recidivism rates were significantly reduced for clients who participated in the program compared to those who had not participated.
McGuire et al., 2008	929 male clients sentenced in 2002 in England and Wales who: (1) completed a structured cognitive-behavioral treatment program, (2) began but did not complete a program, (3) were assigned to a program but failed to start the program, or (4) had not been assigned to a program	Intention-to-treat analysis & treatment received analysis	• When comparing groups that were or were not assigned to a program, there was no significant overall difference between groups in terms of re-conviction outcomes. • Program completion was associated with reduced reconvictions. • Results indicated a potential treatment effect among moderate to high-risk clients.
Palmer et al., 2015	801 female clients in England and Wales who: (1) completed a cognitive skills program, (2) began but did not complete a program, or (3) were not assigned to a program	Quasi-experimental design & regression analyses	• Reconviction rates were not significantly different between (1) those who completed the program and those who were not assigned to a program, or (2) those who completed and those who did not complete. • Clients who did not complete the program had higher reconviction rates compared to those who were not assigned to a program.
Rodriguez & Webb, 2007	2,840 clients from Arizona probation departments	Regression analyses	• Within the courtroom workgroup, probation officers had the largest impact on probation revocation cases.

Note: Study descriptions do not necessarily include all methods, data sources, and/or findings. Instead, the study description is focused on elements relevant to the influence of each factor (e.g., probation officer behavior, monetary sanctions) on probation revocation, success, and/or recidivism. The term "clients" refers to probation clients unless otherwise specified.

have had negative effects, specific PO actions measured had none (Morash et al., 2016). More research is needed to clarify both whether PO decision-making is driving revocation rates as well as what influences decision-making in situations of client noncompliance (i.e., whether to reprimand informally or formally).

A handful of studies have also examined the nature and impact of the PO-client relationship on violations. Seminal work by Andrews and Bonta (2015) on the Risk Needs Responsivity model (RNR) emphasizes the importance of high-quality interpersonal relationships to reduce criminogenic needs.

Research has indicated that PO-client relationships characterized by respect, supportiveness, empathy, and trust appear to be associated with improved outcomes. For instance, one study utilized focus groups and administrative data to compare outcomes for clients with mental health treatment mandates, who were either assigned to traditional probation agencies or to specialty agencies (Skeem et al., 2003). The study found that clients had better treatment outcomes when supervised by specialty agencies, which emphasized rehabilitation (rather than only community safety) and utilized a respectful, personal relationship with clients.

A later longitudinal study explored the impact of the relationship between female probation and parole clients and their officers regarding how clients respond to supervision actions (Morash et al., 2014). The study utilized interview data from 330 female clients in Michigan and found that clients with POs who utilized supportive (rather than punitive) behaviors had less anxiety and less tendency toward reactive behaviors (i.e., doing the opposite of what the PO asks of her).

In a similar vein, researchers in California examined the effects of "empathetic supervision" on probation and parole violations (Okonofua et al., 2021). A total of 216 probation and parole officers were given empathetic supervision exercises geared toward increasing empathy and reducing "collective blame" toward clients. Compared to the control group, clients receiving "empathetic supervision" experienced a 13% reduction in violations and recidivism.

Another study in that year examined the effects of the PO-client relationship through the lens of the Working Alliance with Mandated Clients Inventory (WAMCI), developed from modern psychotherapy research which explores the "working alliance" between therapists and patients (Sturm et al., 2021). Using a sample of 199 individuals sentenced to community supervision in the Netherlands, researchers used the WAMCI tool to measure the officer-client relationship on subscales such as "Trust" and "Reactance," and found that clients that reported greater trust in their POs were less likely to recidivate within the four-year follow up period.

In contrast to studies which have found that PO-client relationships characterized by elements like trust and empathy are associated with improved outcomes, a recent study has found that authoritative supervision styles may be more effective than those that are procedurally just. Smith et al. (2020) examined the relationship between PO supervision styles and female probation and parole client outcomes. Using interviews and surveys, researchers captured perceptions about officers' background, caseload characteristics, and supervision styles, such as "procedurally fair" or "authoritative." Data suggested that female clients whose POs used procedurally fair supervision styles were more likely to be rearrested, while those with more authoritative supervision styles were less likely to be rearrested.

In summary, research on the impacts of PO behaviors and the PO-client relationship suggests that these dynamics may have important implications for probation outcomes. While some research has found little to no evidence that PO actions influence client behavior or success, other studies have found that POs' decisions are consequential in impacting case outcomes and that POs use of sanctions and rewards have the potential to reduce revocation rates. Research on the PO-client relationship generally suggests that relationships characterized by respect, supportiveness, empathy, and trust have a positive impact on supervision outcomes.

Effects of supervision intensity and specialized caseloads on probation revocations

Intensive supervision programs (ISPs) are often integrated into probation departments. ISP clients are monitored more closely (e.g., more frequent reporting), and their release conditions are more stringent (e.g., more programming) than those for clients on a traditional caseload. The rationale behind ISPs assumes that clients who are more closely supervised will have less misconduct and better outcomes. However, a majority of studies have found ISPs to have worse client outcomes than traditional probation. A 2002 review of 15 studies on ISPs from 1960 to 1998 found that ISPs elicited either no difference in recidivism or higher incidence of recidivism compared to traditional probation (Taxman, 2002).

Findings from several more recent studies are consistent with Taxman's 2002 review in that they have found either no difference or higher rates of revocation and incarceration for ISP clients. For example, a 2010 study utilized administrative data collected on 8,878 probation clients from the Iowa Department of Correction from 2001 to 2007 to examine ISP outcomes. Data suggests that ISP reduced the likelihood of recidivism (i.e., new arrests during or after the probation period) by 25.5% in the first six months after release. However, researchers emphasized that ISP had no significant effect on revocations for non-arrest related violations (e.g., positive drug screens; Jalbert et al., 2010).

In a 2016 study, Buttars, Huss, and Brack found that ISP probation clients were more likely to be revoked than individuals receiving standard probation. After controlling for propensity score, residential treatment and standard probation were the only significant predictors of revocation (Buttars et al., 2016). Another study by Hyatt and Barnes (2017) details an experimental evaluation of an ISP and its effects on probation client recidivism, absconding, technical violations, and incarceration. Clients were randomly assigned to either ISP (N = 447) or a traditional caseload (N = 385). After 12 months, no differences in recidivism were found; ISP clients had significantly more technical violations and incarcerations; they also absconded at significantly higher rates. The authors posit that these high failure rates may signal that the enhanced requirements of ISPs are simply too much for some high-risk clients to endure.

A recent study by Frailing et al. (2020) contrasts the findings of negative ISP outcomes from other research. The study examines the Swift and Certain (SAC) Probation Program in Jefferson Parish, Louisiana, an intensive supervision program for high-risk clients. In the study's first two years, researchers found that the majority of the program's goals were being met, including measurable reductions in new crime, substance use, and jail overcrowding. However, researchers indicated that SAC programs present their own set of challenges and advocate exploring these, particularly through the use of probation client perceptions surveys.

As opposed to ISPs, a study by Duru et al. (2020) explored how reducing, rather than enhancing, supervision intensity impacts low-risk probation clients. A total of 2,999 low-risk clients in a large U.S. probation department were assigned to either a low-risk or a regular caseload (i.e., mixed low, moderate, and high-risk clients). A low-risk caseload reduced supervision intensity in terms of face-to-face contacts, urine drug screens, and overall volume of case notes. Researchers found that clients on the low-risk caseload were significantly less likely to be revoked. Further, rates of rearrest were similar across both groups, indicating that the reduced supervision intensity did not negatively influence criminal behavior. Duru et al.'s findings are consistent with an earlier randomized controlled trial which utilized a sample of 1,559 low-risk probation and parole clients (Barnes et al., 2010). Clients were assigned either to a standard intensity or a low-intensity supervision group and the study found no significant differences in arrests between the groups during a one year follow up period.

Another line of research suggests that smaller probation caseloads may promote positive client outcomes. For example, a multi-site study in 2011 found that clients on smaller caseloads had fewer arrests for new crimes and were more likely to receive correctional interventions; however, technical violations were slightly higher than those on larger caseloads (Jalbert et al., 2011). The authors emphasized that these positive effects were only seen in agencies whose officers had correctly implemented evidence-based practices in their casework.

A later, longitudinal study by Manchak et al. (2014) examined differences between smaller, specialty caseloads in terms of officer practices, probation client treatment, and rule violations. Specialty mental health caseloads (n = 183 clients) were compared to larger, traditional caseloads (n = 176 clients). Results suggested that smaller, specialty caseloads yielded significantly more effective officer practices (problem solving vs. sanction threats), greater treatment involvement, and fewer rates of violation reports than traditional caseloads.

Recently, Fox et al. (2022) conducted a Rapid Evidence Assessment on studies examining the impact of probation caseload sizes on client outcomes. A total of five relevant studies were identified for this review. Although researchers anticipated that small caseload sizes would result in more intensive supervision and therefore more probation violations, the studies reviewed did not find this effect; instead, the studies found that smaller caseload sizes had lower rates of technical violations as well as new arrests and reconvictions.

A randomized control trial in 2022 examined the effects of a specialty mental health probation (SMHP) caseload on probation client outcomes in two southeastern U.S. counties (Van Deinse et al., 2022). For a total of 100 clients with serious mental illnesses on either a standard or SMHP caseload, researchers examined outcomes in terms of mental health treatment engagement and crime violations. Results suggest that clients on SMHP had higher rates of mental health treatment engagement but also had higher rates of new crime violations.

Overall, ISPs are largely unsuccessful and unlikely to reduce revocations due to enhanced detection of problematic behavior. On the other hand, reduced supervision intensity for low-risk clients may successfully reduce revocations without having a negative impact on criminal behavior. Further, smaller caseload sizes may improve supervision outcomes in terms of violations, new arrests, and reconvictions.

Effects of monetary sanctions on probation revocations

Probation revocations can also stem from nonpayment of monetary sanctions, which are also frequently referred to as "legal financial obligations," and may include court costs, fines, fees, restitution, and surcharges (Harris, 2016; Vallas & Patel, 2012). Monthly user fees are often assessed for individuals on probation but monetary sanctions that are accumulated at other points of criminal justice contact (e.g., court costs, cost of treatment) inflate criminal debt and can have far reaching effects (Harris, 2016).

In 1971, the Supreme Court held that imposing a jail sentence due to an indigent individual's unpaid fines is unconstitutional (*Tate v., Short*, 1972). Additionally, in 1983 the Supreme Court ruled in Bearden v. Georgia that an individual cannot be revoked from probation if the court has not evaluated the individual's ability to pay and has not weighed alternative options to incarceration (*Bearden v. Georgia*, 1983). The ruling specified that an individual cannot be imprisoned for failure to pay unless the individual possesses the resources to make payments but willfully refuses to do so. Notwithstanding such legal protections, there is evidence that policies and practices regarding nonpayment of monetary sanctions in many jurisdictions still leads to revocations (Bannon et al., 2010).

Some research based on policy and qualitative analyses has documented policies and practices which influence revocations. For instance, Alexes Harris (2016) provided a detailed illustration of how legal financial obligations (LFOs) are implemented in the U.S. Harris found that relatively recent modifications in state penal codes, adding and modifying existing LFOs, have contributed to a dramatic increase in the both the regularity with which they are imposed as well as the total amount imposed in recent years. Harris found that a total of 44 states as well as the District of Columbia have statutes which permit judges to impose imprisonment for nonpayment of LFOs. In evaluating the LFO practices in five Washington State counties, Harris found an explanation for how nonpayment may still lead to probation revocations, despite the legal protections previously mentioned. By observing court proceedings and interviewing court officials and defendants, Harris discovered that court officials conceived of their own varied interpretations of legal concepts like "willfulness" and "indigent." For instance, individuals who were homeless were still expected to pay LFOs in some counties.

The Harvard Law School Criminal Justice Policy Program also recently published a report on financial sanctions for individuals on probation which relied on a review of state statutes and local policies as well as interviews with various stakeholders such as probation officers and judges (Brett et al., 2020). The report assessed state statutes relevant to revocation for nonpayment of LFOs and found wide variation. Statutes in eight states allow revocation or incarceration due to delinquent fines, fees, and/or restitution and these statutes do not reference the individual's ability to pay. However, in twenty-three states, there are statutes which outline the requirements of assessing ability to pay under *Bearden*. Just three states have statutes which prohibit revocation or incarceration due to nonpayment alone. While the other fifteen states do not have statutes on the topic of revoking probation for nonpayment, a number of them do have statutes allowing revocation based on violation of any condition of probation which could include a nonpayment violation. Attorneys reported that nonpayment increases the odds of revocation (Brett et al., 2020). The authors also found that while revocations based on nonpayment alone are rare, probation officers may accumulate violations including nonpayment, to make a stronger case when filing for revocation. Importantly, interviews indicated that when nonpayment violations are included among other violations, ability to pay is not often assessed.

While such practices have been documented, empirical research on the influence of monetary sanctions on adult probation revocations is limited. In 1991, Gordon and Glaser evaluated the use and effects of financial penalties in the Los Angeles County municipal courts. The authors found that individuals who were assigned probation, jail, and financial penalty had higher odds of revocation compared to those who were only assigned financial penalties. Also, the extent of the financial penalty reduced the odds that the amount would be paid in full but increased the chances of probation being revoked. Thus, greater financial penalties appeared to be linked with revocation.

On the other hand, some scholars have found that only certain types of monetary sanctions result in negative probation outcomes. Ruhland et al. (2020) investigated the association between fines and fees and probation revocation. The authors conducted regression analyses on a sample of 1,257 clients from one probation department in Texas. Results indicated that, compared to fines (used for punitive purposes), fees (used to pay for services) had a larger influence on revocations. Clients with larger fee assessment amounts, but not fine assessment amounts, had a significantly greater likelihood of revocation. Aside from what clients were charged, the study also found that those with a greater percentage of unpaid fines and fees were more likely to be revoked (Ruhland et al., 2020).

Other empirical research has failed to find a significant association between monetary sanctions and probation outcomes. Minor et al. (2003) examined two types of LFO's, fines and restitution, and did not find a significant impact on violations in a sample of 200 individuals, on federal probation in Kentucky, from 1996 to 1999. This study's analysis was limited to fines and restitution, ignoring fees, which Ruhland et al. (2020) recently found to have a larger influence on probation revocations compared to fines. Iratzoqui and Metcalfe (2017) assessed the relationship between several monetary sanctions and probation violations in a sample of 358 indigent adults with felony probation cases in a public defender's office in Florida. The study found that monetary sanctions did not significantly influence the chances of probation violation but did produce effects in the anticipated direction.

Qualitative research has also indicated that while POs report that revocations based solely on nonpayment are rare, probation clients often express fear of such revocation which may indirectly lead to incarceration. Probation officers (n = 11) from three judicial circuits in Georgia reported that clients were never revoked only due to nonpayment (Shannon, 2020). Instead, they suggested that clients could be revoked based on nonpayment in addition to other kinds of noncompliance. However, many clients (n = 60) supervised in the same judicial districts reported that they were threatened by POs and were fearful of incarceration based on nonpayment. One PO explained that in some cases, clients would fail to appear for probation meetings because they are fearful of revocation solely based on nonpayment. In these cases, a client could be revoked for the technical violation of failure to appear which was rooted in nonpayment.

Taken together, empirical research generally finds that monetary sanctions increase rates of probation failure, particularly when the rates are higher and even more so when individuals cannot pay them and receive violations. Explaining why this is the case, a 2020 study found that court processes related to LFO collection (e.g., court appearances) destabilize individuals' lives, making it more difficult to maintain stable employment or housing and therefore more difficult to remain compliant with probation requirements (Cadigan & Kirk, 2020). Therefore, LFOs influence probation failure indirectly through financial hardship and procedural hassle.

Effects of probation client characteristics on probation revocations

Sex

Several studies examine the effects of probation client demographics or characteristics on revocations. In terms of sex, literature on probation outcomes is mixed. Some studies find that male clients are more likely to be revoked (Steinmetz & Henderson, 2016) and/or to be unsuccessful on probation (Morgan, 1994; Sims & Jones, 1997; Turner et al., 2022). Other research has not found a significant relationship between sex and probation revocations, technical violations, or new crimes (Gray et al., 2001; Olson & Lurigio, 2000). There is some evidence to suggest that the influence of sex and age on probation success is explained by probation clients' prior records and lower education levels (Albonetti & Hepburn, 1997). There is also evidence to suggest that men are more likely than women to be revoked for new offenses, but not for technical violations (Ruhland et al., 2020).

Age

Several studies have found that younger probation clients had a greater likelihood of revocation (Gordon & Glaser, 1991; Olson & Lurigio, 2000) or were more likely to be unsuccessful on probation (Sims & Jones, 1997; Turner et al., 2022). Other research has found a weaker relationship between age and probation outcomes. Steinmetz and Henderson (2016) found that age was a poor predictor for probation revocation. The authors suggest this finding could be explained by the mean age of the sample, which was around 34 years old. Ruhland et al. (2020) also found that age did not significantly relate to the revocation odds. Morgan (1994) found that while age did not significantly predict probation success, the relationship was in the predicted direction.

Race & ethnicity

Compared to sex and age, the literature finds a stronger relationship between race and probation outcomes. Gordon and Glaser (1991) found that Black probation clients had more than twice the odds of being revoked. This relationship between race and revocation mirrors findings in the more general context of race and probation success (Gray et al., 2001; Sims & Jones, 1997; Turner et al., 2022; Whitehead, 2006).

In a 2014 study, the Urban Institute investigated whether race affected revocations by examining 105,200 probation clients from four probation departments in Texas, Iowa, Oregon, and New York (Jannetta et al., 2014). The study found that Black clients were significantly more likely to be revoked when compared to Hispanic and White clients. To give context to these findings, 50 probation staff and judges across the four sites were also interviewed. Many respondents expressed the view that racial and ethnic minorities had greater likelihoods of arrest and that minority neighborhoods were more heavily monitored by police resulting in more frequent contact. Consequently, respondents believed that minorities had a greater likelihood of arrest, probation violations, and revocations.

In one recent exception to the literature which has found a relationship between race and probation revocations, Ruhland et al. (2020) found no influence of race or ethnicity on the likelihood of probation revocations in one Texas probation department. Moreover, Ruhland et al. (2020) found that compared to nonwhite individuals, White individuals generally experienced revocation due to technical violations and new criminal offenses more quickly.

Recent research suggests that a mixed-methods approach may help explain discordant findings related to the influence of race and ethnicity on revocation and noncompliance. A mixed-methods study of 347 domestic violence cases from one urban county in the Midwestern U.S. found that there were not differences in the chances of being sanctioned for noncompliance between probation clients of different races and ethnicities (Dagenhardt, 2021). Further, and unexpectedly, relative to White clients, Hispanic and Black clients were given shorter stays in jail for noncompliance. The qualitative data however, indicated that these shorter jail sanctions could be explained by the tendency for judges to sanction Black and Hispanic clients for minor drug use violations with a short jail stay. White clients, by contrast, were given longer jail stays only when more serious violations occurred.

Research has also found that negative probation outcomes may be more severe when race interacts with other demographic characteristics such as gender, age, and employment status. For instance, Steinmetz and Henderson (2016) found that Black probation clients had increased odds of revocation but also that the interaction between being Black and male was a strong predictor of revocation.

Tapia and Harris (2006) similarly found evidence of harsher revocation consequences for young Black men on probation for felony-level offenses. Black probation clients who were unemployed did not have a significantly higher likelihood of revocation when compared to employed Black clients. However, for male, female, White, and Hispanic clients, being unemployed was associated with a higher likelihood of revocation. In other words, the value of employment was reduced for Black clients. Further, compared to all other groups, Black men between the ages of 17 and 29 had the greatest chances of revocation regardless of being employed. Thus, the effect of things outside their control (age and skin color) had a greater impact on probation success than things inside their control (employment status).

The literature comparing probation outcomes of Hispanic and White clients demonstrates a wide range of findings. Steinmetz and Henderson (2016) found that Hispanic clients on probation had a greater likelihood of being revoked in comparison to White clients. In contrast, other research has found that revocation odds for Hispanic clients were similar or not significantly different from those of White clients (Gordon & Glaser, 1991; Ruhland et al., 2020; Tapia & Harris, 2006). The Urban Institute's investigation of disparities in probation revocations in four states also found mixed results in terms of disparities between Hispanic and other probation clients (Jannetta et al., 2014). In New York City, Hispanic clients had higher rates of revocation compared to White clients; however, in two other locations the revocation rate was lower than that for White clients and in one location there was no discernable difference. The revocation rate for Hispanic clients was lower than the rate for Black clients in all study locations. A more recent study also found that Hispanic probation clients were more likely to be successful on probation compared to White clients (Turner et al., 2022).

Education

The literature also examines the effects of education on probation outcomes, which suggests that probation clients with greater educational attainment have better outcomes. Three studies have found that those with greater levels of education had higher odds of probation success and reduced odds of revocation (Morgan, 1994; Turner et al., 2022; Zettler & Martin, 2020). Similarly, another study found that those who had not completed high school had higher revocation odds (Gordon & Glaser, 1991).

In sum, the literature suggests that Black probation clients and those with lower levels of education are more likely to experience negative probation outcomes. Male clients may also experience poorer outcomes than female clients. It is more difficult to summarize the experiences of Hispanic clients using a national lens because they experience a discordant range of outcomes across different settings. Additionally, some studies have found that it is the interaction of demographic factors, such as race, ethnicity and gender that matters more than one factor alone.

Effects of programming and services on probation revocations

Research has explored whether certain types of probation programming or services can reduce revocations. Taken together, research on probation programming consistently shows that the most promising programs incorporate substance abuse treatment and cognitive behavioral therapy (CBT); both seek to address underlying issues that lead to high numbers of technical violations – the leading cause of probation revocations (Gray et al., 2001; Jalbert et al., 2010).

Additionally, research indicates that probation programs yield better outcomes when utilizing a risk-needs-responsivity (RNR) framework under which programming is tailored to the individual needs of each offender (Bonta et al., 2011). Thus, high-risk offenders receive more intensive services than low-risk offenders. Further, the services provided aim to correct factors associated with criminogenic behaviors such as substance abuse, pro-criminal attitudes, and criminal association (Jalbert et al., 2011). RNR research cautions practitioners to avoid over programming, that is, when low-risk offenders receive more or higher-level services than necessary. Essentially, services should target those who are high-risk because they are thought to be the most responsive to treatment (Jalbert et al., 2011; Van Voorhis et al., 2013).

Substance abuse treatment

In evaluating the impact of Arizona's mandatory drug treatment law, Rodriguez and Webb (2007) examined data from 2,840 men on probation for low-level drug offenses. The authors found that most clients (57%) faced revocation of their probation for technical violations. However, the authors suggest that high revocations rates might be due to inadequate programming. That is, because the state mandated all probation clients to receive treatment, practitioners likely did not carefully assess what level of treatment each client needed, resulting in under/over programming for many clients which could have resulted in increased revocations according to the RNR model (Longshore et al., 2004; Rodriguez & Webb, 2007).

Some also contend that involuntary programs yield unfavorable outcomes. The RNR paradigm maintains programming is most effective when individuals are ready to change (Bonta et al., 2011). Thus, when people on probation voluntarily participate in drug treatment, they evidence more favorable results. For example, California's "Proposition 36" provides adults convicted of a nonviolent drug offense the option to be placed on probation and take part in drug treatment. Under the Proposition, those with one or two drug-related violations would only face alterations to their treatment plans, not revocation. A study by Longshore et al. (2004) examined 35,947 probation clients who participated in treatment under Proposition 36 and found that only one in five clients were revoked, a rate lower than typical revocation rates.

A more recent study evaluated the influence of both mental health and substance abuse services on recidivism among a sample of probation clients (N = 772) with either mental health, substance use, or co-occurring disorders (Jacobs et al., 2022). Using Cox proportional hazards models, the authors found that use of mental health services significantly predicted decreased recidivism (i.e., rearrests) among probation clients diagnosed with a mental disorder. The analyses however, revealed no significant relationship between services and recidivism for those with substance abuse and co-occurring disorders. In fact, among those diagnosed with a substance abuse disorder, there was an increased (though not statistically significant) risk of rearrest. The authors suggest this finding may be explained by the nature of substance abuse services which increase the level of surveillance over probation clients.

Findings from another recent study among female probation clients suggests that when engagement in substance abuse treatment is low, group treatment may be counterproductive to recidivism. This supports other literature that suggests individuals must be willing and ready to change for treatment to be effective. Goodson et al. (2020) found that the impact of peer support on recidivism (i.e., technical violations and arrest) differed depending on how engaged clients were in their treatment. Using a sample of about 200 women on probation or parole, the authors found that even though clients had higher levels of peer support, they also had higher levels of recidivism when they were not engaged in treatment.

Cognitive behavioral therapy

Research on the impact of CBT on probation revocations has found promising results. A recent study found that probation clients who received CBT were more likely to successfully complete probation (Kosson et al., 2019). Kosson et al. (2019) evaluated the efficacy of the Lake County, Illinois Thinking for a Change (T4C) program. While groups of 8–12 probation clients typically receive 22 weeks of treatment in T4C, this program reduced the number to 20 weeks and slightly modified the program materials to better suit higher-risk probation clients. The study examined 164 high- and medium-risk probation clients (2002–2004 cohort) and a control group consisting of 103 similarly situated clients (1997–2000 cohort). The evaluation found that only about 18% of probation clients in the control group completed probation in contrast to ~54% of clients who received CBT treatment. In an earlier study comparing the outcomes of 71 treatment group probation clients and 71 control group clients following their voluntary participation in a T4C, Golden (2002) found that program participants were no less likely to be revoked for technical violations. However, revocation for new offenses decreased 33% for participants who completed the program (Golden, 2002).

Research examining the impact of CBT programs on recidivism more generally have also revealed positive results. Studies both in the U.S. and the United Kingdom relying on randomized and quasi-experimental designs have found recidivism rates were significantly reduced among clients who completed a CBT program (Barnes et al., 2017; Hatcher et al., 2012; Hollin et al., 2008; Lowenkamp et al., 2009). One study with more mixed results found that there was no significant overall difference in re-conviction between clients who were or were not assigned to a CBT program (McGuire et al., 2008). However, further analyses did suggest a potential treatment effect among moderate- to high-risk clients. Importantly, one additional study indicates that CBT programs may not produce improved outcomes among female clients (Palmer et al., 2015). The authors suggest that certain CBT programs may not be gender responsive with regard to targeting relevant criminogenic needs or in terms of the method of delivery.

Some programming has also produced successful results using a combination of CBT and other practices like reduced probation caseloads in an evidence-based setting. Several have suggested that the combination of intensified supervision and CBT is key to program success as previous research indicates intensive supervision alone is not effective (Farrington & Welsh, 2005; Gendreau et al., 2000; Lowenkamp & Latessa, 2005). However, a multi-site evaluation of programs in Oklahoma and Iowa has produced mixed results. Jalbert et al. (2011) examination of Oklahoma's program found a statistically significant reduction in recidivism rates for participants, as well as moderately increased revocation rates. Similarly, a 6-month follow-up in Iowa showed program participants in were significantly less likely (26%) to recidivate in the following years; however, they were also more likely to have their probation revoked during their participation (Jalbert et al., 2011). The authors suggest that increased supervision may have resulted in the observed increase in technical violations.

Discussion

Despite increased reliance on probation in recent years as an alternative to incarceration, adult probation clients often end up experiencing incarceration due to revocations. As such, understanding factors which lead to revocations is crucial to informing probation policy and practice. This rapid review examined 50 studies on the effects of probation officer behaviors, PO-client relationships, caseload size and supervision intensity, legal financial obligations, client characteristics, and programming and services on adult probation revocations.

Studies of PO behavior and PO-client relationships suggest that the use of rewards and sanctions and the presence of PO-client relationships which involve trust, respect, supportiveness, and empathy appear to be linked with improved supervision outcomes. However, beyond the use of rewards and sanctions, little research has explored what kinds of PO behaviors may be effective in reducing revocations. Further, we know little about factors which influence PO decision making in response to client noncompliance. For example, what influences a PO to issue a verbal warning rather than a formal violation? Future research in this vein may better inform strategies to reduce revocations.

Research exploring the influence of supervision intensity and caseload size has generally found that intensive supervision programs (ISPs) lead to poorer supervision outcomes due to increased detection of problematic behavior. On the other hand, studies examining the effectiveness of reduced supervision intensity for low-risk clients have found that this strategy can reduce revocations without negatively impacting criminal behavior. Additionally, the use of smaller caseload sizes appears to improve supervision outcomes.

While the body of literature on ISPs is sizable, just two studies in our review explored the use of reduced supervision intensity for low-risk clients. Thus, more research in this area is warranted to confirm the efficacy of this strategy. Further, while several studies indicate that reduced caseload sizes are effective, these studies typically focus on specialty mental health caseloads or small caseloads with intensive supervision. Future research exploring the effectiveness of other smaller, specialty caseloads like substance use disorder, and domestic violence caseloads would also be informative.

Monetary sanctions increase the chances of probation failure, particularly when rates are higher and when clients are unable to pay. Research has also indicated that clients who are Black, male, and those who have lower levels of education are more likely to have negative probation outcomes. Research is lacking however, in terms of how client characteristics interact with other factors to influence probation outcomes. For instance, do monetary sanctions moderate the influence of a client's race on probation revocations? It is possible that low-income clients and clients of color are less able to pay monetary sanctions leading to greater revocation rates. Similarly, future research should investigate whether clients with different racial, ethnic, class, and gender characteristics respond differently to various supervision strategies, programming, and services. Some research for example, has indicated that female probation clients may not benefit from programming which has improved outcomes for male clients (Palmer et al., 2015). Similar results may be found with regard to other client characteristics and in other supervision strategies.

Research on programming and services has found mixed results when investigating whether substance abuse treatment improves probation outcomes. It is unclear to what extent increased surveillance in substance abuse treatment programs explains failure rates. CBT programs however, have generally been shown to have a positive influence on program outcomes. Further investigation into the intensity and duration of CBT needed to produce these positive outcomes would also be useful.

The findings from this review suggest several implications for probation policy and practice. First, given that monetary sanctions are associated with probation failure, particularly when amounts are higher and clients are unable to pay, policies surrounding monetary sanctions should be reconsidered. Courts and supervision agencies should reduce the total amount of monetary sanctions assessed to justice-involved individuals. Criminal justice agencies should also improve ability to pay assessments. Prior research suggests that such assessments are often inadequate, if completed at all (Brett et al., 2020). Reduced monetary sanction assessments, particularly among those who are less able to pay may reduce probation revocations. POs can also work with clients who are struggling to pay by creating budgets, aiding in employment searches, and finding ways to lower payments (e.g., fee waivers) when necessary. POs should also ensure clients are aware that they are unlikely to be revoked for nonpayment alone. Clear communication on this policy would help to prevent situations where a client avoids their PO or the court and accumulates other violations (i.e., FTAs) that are more likely to lead to revocation.

Second, this review implies several key points about specific supervision strategies. Probation agencies should avoid ISPs, except in the context of smaller caseloads. ISPs on their own, appear to increase rates of probation failure via enhanced surveillance and detection of client noncompliance. Further, while more research is warranted on the effectiveness of reduced supervision intensity for low-risk clients, studies which are available suggest that this approach can be effective in reducing revocations without risking increased criminal behavior. Use of this reduced supervision intensity strategy could free up time and energy of POs which may facilitate the use of smaller and specialty caseloads that have been shown to be associated with improved probation outcomes.

Lastly, the research on programming and services suggests that probation agencies should consider using CBT programs and should take thoughtful approaches to substance abuse treatment programs. Studies of CBT programs have largely been associated with improved probation outcomes. Agencies using such programs should, however, consider developing versions of the program that specifically target the criminogenic needs of female clients (Palmer et al., 2015). Agencies utilizing substance abuse treatment programs should also be aware that the increased surveillance associated with these programs may increase violations. It may be beneficial for supervision agencies to be more tolerant of such violations in the interest of the client's successful probation completion. Additionally, based on results of prior research (Rodriguez & Webb, 2007), and RNR principles, substance abuse treatment programs should be primarily targeted toward higher risk clients and those who are willing to engage in treatment.

In all, there remain many unanswered questions about precisely how and why adult probation clients experience revocations and as to the best supervision approaches to prevent revocations. It is our hope that this review helps to synthesize prior research on the factors associated with probation revocations in order to inform probation practices and current critical debates related to criminal legal processing while also helping to guide future research in this area.

Disclosure statement

No potential conflict of interest was reported by the author(s).

Funding

This work was supported by Arnold Ventures;

ORCID

Carmen L. Diaz http://orcid.org/0000-0002-4340-3139
Staci Rising http://orcid.org/0000-0002-4333-4372
Eric Grommon http://orcid.org/0000-0003-4086-3698
Miriam Northcutt Bohmert http://orcid.org/0000-0002-6673-5937
Evan Marie Lowder http://orcid.org/0000-0002-5855-2479

References

Albonetti, C. A., & Hepburn, J. R. (1997). Probation revocation: A proportional hazards model of the conditioning effects of social disadvantage. *Social Problems*, *44*(1), 15. https://doi.org/10.2307/3096877

American Correctional Association. (2006). *Public correctional policy on probation*. (p. 23). http://www.aca.org/ACA_Prod_IMIS/docs/GovernmentAffairs/ACA_PUBLIC_CORRECTIONAL_POLICIES_BOOK.pdf

Andrews, D. A., & Bonta, J. (2015). *The psychology of criminal conduct: Vol. 5th ed.* Routledge. https://proxyiub.uits.iu.edu/login?url=https://search.ebscohost.com/login.aspx?direct=true&db=nlebk&AN=850143&site=eds-live&scope=site

Bannon, A., Nagrecha, M., & Diller, R. (2010). *Criminal justice debt: A barrier to reentry.* Brennan Center for Justice. https://www.criminallegalnews.org/media/publications/brennan_center_for_justice_reentry_report_2010.pdf

Barnes, G. C., Ahlman, L., Gill, C., Sherman, L. W., Kurtz, E., & Malvestuto, R. (2010). Low-intensity community supervision for low-risk offenders: A randomized, controlled trial. *Journal of Experimental Criminology, 6*(2), 159–189. https://doi.org/https://doi.org/10.1007/s11292-010-9094-4

Barnes, G. C., Hyatt, J. M., & Sherman, L. W. (2017). Even a little bit helps: An implementation and experimental evaluation of cognitive-behavioral therapy for high-risk probationers. *Criminal Justice and Behavior, 44*(4), 611–630. https://doi.org/10.1177/0093854816673862

Bonta, J., Bourgon, G., Rugge, T., Scott, T.-L., Yessine, A. K., Gutierrez, L., & Li, J. (2011). An experimental demonstration of training probation officers in evidence-based community supervision. *Criminal Justice and Behavior, 38*(11), 1127–1148. https://doi.org/10.1177/0093854811420678

Brett, S., Khoshkhoo, N., & Nagrecha, M. (2020). *Paying on probation: How financial sanctions intersect with probation to target, trap, and punish people who cannot pay.* Harvard Law School Criminal Justice Policy Program.

Brilliant, J. A. (1989). The modern day scarlet letter: A critical analysis of modern probation conditions. *Duke Law Journal, 1989*(5), 1357. https://doi.org/10.2307/1372521

Bureau of Justice Statistics. (2019). *Prisoners in 2017* (pp. 1). https://www.bjs.gov/content/pub/pdf/p17_sum.pdf

Buttars, A., Huss, M. T., & Brack, C. (2016). An analysis of an intensive supervision program for sex offenders using propensity scores. *Journal of Offender Rehabilitation, 55*(1), 51–68. https://doi.org/10.1080/10509674.2015.1107003

Cadigan, M., & Kirk, G. (2020). On thin ice: Bureaucratic processes of monetary sanctions and job insecurity. *RSF: The Russell Sage Foundation Journal of the Social Sciences, 6*(1), 113–131. https://doi.org/10.7758/RSF.2020.6.1.05

Crutchfield, R. D., Fernandes, A., & Martinez, J. (2010). Racial and ethnic disparity and criminal justice: How much is too much? *The Journal of Criminal Law and Criminology (1973), 100*(3), 903–932. https://www.jstor.org/stable/25766112

CUNY Institute for State & Local Governance (ISLG). (n.d.). *Case Study: Reducing Revocations Challenge.* Retrieved July 13 2022, from https://islg.cuny.edu/case-study-reducing-revocations-challenge

Dagenhardt, R. (2021). "You know baseball? 3 strikes": Understanding racial disparity with mixed methods for probation review hearings. *Social Sciences, 10*(6), 235. https://doi.org/10.3390/socsci10060235

Duru, H., Lovins, L. B., & Lovins, B. (2020). Does reducing supervision for low-risk probations jeopardize community safety? *Federal Probation, 84*(1), 21–27. https://heinonline.org/HOL/P?h=hein.journals/fedpro84&i=23

Farrington, D. P., & Welsh, B. C. (2005). Randomized experiments in criminology: What have we learned in the last two decades? *Journal of Experimental Criminology, 1*(1), 9–38. https://doi.org/10.1007/s11292-004-6460-0

Fox, C., Harrison, J., Hothersall, G., Smith, A., & Webster, R. (2022). A rapid evidence assessment of the impact of probation caseloads on reducing recidivism and other probation outcomes. *Probation Journal, 69*(2), 138–158. https://doi.org/10.1177/02645505211025595

Frailing, K., Rapp, V., & Taylor, R. (2020). Swift and certain probation as a HOPE-like model: Progress toward goals and lingering challenges. *Corrections*, 1–16. https://doi.org/10.1080/23774657.2020.1807425

Ganann, R., Ciliska, D., & Thomas, H. (2010). Expediting systematic reviews: Methods and implications of rapid reviews. *Implementation Science, 5*(1), 56. https://doi.org/10.1186/1748-5908-5-56

Gendreau, P., Goggin, C., & Fulton, B. (2000). Intensive probation in probation and parole settings. *Handbook of Offender Assessment and Treatment*, 195–204.

Glaze, L. E., & Bonczar, T. P. (2009). *Probation and Parole in the United States, 2008* (pp. 61). Bureau of Justice Statistics. http://bjs.ojp.usdoj.gov/content/pub/pdf/ppus08.pdf

Golden, L. S. (2002). *Evaluation of the efficacy of a cognitive behavioral program for offenders on probation: Thinking for a Change*. [University of Texas]. https://secure.ce-credit.com/articles/102109/018190.pdf

Goodson, M. V., Morash, M., & Kashy, D. A. (2020). The moderating effect of substance abuse treatment engagement on the connection between support from program participants and substance-related recidivism for justice-involved women. *International Journal of Offender Therapy and Comparative Criminology*, *64*(12), 1217–1235. https://doi.org/10.1177/0306624X19863218

Gordon, M. A., & Glaser, D. (1991). The use and effects of financial penalties in municipal courts. *Criminology*, *29*(4), 651–676. https://doi.org/10.1111/j.1745-9125.1991.tb01083.x

Gray, M. K., Fields, M., & Maxwell, S. R. (2001). Examining probation violations: Who, what, and when. *Crime and Delinquency*, *47*(4), 537–557. https://doi.org/10.1177/0011128701047004003

Harris, A. (2016). *A pound of flesh: Monetary sanctions as punishment for the poor*. Russell Sage Foundation.

Hatcher, R. M., McGuire, J., Bilby, C. A. L., Palmer, E. J., & Hollin, C. R. (2012). Methodological considerations in the evaluation of offender interventions: The problem of attrition. *International Journal of Offender Therapy and Comparative Criminology*, *56*(3), 447–464. https://doi.org/10.1177/0306624X11403271

Hollin, C. R., McGuire, J., Hounsome, J. C., Hatcher, R. M., Bilby, C. A. L., & Palmer, E. J. (2008). Cognitive skills behavior programs for offenders in the community: A reconviction analysis. *Criminal Justice and Behavior*, *35*(3), 269–283. https://doi.org/10.1177/0093854807312234

Hyatt, J. M., & Barnes, G. C. (2017). An experimental evaluation of the impact of intensive supervision on the recidivism of high-risk probationers. *Crime and Delinquency*, *63*(1), 3–38. https://doi.org/10.1177/0011128714555757

Iratzoqui, A., & Metcalfe, C. (2017). Set up for failure? Examining the influence of monetary sanctions on probation success. *Criminal Justice Policy Review*, *28*(4), 370–393. https://doi.org/10.1177/0887403415586595

Jacobs, L. A., Branson, Z., Greeno, C. G., Skeem, J. L., & Labrum, T. (2022). Community behavioral health service use and criminal recidivism of people with mental, substance use, and co-occurring disorders. *Psychiatric Services*, https://doi.org/10.1176/appi.ps.202100530

Jalbert, S. K., Rhodes, W., Flygare, C., & Kane, M. (2010). Testing probation outcomes in an evidence-based practice setting: Reduced caseload size and intensive supervision effectiveness. *Journal of Offender Rehabilitation*, *49*(4), 233–253. https://doi.org/10.1080/10509671003715987

Jalbert, S. K., Rhoes, W., Kane, M., Clawson, E., Bogue, B., Flygare, C., Kling, R., & Guevara, M. (2011). *Multi-site evaluation of reduced probation caseload size in an evidence-based practice setting in Oklahoma City Oklahoma, Polk County, Iowa, and Colorado, 1997-2010: Archival version* [Data set]. ICPSR - Interuniversity Consortium for Political and Social Research. https://doi.org/10.3886/ICPSR31961

Jannetta, J., Breaux, J., Ho, H., & Porter, J. (2014). *Examining racial and ethnic disparities in probation revocation: Summary findings and implications from a multisite study*. Urban Institute. https://www.urban.org/research/publication/examining-racial-and-ethnic-disparities-probation-revocation

Kosson, D. S., Walsh, Z., Anderson, J. R., Brook, M., Swogger, M. T., & Verborg, R. (2019). Evaluation of a cognitive-behavioral intervention for high- and medium-risk probationers. *Behavioral Sciences & the Law*, *37*(4), 329–341. https://doi.org/10.1002/bsl.2394

Longshore, D., Urada, D., & Hawken, A. (2004). *Evaluation of the substance abuse and crime prevention act: 2003 report*. Department of Alcohol and Drug Programs. https://nyuscholars.nyu.edu/en/publications/evaluation-of-the-substance-abuse-and-crime-prevention-act-2003-r

Lowenkamp, C. T., Hubbard, D., Makarios, M. D., & Latessa, E. J. (2009). A quasi-experimental evaluation of thinking for a change: A "real-world" application. *Criminal Justice and Behavior, 36* (2), 137–146. https://doi.org/10.1177/0093854808328230

Lowenkamp, C. T., & Latessa, E. J. (2005). Increasing the effectiveness of correctional programming through the risk principle: Identifying offenders for residential placement. *Criminology & Public Policy, 4*(2), 263–290. https://doi.org/10.1111/j.1745-9133.2005.00021.x

MacKenzie, D. L., Browning, K., Skroban, S. B., & Smith, D. A. (1999). The impact of probation on the criminal activities of offenders. *Journal of Research in Crime and Delinquency, 36*(4), 423–453. https://doi.org/10.1177/0022427899036004004

Manchak, S. M., Skeem, J. L., Kennealy, P. J., & Louden, J. E. (2014). High-fidelity specialty mental health probation improves officer practices, treatment access, and rule compliance. *Law and Human Behavior, 38*(5), 450–461. https://doi.org/10.1037/lhb0000076

McGuire, J., Bilby, C. A. L., Hatcher, R. M., Hollin, C. R., Hounsome, J., & Palmer, E. J. (2008). Evaluation of structured cognitive–behavioural treatment programmes in reducing criminal recidivism. *Journal of Experimental Criminology, 4*(1), 21–40. https://doi.org/10.1007/s11292-007-9047-8

Minor, K. I., Wells, J. B., & Sims, C. (2003). Recidivism among federal probationers: Predicting sentence violations. *Federal Probation, 67*, 31. https://heinonline.org/HOL/Page?handle=hein.journals/fedpro67&id=33&div=&collection=

Morash, M., Kashy, D. A., Smith, S. W., & Cobbina, J. E. (2014). The effects of probation or parole agent relationship style and women offenders' criminogenic needs on offenders' responses to supervision Interactions. *Criminal Justice and Behavior*. https://doi.org/10.1177/0093854814551602

Morash, M., Kashy, D. A., Smith, S. W., & Cobbina, J. E. (2016). The connection of probation/parole officer actions to women offenders' recidivism. *Criminal Justice and Behavior, 43*(4), 506–524. https://doi.org/10.1177/0093854815626490

Morgan, K. D. (1994). Factors associated with probation outcome. *Journal of Criminal Justice, 22*(4), 341–353. https://doi.org/10.1016/0047-2352(94)90081-7

Okonofua, J. A., Saadatian, K., Ocampo, J., Ruiz, M., & Oxholm, P. D. (2021). A scalable empathic supervision intervention to mitigate recidivism from probation and parole. *Proceedings of the National Academy of Sciences, 118*(14), e2018036118. https://doi.org/10.1073/pnas.2018036118

Olson, D. E., & Lurigio, A. J. (2000). Predicting probation outcomes: Factors associated with probation rearrest, revocations, and technical violations during supervision. *Justice Research and Policy, 2*(1), 73–86. https://doi.org/10.3818/JRP.2.1.2000.73

Palmer, E. J., Hatcher, R. M., McGuire, J., & Hollin, C. R. (2015). Cognitive skills programs for female offenders in the community: Effect on reconviction. *Criminal Justice and Behavior, 42*(4), 345–360. https://doi.org/10.1177/0093854814552099

Petersilia, J., & Cullen, F. T. (2014). Liberal but not stupid: Meeting the promise of downsizing prisons. *SSRN Electronic Journal*. https://doi.org/10.2139/ssrn.2458024

Petersilia, J., Turner, S., & Peterson, J. E. (1986). Rand Corporation. *Prison versus probation in California: Implications for crime and offender recidivism*. https://www.rand.org/pubs/reports/R3323.html

Rodriguez, N., & Webb, V. J. (2007). Probation violations, revocations, and imprisonment: The decisions of probation officers, prosecutors, and judges pre- and post-mandatory drug treatment. *Criminal Justice Policy Review, 18*(1), 3–30. https://doi.org/10.1177/0887403406292956

Ruhland, E., Holmes, B., & Petkus, A. (2020). The role of fines and fees on probation outcomes. *Criminal Justice and Behavior*, 0093854820918877. https://doi.org/10.1177/0093854820918877

Shannon, S. (2020). Probation and monetary sanctions in Georgia: Evidence from a multi-method study. *Georgia Law Review, 54*(4), 1213–1234. https://heinonline-org.proxyiub.uits.iu.edu/HOL/Page?handle=hein.journals/geolr54&div=35

Sims, B., & Jones, M. (1997). Predicting success or failure on probation: Factors associated with felony probation outcomes. *Crime and Delinquency, 43*(3), 314–327. https://doi.org/10.1177/0011128797043003005

Sirdifield, C., Brooker, C., & Marples, R. (2020). Suicide and probation: A systematic review of the literature. *Forensic Science International: Mind and Law, 1*, 100012. https://doi.org/10.1016/j.fsiml.2020.100012

Skeem, J. L., Encandela, J., & Louden, J. E. (2003). Perspectives on probation and mandated mental health treatment in specialized and traditional probation departments. *Behavioral Sciences & the Law, 21*(4), 429–458. https://doi.org/10.1002/bsl.547

Skeem, J. L., & Manchak, S. (2008). Back to the future: From Klockars' model of effective supervision to evidence-based practice in probation. *Journal of Offender Rehabilitation, 47*(3), 220–247. https://doi.org/10.1080/10509670802134069

Smith, M., Gartner, N. R., & Cooley, B. N. (2020). Officer supervision styles and female probationer/parolee recidivism. *Corrections*, 1–27. https://doi.org/10.1080/23774657.2020.1833793

Steinmetz, K. F., & Henderson, H. (2016). Inequality on probation: An examination of differential probation outcomes. *Journal of Ethnicity in Criminal Justice, 14*(1), 1–20. https://doi.org/10.1080/15377938.2015.1030527

Sturm, A., de Vogel, V., Menger, A., & Huibers, M. J. H. (2021). The price of mistrust: A study into the working alliance as predictor for recidivism. *Journal of Police and Criminal Psychology.* https://doi.org/10.1007/s11896-021-09450-1

Tapia, M., & Harris, P. M. (2006). Race and revocation: Is there a penalty for young, minority males? *Journal of Ethnicity in Criminal Justice, 4*(3), 1–25. https://doi.org/10.1300/J222v04n03_01

Taxman, F. S. (2002). Supervision: Exploring the dimensions of effectiveness. *Federal Probation, 66* (2), 14–27. https://heinonline.org/HOL/LandingPage?handle=hein.journals/fedpro66&div=25&id=&page=

Turner, H. C., Scheyett, A. M., & Allen, L. D. (2022). Legal and extralegal factors associated with success on misdemeanor probation. *Open Journal of Social Sciences, 10*(3), 257–272. https://doi.org/10.4236/jss.2022.103019

Vallas, R., & Patel, R. (2012). Sentenced to a life of criminal debt: A barrier to reentry and climbing out of poverty. *Clearinghouse Review, 46*, 131. https://heinonline.org/HOL/Page?handle=hein.journals/clear46&id=139&div=&collection=

Van Deinse, T. B., Givens, A., Cowell, M., Ghezzi, M., Murray-Lichtman, A., & Cuddeback, G. S. (2022). A randomized trial of specialty mental health probation: Measuring implementation and effectiveness outcomes. *Administration and Policy in Mental Health and Mental Health Services Research, 49*(3), 415–428. https://doi.org/10.1007/s10488-021-01172-0

Van Voorhis, P., Spiropoulos, G., Ritchie, P. N., Seabrook, R., & Spruance, L. (2013). Identifying areas of specific responsivity in cognitive-behavioral treatment outcomes. *Criminal Justice and Behavior, 40*(11), 1250–1279. https://doi.org/10.1177/0093854813494182

Watt, A., Cameron, A., Sturm, L., Lathlean, T., Babidge, W., Blamey, S., Facey, K., Hailey, D., Norderhaug, I., & Maddern, G. (2008). Rapid reviews versus full systematic reviews: An inventory of current methods and practice in health technology assessment. *International Journal of Technology Assessment in Health Care, 24*(2), 133–139. https://doi.org/10.1017/S0266462308080185

Whitehead, J. T. (2006). The effectiveness of felony probation: Results from an eastern state. *Justice Quarterly, 8*(4), 525–543. https://doi.org/10.1080/07418829100091201

Wodahl, E. J., Garland, B., Culhane, S. E., & McCarty, W. P. (2011). Utilizing behavioral interventions to improve supervision outcomes in community-based corrections. *Criminal Justice and Behavior, 38*(4), 386–405. https://doi.org/10.1177/0093854810397866

Zettler, H. R., & Martin, K. D. (2020). Exploring the impact of technical violations on probation revocations in the context of drug court. *American Journal of Criminal Justice, 45*(6), 1003–1023. https://doi.org/10.1007/s12103-020-09529-1

Evaluating the Effectiveness of Electronic Monitoring with Probationers

Jeff A. Bouffard and H. Daniel Butler

ABSTRACT
Despite growth in the use of electronic monitoring (EM), and Global Positioning Satellite (GPS) tracking in particular over the last 20 years, limited research has examined the effectiveness of these approaches on community supervision outcomes (e.g. likelihood of failure on community supervision). This study makes use of data from over 59,000 probation cases collected over a 40-year time span in a midwestern state. Using Propensity Score Matching (PSM), the study compares the rates of unsuccessful sentence completion among those who were supervised with and without any EM (and also GPS specifically). Results reveal that after matching cases on a variety of relevant controls (e.g. demographics, risk level, current offense type), those receiving EM while on probation were significantly more likely to fail to complete their term of supervision, with similar results for those who received GPS, specifically. Limitations of the study and implications for the use of EM/GPS with probationers as a potential alternative to prison are discussed.

Introduction

The "Get Tough" era of the 1970s and 1980s included to a number of policy changes related to both sentencing and correctional administration that lead to increases in the likelihood of receiving an incarceration sentence, and the length of those sentences (Blumstein, 2002; Travis et al., 2014). At the same time, changes to correctional practices such as elimination of earned good time, and in some cases the elimination of parole also lead to increased prison populations. These policies also had the effect of reducing the ability of prison authorities to regulate the number of people incarcerated using these "back-end" strategies (Tonry, 1996). After decades of policies that lead to mass incarceration, the 1990s saw a move to develop alternatives to the existing dichotomy of either incarceration or traditional probation (Morris & Tonry, 1990; Renzema & Mayo-Wilson, 2005). A number of such alternative (or intermediate) sanction programs were developed or their use was expanded, during this timeframe, with one of the goals being the reduction of prison crowding. These interventions included programs such as intensive supervision probation and parole, halfway houses, day reporting centers, home confinement, and electronic monitoring (Morris & Tonry, 1990).

The use of Electronic Monitoring (EM) within the U.S. criminal justice system began in the 1980s. One form of this early Radio Frequency (RF) technology required the individual to wear a small transmitter, usually on the ankle, which sent a constant radio signal to a receiver that was typically connected to a central computer via a telephone line. This type of "active" system was usually used as part of a home confinement sanction, at least in part because it depended on the use of a landline phone. Other early forms of RF technology, known as "passive" systems, required the individual to place the transmitter near a receiver (often in response to a randomly timed phone call to their residence) in order to signal to the central computer monitoring system that the person was where they were expected to be (Belur et al., 2020; Hawkes et al., 2023; Lab, 2020; Renzema & Mayo-Wilson, 2005).

Advancements in technology in the 1990s lead to the more widespread use of *Global Positioning Satellite* (GPS) systems that could provide near real-time monitoring of individuals and allow tracking over greater distances (Belur et al., 2020; Hawkes et al., 2023; Lab, 2020; Renzema & Mayo-Wilson, 2005). GPS monitoring typically also involves the individual wearing a device on their ankle, which can be tracked either continuously, or intermittently by GPS satellites. Beginning in about the year 2000, the use of other forms of EM have reportedly declined as more agencies move to the use of GPS tracking (Lilly, 2006; Pew Charitable Trusts, 2016; Zhang et al., 2024).[1]

Despite increasing use of EM, and GPS in particular over the last 20 years (Bartles & Martinovic, 2017; Hawkes et al., 2023), relatively few well-designed studies have examined their effectiveness. This is especially true among samples of generic offenders (as opposed to sex offenders) and in terms of outcomes of interest to correctional administrators (i.e., beyond re-arrests; Belur et al., 2020). In light of these gaps in the existing research, the current study was designed to address three specific research questions. In particular, we examine whether receiving any form of EM while on probation supervision is related to the likelihood of a person receiving an unsuccessful probation outcome (i.e., person has their probation revoked due to repeated technical violations, a new criminal offense, or because the person absconded from supervision). Likewise, we also examine whether receiving GPS supervision while on probation is related to receiving an unsuccessful outcome. Finally, given the differences in the intensity of supervision that is possible with GPS, as compared to other forms of EM (which do not track individuals in near real-time), we also examine whether these two types of EM (any EM vs. any GPS) produce different probabilities of unsuccessful case outcomes relative to one another.

Goals of electronic monitoring

While EM began its use as an adjunct to home confinement (HC), and is often still used in this context, its use has expanded in the last two decades to include greater supervision of those awaiting trial (i.e., pre-trial releases), as an alternative to prison (i.e., probationers) and as a means to increase supervision of those released from prison (i.e., parolees; Brown et al., 2007; Hawkes et al., 2023). A recent estimate suggests that roughly 250,000 adults were supervised by the criminal justice system using EM in 2021. This amounted to an approximately 500% increase from 2005 levels (Zhang, et al., 2024). Relative to the 3,745,000 individuals supervised in the community in 2021, this number indicates that roughly 6.7% of adults on community supervision were subject to EM. These authors also note that there is no national system in place to accurately record the extent of EM use in the U.S. (Zhang, et al., 2024), which limits our ability to assess the extent to which individuals on different types of supervision (i.e., pre-trial release, probation, parole) may be subject to EM.

In general, EM is anticipated to improve the intensity and quality of supervision provided to various individuals under correctional control. This is then hypothesized to lead to increased deterrence and incapacitation of the individual, while still allowing them to be managed in the community (Hawkes et al., 2023). Supporters of EM would suggest that this in turn creates cost savings by reducing the number of individuals who are incarcerated in more costly secure facilities. At the same time, EM should conceivably also lead to improvements in public safety relative to more traditional forms of community supervision that do not include the enhanced ability to monitor and track individuals as closely as does EM (Belur et al., 2020; Renzema & Mayo-Wilson, 2005). In addition, it has also been suggested EM may facilitate rehabilitation efforts by providing structure for the individual and supporting their participation in rehabilitation efforts, employment and family relationships (Bonta et al., 2000a; Gendreau et al., 2000; Hawkes et al., 2023).

Effectiveness of EM

A number of studies have examined the effectiveness of EM when used in conjunction with home confinement (Omori & Turner, 2015; Sugg et al., 2001; see also a meta-analysis of these combined programs by Bouchard & Wong, 2018). For example, Yeh (2010) examined the cost-effectiveness of HC/EM among a national sample of probationers and parolees. Yeh determined that EM, when combined with HC could be a cost-effective alternative to incarceration. A similar meta-analysis of 11 studies of EM in conjunction with HC by Bouchard and Wong (2018) found that HC with EM lead to lower chances of being re-arrested and re-convicted. They also reported that there were no significant effects on re-incarceration outcomes. Of note, only four of the studies examined by Bouchard and Wong (2018) included GPS supervision specifically (with three of those focused on sexual offenders, and only one on general offenders).

Some individual studies show positive effects of the use of EM with HC (see Bales et al., 2010; Padgett et al., 2006) or when used in conjunction with Cognitive-Behavioral Treatment (see Bonta et al., 2000a). For the most part however, the existing literature seems to conclude that EM by itself may have limited or no effects (Bonta et al., 2000b; Finn & Muirhead Steves, 2002; Omori & Turner, 2015; Petersilia & Turner, 1992; Sugg et al., 2001). In addition, several systematic reviews and meta-analyses have concluded that EM in general has had no significant effects on recidivism outcomes (Aos et al., 2007; Belur et al., 2020; Bouchard & Wong, 2018; Gendreau et al., 2000; MacKenzie, 1997; Renzema & Mayo-Wilson, 2005). For example, a recent systematic review by Belur et al. (2020) showed no effects of EM on the likelihood of recidivism, though it did seem to increase the length of time until a new offense.

Most early EM programs, and thus most of the early research, focused on lower-risk offenders. Over time though, the focus has shifted to the use of EM with more serious offenders (including sex offenders) and even some use with other kinds of high-risk, violent offenders (Finn & Muirhead Steves, 2002) including gang-involved individuals (S. V. Gies et al., 2013). The rationale for use of EM with these more serious, high-risk groups of individuals is that EM may serve as a useful front-end (i.e., an alternative to prison for some moderate to higher risk offenders) or back-end strategy (i.e., with parole supervision) to control prison crowding (Hawkes et al., 2023).

Research on EM for sexual offenders

A number of studies examining the effectiveness of EM on more serious offenders have looked specifically at its effects when used with individuals convicted of sexual offenses (S. Gies et al., 2016; Yeh, 2010). These individuals have been the subject of increased supervision using EM in many jurisdictions, particularly since the widespread availability of GPS technology, and legislation in a number of states to mandate the use of GPS tracking for such offenders (S. Gies et al., 2016; Yeh, 2010). These evaluations have generally produced mixed results. For instance, among sex offenders in their study, Padgett et al. (2006) found a reduction in the likelihood of committing a new offense (about 45% less likely than those not on GPS). Among other types of violent offenders however, there was a 92% lower risk of a new offense among those on GPS, compared to those not supervised this way. Thus, while GPS supervision did seem to reduce re-offense risk among high-risk sex offenders, the reduction was considerably larger among other kinds of violent offenders. On the other hand, S. Gies et al. (2016) found that sex offenders in their control group (not supervised using GPS) were about twice as likely to be re-arrested (and twice as likely to be convicted) for a new offense, in their first year on parole than those not supervised using GPS. These kinds of positive results for sex offenders supervised in the community using EM (especially GPS) provide support for the notion that the use of EM may increase public safety by providing for more comprehensive monitoring (and thus deterrence and incapacitation) of offenders in the community.

EM effectiveness among other offenders and on other outcomes

While most of the research on the effectiveness of EM in general has examined its impact on new arrest rates, Belur et al. (2020) reviewed seven studies of the effectiveness of EM on the likelihood of violating conditions of release. They found that EM did not produce a significant reduction in the likelihood of such violations. In fact, the average effect size (ES) among seven such studies was 1.04. In addition, they found that EM did not produce significant reductions in the likelihood of recidivism among those on pre-sentence EM (average ES among two studies was 0.88). Nor was there a significant effect among those more serious offenders who had been in prison and received EM supervision post-prison (average ES among seven such studies was 1.46). On the other hand, among those receiving EM post-sentence (i.e., in lieu of prison; four studies) the average ES was 1.41 and indicated a significant reduction in the odds of recidivism (Belur et al., 2020). Finally, among only eight studies that had specifically examined the effectiveness of GPS monitoring, meta-analytic results from Belur et al. (2020) revealed no significant effect of this form of supervision on recidivism odds.

While a number of systematic reviews and meta-analyses have attempted to summarize the existing research on the effectiveness of EM (Aos et al., 2007; Gendreau et al., 2000; MacKenzie, 1997; Renzema & Mayo-Wilson, 2005) many of them have used relatively restrictive criteria for those evaluations that the researchers decided to include. As such, these reviews have found small numbers of studies to summarize. For instance, while Gendreau et al. (2000) reviewed the effectiveness of 140 studies in their meta-analysis of correctional treatment program effectiveness, only six of these were studies of EM programs. MacKenzie (1997) could only locate two reasonable evaluations, and Renzema and

Mayo-Wilson (2005) were only able to identify three evaluations that met the rigorous inclusion criteria in their meta-analysis.

Beyond their formal meta-analysis of 18 EM studies, Belur et al. (2020) also conducted what they called a "realist-inspired qualitative synthesis" (involving a larger sample of 34 studies; p. 1). Even with Belur and colleagues' more relaxed criteria for study inclusion they were able to identify relatively few studies to review. In fact, similar attempts to synthesize this literature have also revealed only a few available studies of even modest methodological rigor to be examined. This is especially true in terms of the use of EM for non-sex offenders, and of the use of EM for individuals not on some form of post-prison supervision (i.e., parole).

In addition, despite the growth in the use of GPS specifically in the last several years (Bales et al., 2010; Kilgore, 2018), our review of the existing literature suggests the same conclusion, that there has been comparatively little empirical research on the effectiveness of GPS with various types of offenders beyond its use with sexual offenders. Bales et al. (2010), p. did examine the impact of GPS monitoring (relative to other forms of Radio Frequency monitoring) on the likelihood of failures while on supervision. These authors found that GPS specifically produced a significant, but small (6%) reduction in failure likelihood relative to RF supervision. S. V. Gies et al. (2013) also examined rates of return to prison for violations of conditions of release (as well as re-arrest rates), by high-risk gang offenders (HRGO) on post-release supervision. Using propensity score matching and an intent-to-treat design, they examined a group of 784 HRGO in California. They found that among HRGO's, being supervised using GPS was related to significantly lower likelihood of re-arrest for new crimes in general (46.7% vs. 56.1%), and for violent offenses specifically (12.5% vs. 19.6%), during a two-year follow-up period. They also reported that HRGOs supervised using GPS had statistically similar rates of technical violations (43.9% vs. 42.6%, n.s.) relative to the matched controls over the same two-year follow-up period. On the other hand, Finn and Muirhead Steves (2002) examined a sample of high-risk violent offenders placed on parole and found no effect of EM (RF type) on either the rate of return to prison, or on the time to failure, up to four years following release from prison.

Overall then, the existing research on the effectiveness of EM (and GPS specifically) demonstrate an inconsistent set of results. Home confinement with EM may produce beneficial outcomes, but when used by itself research seems to suggest EM has had limited if any impacts on outcomes such as criminal recidivism or rates of technical violations. The use of GPS for sexual offenders has also produced a mixed set of results, with some studies showing reduced recidivism and other no effects. Among the few studies that have examined EM among other types of serious offenders, results are once again mixed. Some of these studies show no effects on technical violation rates, returns to prison or criminal recidivism, while some results suggest GPS may be useful in reducing recidivism, including for violence among serious, gang-involved offenders.

Current study

Beyond the generally inconsistent results across several studies of the effects of EM and GPS, relatively few studies have examined the impacts of either form of EM on outcomes of interest to correctional administrators (e.g., violations of conditions that lead to revocation, return to secure facilities). Thus, there is a need in the empirical literature for well-designed, large-scale studies of the effectiveness of EM, and GPS specifically, among more generic offenders (non-sexual offenders) who have been sentenced to probation rather than prison. Moreover, there is a need to examine whether the use of EM for these individuals will lead to increased rates of violations and subsequent revocation that would then lead to incarceration of the supervised individual; an outcome which the use of electronic monitoring is intended to avoid.

The current study makes use of four decades worth of correctional services data (1980–2020) on the use of various forms of electronic monitoring from the corrections agency in a midwestern state. Using this data, we examine the impact of receiving both *any form of EM*, and *GPS monitoring* specifically, on the likelihood of the individual failing to complete their sentenced term of probation supervision (e.g., revocation, absconding). Our total dataset of 94,158 cases assigned to probation represents all such cases in the state over the years in question.

We also use a propensity score matching (PSM) technique to examine the impact of our two measures of EM (*any EM* and *GPS*, specifically) controlling for a number of other potentially relevant confounds that could impact the likelihood of unsuccessful probation completion. These controls include demographic factors (age, sex, race, ethnicity), education level, employment, current offense type, assessed risk level, the imposition of other supervision requirements, and overall length of supervision. Importantly, the data available for this study provides an opportunity to examine the effectiveness of EM (and GPS, in particular) on outcomes of particular relevance to court and correctional administrators (i.e., the likelihood of failure on probation supervision) among a large and representative sample of adult individuals convicted for a variety of offenses.

The existing research on the use of EM technologies (and GPS specifically) paints an inconsistent picture in terms of their expected effectiveness in reducing the chances of failure on community supervision. As such, rather than advancing specific directional hypotheses, we propose merely a set of exploratory research questions. First, we seek to determine whether the addition of *any form of EM* during a term of probation supervision is related to the likelihood of receiving an unsuccessful outcome for that sentence. Second, we seek to determine whether spending some amount of time on *GPS supervision* specifically, during a probation sentence has any relationship to the individual's likelihood of receiving an unsuccessful completion of that sentence. Finally, given that monitoring with GPS provides more intense supervision of individuals, we also examine whether there are any differences in the likelihood of an unsuccessful case outcome between those who received *some form of EM other than GPS* relative to those who received *GPS* supervision, specifically.

Methods

Procedures

After receiving human subjects approval from the IRB at the researchers' university, the researchers received a series of data files from a midwestern state corrections agency. These data files included data on the convicted individual's demographic characteristics (age, sex, race, ethnicity), current offense(s), sentence type and length, educational level, employment status during the period of supervision, any services received during the sentence (e.g., education, drug treatment). These files also included data on any probation supervision enhancements received (e.g., any form of EM such as GPS, RF, ignition interlocks), and the individual's risk level (based on the department's formal risk assessment tools). These data files contained information on all individuals sentenced to the department during the years 1980 through the end of 2020.

In the state in question, there was no use of GPS for those under correctional supervision prior to 2005, though there were other forms of EM used (e.g., RF and SCRAM, or Secure Continuous Remote Alcohol Monitor). In this state, most individuals convicted of sexual offenses after 2005 were, by statute subjected to long periods of community supervision including the mandatory use of EM. In light of this, the researchers decided to exclude all individuals whose most serious current offense was a sexual crime from our analysis (n = 729), since there would be very few contemporary sexual offenders not receiving EM that could be used as potential "comparison" cases. Finally, the researchers also excluded individuals assigned to a number of specialized supervision programs (e.g., specialty courts for drug offenders or drunk drivers) or those with special statuses (e.g., those with Federal Detainers). In general, these types of individuals (n = 2,281) are receiving a number of unique services which could confound an assessment of the impact of EM itself on their likelihood of success.

Samples

The final overall population of cases (excluding sexual offenders, and those in other special programs and statuses) on probation during the 40 years of provided data included 91,148 individuals. Given the lengthy time period covered by this data, a considerable number of individuals appeared multiple times. As such, the researchers made the decision to examine only the *most recent offense* that lead to a conviction and term of probation supervision for each individual in the dataset. In addition to creating a more manageable dataset, this procedure also allows for the assumption of independence of each individual case, rather than examining repeated instances of supervision of the same individual over time. About 95% (n = 86,728) of the total population of cases had started their *most recent* term of probation supervision between the years 2012 to 2020. In particular, there were only 4,420 cases in the provided data who had started their most recent term of supervision prior to 2012 (mean = 138 per year, with a high of 951 in 2011). During the 2012–2020 time period, the average number of probation cases per year was 9,636. Case numbers generally increased each year during this time, and ranged from 1,869 on probation in 2012, to a high of 13,153 in 2019. In 2020 there was a drop to 11,420 cases, possibly related to the overall slowdown in court operations during the early COVID-19 pandemic. Over the entire 40-year time period only about 2.3% (n = 2,061) of those on probation had been assigned to some form of EM (for at least some period of time) while they were being supervised in the community. In addition, about half of those who received some form of EM while being supervised (50.5%, n = 1,040) were supervised with GPS specifically (1.1% of the total probation population).

Across the entire 40-year time period, individuals being supervised on probation had an average age of 33.5 years. About 71% of the sample were men and 74% were identified as White, with 14.9% identified as Black and 7.4% identified as Hispanic. Among probationers for whom data was available, 73.6% had a GED or High School Diploma, although there was considerable missing data on this item (19,886, or 21.1% of cases did not have education level data). In terms of current offenses, 16.7% of this group had been convicted of a violent offense, 21.2% of a property offense, 23.9% a drug offense and 37% some form of public order offense (e.g., operating a vehicle while intoxicated or without a license, other traffic offenses, public intoxication, illegally carrying a weapon, failure to appear). These individuals spent an average of 604 days on probation supervision, and among those with outcome data available, 16% of them eventually received an "unsuccessful" outcome for their probation supervision sentence. Unsuccessful case outcomes were determined based on the criteria from the Department of Corrections, and included individuals who had their probation revoked for behaviors such as repeated technical violations, commission of new crimes, and absconding from supervision.

A number of cases did not have an *educational level* recorded in agency records, as noted. These cases were excluded from our final sample used in the propensity score matching procedure described below, however we did examine whether there were any substantive demographic differences (i.e., age, race, ethnicity, gender) between those probation cases for whom educational level was available and those for whom it was missing. In general, the missing cases did not appear to be substantially different from those which were included in our final sample. For instance, the average age of those included cases was 31.8 years, while among those who did not have educational data available, the average age was 33.9 years. Likewise, the samples were similar in terms of the proportion of women (28.7% among the included cases, 29.6% among the excluded cases), the proportion of African Americans (15.6% among the included cases, 12.2% among the excluded cases), and the proportion of Hispanics (6.7% in the included cases, 9.8% in the excluded cases). Overall then, the omission of cases that lacked education data does not seem to have impacted how well the final sample represents the entire population of probation cases.

Measures

Electronic monitoring indicators

The corrections agency's database contains information on whether individuals on probation were subject to any "special" forms of supervision. Essentially this data field denotes individuals who receive some type of supervision enhancement (like GPS or some other form of EM), or who are participating in some form of specialized program (e.g., specialty courts for drug offenders, drunk drivers, those with mental illness or veterans). Recall that we omitted cases participating in such specialized treatment programs to avoid confounding their potential treatment effects with the potential effect of EM/GPS supervision enhancements. Our main treatment indicator variable then (any EM) was scored as "1" if records indicated the individual had been assigned to be supervised using any form of EM (e.g., GPS, RF, SCRAM), during their probation term (and 0 if not). The same is true for our second indicator variable used in our GPS analysis. Specifically, we examine those who were ordered to any amount of time on GPS tracking (1 = any GPS, 0 = no GPS or any other form EM was used). In particular then, our examination of the impact of GPS supervision examines its effectiveness relative to no EM of any kind. We also conducted a simple bivariate comparison of failure rates between those on other forms of EM and those on GPS specifically, using a difference of means test, rather than another PSM analysis. The numbers of individuals whose most recent term of probation involved them being assigned to some amount of time being supervised with RF ($n = 59$) and SCRAM ($n = 184$) technologies were so small as to preclude examination of any possible effects for these specific forms of EM.

Demographics

Data on probationers' demographic characteristics was also provided by the Department of Corrections, including their year of birth (but not full date of birth, to limit the ability to identify individuals). Our variable representing age was estimated by subtracting the year of birth (with January 1 added for each case) from the date that each person's most recent probation supervision started. Probationers' sex was coded by the department as male and female. Data on individuals' race and ethnicity were coded by the department on a single variable, with options for White, Black, Hispanic, Asian Pacific Islander, Native American and Unknown.

Education and employment

Department records included a text field to describe each probationer's highest level of education achieved. From this the researchers created a dichotomous variable to indicate whether the individual had at least completed High School or earned a General Education Diploma (GED). Probation records also indicated whether the individual had been fired at any point during their most recent term of supervision and we created a dichotomous variable to indicate this, with the rationale that being fired during supervision could be an indicator of adjustment problems that could lead to an eventual unsuccessful outcome. Probation records indicated that in 7.1% of the total population of probation cases ($n =$ 6,460 of the 91,148 cases), the person had been fired from their current employment during their term of supervision.

Risk level

The Department of Corrections had used a number of risk assessment tools over the years. Each of these risk assessment tools collected information on criminogenic factors such as antisocial peers, antisocial attitudes, substance abuse and mental health issues, employment history, and social supports. Since these various risk tools produced differing numerical summary scores to indicate varying levels of risk across probationers, it was not possible to use these "raw scores" as our control variable for the assessed risk levels of individuals from different time periods within the data. The Department of Corrections did however use the scores from these disparate numerical risk tools to classify participants into one of five risk levels, and these risk-level categories were consistent over time (i.e., 5 = Intensive, 4 = High Normal, 3 = Low Normal, 2 = Minimum, 1 = Administrative, and 0 = No Recent Assessment). As such, in order to control for assessed risk levels for individuals from different time periods (based on results from different assessment tools), we used the *risk level categories* assigned to each probationer at the time their most recent probation term started. We also estimated some supplemental analyses to determine whether our findings for unsuccessful probation outcome would differ substantively when individuals with no recent assessment score were removed from the sample. The findings were substantively identical with or without these *No Recent Assessment* cases included (results not presented, but available from the authors).

Current offense type

In many cases, an individual was charged with, and convicted of multiple offenses within a given criminal arrest event. In light of this, in coding the "current offense type" for each case the researchers used only the most serious current offense type where a violent current offense = 1 and a nonviolent offense = 0. Violent offenses were those that had be classified as such in the Department of Corrections data, and included crimes such as various forms of assault, child endangerment, attempted murder and murder. Nonviolent offenses were those the department had classified as either Property crimes (e.g., theft, forgery/fraud), Drug crimes (e.g., drug possession, drug trafficking), or Public Order (e.g., traffic and weapons offenses, public intoxication).

Sentence length and services received during supervision

The total length of time on probation to which each individual was sentenced was calculated as the difference between the recorded start date and end date for that term. On average, probationers in this dataset spent 604 days being supervised (S.D. = 658, range = 0 to 13,882 days) on probation.[2] Department records also contained information about any additional services that the individual started during their probation term, as well as the date they started the services. In particular, department records included information on three categories of services, including any "educational" programming, any "treatment" services (e.g., anger management, substance abuse treatment) and any "activities" that the probationer might have been referred to (e.g., social support groups, legal services, life skills, employment services). Overall, among this group of probationers, 25% had started some form of *treatment* intervention during their supervision term, while only 4% had started some form of *educational programming* during their term, and about 10% had started some *other form of activity* during the time on probation.

Analytical strategy

The purpose of this study is to understand whether individuals who receive EM fare differently on community supervision than individuals who do not receive EM. Likewise, we also examine whether those who receive GPS monitoring specifically, may differ from those who do not. However, a simple descriptive examination of these two groups (i.e., EM/GPS or not) would not adequately answer this question, as individuals who receive EM/GPS may differ in important ways (e.g., criminal history or commitment offense) from those individuals who do not receive EM. In fact, comparisons of the pre-matched samples of EM and No EM groups (and likewise, comparisons of the GPS and No GPS groups) reveal that those who received these supervision enhancements are more likely to be current violent offenders and have higher risk scores, among other significant differences (see Table 1). Thus, it appears that the Department of Corrections is using these electronic supervision tools on individuals who may well be at a higher risk of negative outcomes as a means to provide them with more intensive supervision than would be possible otherwise.

In light of these differences, we use propensity score matching (PSM) as described below. This approach is useful for determining whether individuals who receive EM (GPS) are differentially likely to be unsuccessful on community supervision relative to those who do not receive EM (GPS). In addition, we conclude the analyses by examining whether individuals who received *GPS* while on community supervision differed significantly in

Table 1. Descriptive statistics for unmatched and matched sample for EM versus No EM.

	Pre-Matching					Post-Matching				
	EM		No EM			EM		No EM		
	Mean	(*SD*)	Mean	(*SD*)	SBS[a]	Mean	(*SD*)	Mean	(*SD*)	SBS[a]
Outcome Variables										
Unsuccessful	.38	(.49)	.16	(.37)						
Independent Variables										
Age (in years)	33.02	(11.34)	33.99	(12.08)	−8.28	33.02	(11.34)	33.32	(11.35)	−2.64
Female	.16	(.36)	.30	(.46)	−33.90	.16	(.36)	.16	(.37)	0
Black	.19	(.39)	.14	(.35)	13.49	.19	(.39)	.18	(.39)	2.56
Hispanic	.07	(.25)	.06	(.25)	4.00	.07	(.25)	.06	(.24)	4.08
Other Race/Ethnicity	.02	(.15)	.03	(.17)	−6.24	.02	(.15)	.02	(.15)	0
Highschool/GED	.75	(.43)	.75	(.43)	0.00	.75	(.43)	.76	(.43)	−2.33
Fired	.20	(.40)	.08	(.27)	35.17	.20	(.40)	.18	(.39)	5.06
Employed	.73	(.44)	.51	(.50)	46.71	.73	(.44)	.73	(.44)	0
Risk level	2.98	(1.59)	1.56	(1.36)	95.98	2.98	(1.59)	2.99	(1.48)	−.65
Violent current offense	.32	(.47)	.18	(.38)	32.76	.32	(.47)	.33	(.47)	−2.13
Months on supervision	23.61	(16.44)	20.65	(18.22)	17.06	23.61	(16.44)	23.43	(19.40)	1.01
Education programming	.09	(.28)	.03	(.17)	25.90	.09	(.28)	.07	(.26)	7.40
Treatment programming	.58	(.49)	.23	(.42)	76.70	.58	(.49)	.58	(.49)	0
Activities programming	.23	(.42)	.09	(.29)	38.79	.23	(.42)	.22	(.41)	2.41
N =	1,514		59,158			1,514		1,514		

[a]The standardized bias statistic illustrates whether differences exist between treatment recipients and treatment non-recipients. Values greater than ± 20 indicate a significant difference.

their likelihood of being unsuccessful from those who received some *other form of EM* (i.e., we compare the two electronic monitoring strategies to one another, GPS vs. Other EM). This comparison is a simple difference in means test, rather than a formal PSM analysis.

An important limitation when using observational data is the inability to make causal conclusions relative to the effects of a given treatment (Hernán & Robins, 2020). This is because the treatment effect may be due to factors not accounted for within a study design, such as selection bias, or other internal threats to validity. In corrections research in particular, randomized experiments are often not feasible due to ethical concerns (e.g., randomly assigning people to a treatment may invoke unacceptable harms). In this study, it was not possible to randomly assign individuals to receive EM on community supervision, due to the retrospective nature of the data available (i.e., cases already assigned to various forms of supervision). Therefore, we relied upon propensity score matching (PSM) to examine whether there were significant differences in the likelihood of being unsuccessful on community supervision while receiving a treatment (EM) as compared to no treatment (No EM). PSM is a quasi-experimental design that relies on the inclusion of covariates to match individuals in a treatment group to individuals in a comparison group. Ideally, after "matching" the individuals closely approximate one another with the exception of being in the treatment group or not. It is crucial that theoretical and practical considerations are made when determining what covariates may predict not only selection into the treatment group but also the outcome (Guo & Fraser, 2010; Rosenbaum & Rubin, 1984).

When conducting PSM, the estimation of a propensity score proceeds as follows: 1) include theoretically informed covariates, 2) estimate a logistic regression with the treatment variable as the outcome with the aforementioned covariates, 3) obtain the propensity scores (e.g., the odds of being in the treatment group) after performing the logistic regression. In our propensity score model, we used one-to-one nearest-neighbor matching

Table 2. Descriptive statistics for unmatched and matched sample for GPS versus No GPS (excluding EM).

	Pre-Matching					Post-Matching				
	GPS		No GPS			GPS		No GPS		
	Mean	(*SD*)	Mean	(*SD*)	SBS[a]	Mean	(*SD*)	Mean	(*SD*)	SBS[a]
Outcome Variables										
Unsuccessful	.53	(.50)	.16	(.37)						
Independent Variables										
Age (in years)	30.98	(10.78)	33.99	(12.08)	−26.29	30.98	(10.78)	31.24	(10.29)	−2.47
Female	.12	(.32)	.30	(.46)	−45.43	.12	(.32)	.12	(.32)	0
Black	.24	(.42)	.14	(.35)	25.87	.24	(.42)	.22	(.41)	4.82
Hispanic	.08	(.27)	.06	(.25)	7.69	.08	(.27)	.09	(.28)	−3.64
Other Race/Ethnicity	.03	(.16)	.03	(.17)	0	.03	(.16)	.03	(.16)	0
Highschool/GED	.71	(.46)	.75	(.43)	−8.98	.71	(.46)	.69	(.46)	4.35
Fired	.26	(.44)	.08	(.27)	49.31	.26	(.44)	.25	(.43)	2.30
Employed	.80	(.40)	.51	(.50)	64.05	.80	(.40)	.80	(.40)	0
Risk level	3.44	(1.51)	1.56	(1.36)	130.83	3.44	(1.51)	3.47	(1.33)	−2.11
Violent current offense	.37	(.48)	.18	(.38)	43.89	.37	(.48)	.38	(.49)	−2.06
Months on supervision	23.05	(16.65)	20.65	(18.22)	13.75	23.05	(16.65)	22.27	(15.47)	4.85
Education programming	.09	(.29)	.03	(.17)	25.24	.09	(.29)	.07	(.26)	7.26
Treatment programming	.61	(.49)	.23	(.42)	83.27	.61	(.49)	.62	(.49)	−2.04
Activities programming	.30	(.46)	.09	(.29)	54.61	.30	(.46)	.28	(.45)	4.40
N =	729		59,158			729		729		

[a]The standardized bias statistic illustrates whether differences exist between treatment recipients and treatment non-recipients. Values greater than ± 20 indicate a significant difference.

without replacement, which means only one individual in the treatment group is matched to one individual in the comparison group. This is done for everyone in the treatment group until everyone is matched within a caliper range that represents .25 of the standard deviation of the propensity score.

Sometimes this matching may be inefficient or lead to post-matching differences in the treatment and comparison groups.[3] One method to measure whether the groups approximate one another is through the standardized bias statistic (SBS). A SBS greater than 20 indicates that the groups are significantly different from one another. The pre- and post-matching values of the SBS for our samples are provided in Tables 1 and 2. Across both samples, the post-matching groups do not have SBS values greater than 20, which indicates the groups are similar to one another on the included covariates. The final step includes an examination of the difference of means between the treated group and the comparison group.

Results

The descriptive statistics for the pre-matching comparison between individuals who received EM (treatment) versus No EM (comparison) revealed several covariates did exceed an SBS of 20 (see Table 1). In total, 8 covariates were not balanced prior to matching the samples on propensity scores. This indicates there are significant differences between the groups that may bias estimates of a treatment effect. In particular, prior to matching, approximately 38% of the EM group was unsuccessful on community supervision as compared to 16% of individuals not on EM. After matching, all included covariates were balanced (e.g., SBS less than 20). Examining the matched samples, descriptive statistics revealed that most probationers were in their early 30s, male, white, had a high school diploma/GED, and were employed during their supervision.

The descriptive statistics for the GPS versus no GPS samples are provided in Table 2. In total, 10 covariates were not balanced across the groups prior to using propensity score matching (SBS >20), but after matching, all covariates were balanced (SBS <20) across samples. Examining the matched descriptive statistics showed that the GPS sample was largely similar to the EM group where most individuals are in their early 30s, male, white, had a high school diploma/GED, and were employed during their supervision.

The post-matching difference-of-means test between individuals who received EM versus no EM is provided in Table 3. In total, 1,514 persons received EM, and 1,514 persons who did receive any EM while on probation were matched to this group. After matching, approximately 38% of the EM group was unsuccessful on probation, as compared to 28% in the No EM group, which is a significant difference (Z = 5.86). In other words, individuals who received EM were more likely to be unsuccessful on probation supervision as compared to the matched group that did not receive any enhanced supervision using some form of EM.

The difference-of-means test between individuals who received GPS supervision as compared to the No GPS group (also excluding anyone who received any other form of EM) is provided in Table 4. Individuals who received GPS supervision while on probation were 19% more likely than individuals who did not receive GPS to be unsuccessful on probation supervision (53%; 34% respectively; Z = 7.24).

The final difference-of-means test examines whether individuals who received GPS specifically, differed in their likelihood of being unsuccessful on probation supervision as compared to those who received some other form of EM. This difference-of-means test excludes anyone who did not receive either GPS or some other form of EM. The findings provided in Table 5 reveal that individuals who received GPS supervision were significantly more likely to be unsuccessful on probation supervision (53%) than were individuals who received other forms of EM (25%; Z = 11.14).

Table 3. Average treatment effect among the treated for the EM versus No EM Sample (*N* = 3,028).

	EM	No EM	Difference	Standard Error	*Z*-Test
Unsuccessful	.38	.28	.10	.02	5.86*

Z-Test values greater than ±1.96 indicates a statistically significant difference. Due to one-to-one nearest neighbor matching there are 1,514 participants in the EM group and 1,514 non-EM participants in the comparison group.
*$p < 0.05$.

Table 4. Average treatment effect among the treated for GPS versus No GPS sample (*N* = 1,458).

	GPS	No GPS	Difference	Standard Error	*Z*-Test
Unsuccessful	.53	.34	.19	.03	7.24*

Z-Test values greater than ±1.96 indicates a statistically significant difference. Due to one-to-one nearest neighbor matching there are 729 participants in the GPS group and 729 non-GPS participants in the comparison group.
*$p < 0.05$.

Table 5. Difference in proportional odds test for GPS versus non-GPS EM (*N* = 1,514).

	GPS	EM	Difference	Standard Error	*Z*-Test
Unsuccessful	.53	.25	.28	.02	11.14*

Z-Test values greater than ±1.96 indicates a statistically significant difference.
*$p < 0.05$.

Discussion

In relation to our original research questions, results suggest that those probationers who spent some amount of time being supervised with some form of EM enhancement were more likely to receive an unsuccessful case outcome (about 10% points more) than those who did not. Likewise, those who received some period of time on GPS supervision while on probation were also significantly more likely to experience an unsuccessful case outcome, and in this case the difference was even more pronounced (about 20% points more likely). In addition, the results were obtained using a rigorous propensity score matching technique that controlled for a number of potential predictors of probation failure, including socio-demographic variables, current violent offense, time on supervision, rehabilitative services received, and assessed risk level at the start of the probation term.

Moreover, these results were robust to a number of alternative statistical models. As such, it does not appear that the increased risk of failure on probation is related to a potential selection effect (e.g., simply because the agency used EM/GPS for only the most high-risk offenders). While it is possible that other unmeasured factors could still account for the increased risk of failure seen among those on EM/GPS, our current PSM approach does seem to address a number of important and theoretically relevant potential confounds. Finally, a simple comparison of the sub-sample of probationers who received GPS relative to those who received some other form of EM, reveals that those receiving GPS were more than twice as likely to fail on their probation term as were those who received some other form of EM.

Much of the existing research on the use of EM and GPS has found either small reductions in outcomes such as new arrests or technical violations, or no significant differences in outcomes for those on EM/GPS. Thus, in one sense our results showing a significant increase in the risk of probation failure, even controlling for potential confounds, stand out from the existing pattern of results. On the other hand, we examined a somewhat understudied population (generic offenders, not sexual offenders), who were sentenced to probation rather than parole, where EM use has received more research attention. We also examined a less commonly studied outcome measure, the likelihood of an unsuccessful completion of probation. In fact, we offered only exploratory research questions in this study specifically because our study population and the form of supervision under examination were relatively unique in the existing literature. At the same time, when considering the broader research literature on the effectiveness of increased supervision approaches, whether that involves the use of EM or simply programs such as Intensive Supervision Probation (ISP), our results would not be that unexpected. For example, the finding that increased levels of community supervision are related to increased rates of technical violations can be seen in some of the earliest evaluations of ISP programs (Petersilia & Turner, 1992).

Implications

Some of the existing evaluation research has demonstrated improvements in case outcomes for those on EM/GPS (see Bales et al., 2010), while others have found no significant differences in the likelihood of rates of technical violations or returns to prison (see Finn & Muirhead Steves, 2002; S. V. Gies et al., 2013). Our current results are more in line with the latter set of findings, though here we do not see *insignificant* differences. Instead, our data revealed sizable *increases* in the risk of unsuccessful case outcomes for those supervised with EM/GPS. This outcome however, is not completely unexpected (in light of past research on programs like ISP; see for instance Petersilia & Turner, 1992) that the increased intensity of supervision when these enhancements are used could lead to increased chances of being caught violating conditions of release.

If this result is replicated it would suggest that corrections departments will need to consider how to manage these increased rates of violations among those placed on probation in conjunction with EM. For instance, departments might need to develop a robust graduated sanctions process to be used in response to these individuals' technical violations and potential revocations leading to reincarceration. Otherwise, they may risk incarcerating individuals whom they (or the courts) were initially trying to divert from prisons with the use of community supervision. Departments might also need to consider more comprehensive assessments of potential probationers' risk and needs in order to know what obstacles to successful completion each probationer may face. Along with this, departments may also need to put in place either better supervision, or more intensive support services tied to those assessed risk and need areas. For instance, a more rigorous assessment protocol might identify individuals at elevated risk of failure, who need home confinement with EM, rather than simply probation with EM. Other individuals might need the enhanced supervision provided by the use of EM, but also require intensive therapeutic/social services (i.e., intensive outpatient drug treatment, development of additional informal social supports) to help them successfully complete their community supervision sentences. These types enhanced assessments, along with improvements in supervision (including graduated sanctions) and the provision of indicated treatment services would likely be needed, since the results from the current study at least, seem to suggest that the use of EM/GPS technology itself may not sufficiently promote successful completion of the probation sentence.

In addition, our current results to not include an examination of the relationship between these forms of EM and the likelihood of new offending. As such, additional research should examine these questions using similar generic samples of individuals supervised on probation (i.e., non-sex offenders). Such research would allow an examination of the potential risks to public safety (if rates of new crime are also found to be elevated) as opposed to a risk of increased technical violations and unsuccessful probation outcomes seen here. The current study also only examined the impact of any amount of time on EM (or GPS, specifically) during the probation term. Future research should examine whether the use of EM (or GPS) is any more effective if it is started at the beginning of a probation sentence, as well as whether there may be other effects that depend on the timing or duration of EM use. The existing research on the use of EM with home confinement is generally positive, though usually this research has examined low level offenders. Additional research examining the impact of combining EM/GPS with other enhanced supervision tools is also needed, especially among sample of more generic offenders.

The other important procedural question for probation departments revolves around what to do with the large volume of supervision data produced by various forms of EM (GPS in particular, with its near constant tracking capabilities), and as above, how agencies should respond to that data. This question is not a new one, and in fact has been considered since the earliest uses of these technologies (Morris & Tonry, 1990). These huge amounts of detailed supervision data mean agencies have to decide how to respond to sometimes minor violations of the conditions of release. Any decision not to respond to identified violations potentially risks public safety, while over-responding (e.g., incarcerating probationers for any minor violation) risks increasing prison populations and costs, by funneling individuals initially managed in the community into correctional facilities.

If the pattern of results identified in this dataset is replicated in other samples of similar probationers (i.e., non-sexual offenders), it would appear even more important that probation agencies carefully consider how to manage the large volume of data produced by EM/GPS, and how they will respond to this increased supervision data (i.e., through the use of graduated sanctions, short of incarceration in response to violations). Without some planning for the implementation of appropriate and feasible responses/sanctions for violations, departments will risk incarcerating large numbers of individuals they had intended to divert from prison, because they are more likely to be unable to successfully complete probation supervision when on EM/GPS.

Limitations and future directions

While the PSM technique used here is appropriate for evaluations when true random assignment is not possible, it is not without limitations. For instance, while we controlled for a number of important potential confounding influences (e.g., demographics, assessed risk level, current violence offense), a number of other measures were not available. For instance, it would have been useful to control for factors such as known substance abuse or mental health issues, more complete indicators of employment history, prior performance on community supervision, and assessments of individual motivation. Future research should attempt to examine the potential utility of EM/GPS supervision among probationers including additional control variables, and ideally using random assignment when possible. Likewise, due to limitations in the available data, our analyses did not control for the exact amount of time that probationers spent being supervised with EM or GPS. It will be important for future research to examine potential dosage effects from the use of these enhanced electronic supervision methods. Finally, while our models did control for the number of treatment and educational services that individuals were referred to, it would be useful for future research to more thoroughly examine the potential use of EM/GPS to specifically support rehabilitative efforts by providing needed structure to the individual's life (see Bonta et al., 2000a; Gendreau et al., 2000).

Supporters of the use of enhanced supervision using various technologies argue that these approaches could be useful in reducing prison populations and costs, and maybe even promote rehabilitation. Despite their growth in recent decades the existing research has yet to establish whether these goals have been achieved. Clearly there is a need for more rigorous examination of these programs and their outcomes, especially among specific types of individuals (sexual offenders, higher risk violent offenders and so on) and in different parts of the criminal justice system (pre-trial, post-adjudication and post-incarceration). The authors hope our current effort will spur such additional empirical explorations.

Notes

1. Other more recently developed forms of EM include *Secure Continuous Remote Alcohol Monitoring* (SCRAM) first implemented in 2003. The use of SCRAM technology typically requires the individual to wear a monitoring device attached to their ankle which can periodically analyzes their perspiration to assess the person's use of alcohol. These monitors may also include GPS tracking capabilities in addition to assessing alcohol consumption (SCRAM Systems, 2024). We do not examine the impact of SCRAM separately in this study because there were relatively few such individuals available in our data.
2. We examined whether the outliers in time of probation supervision influenced the findings presented in Tables 3 and 4. We "top coded" time on probation to the 95th percentile and re-estimated the propensity scores. The findings are substantively identical when the effect of the outliers is constrained.
3. We performed several checks for the robustness of the findings. These findings are presented in the Appendix. We first examined whether the large sample size influenced the matching of individuals in the treatment group to the comparison group. One concern is that a large sample size may bias estimates of a treatment effect because the likelihood of finding a nearest-neighbor match based upon the propensity score increases as the sample size increases (see King & Nielsen, 2019 for a review of criticisms of PSM). We used a set seed in Stata 14.2 and randomly selected a sample size that is approximately 3 times as large as the treatment group to examine whether the findings are influenced by sample size. Appendix A and Appendix B reveal that the findings are substantively identical as those presented in Tables 3 and 4. Next, we examined whether receiving EM influences the odds of being unsuccessful by method of a multivariable logistic regression. Appendix C and Appendix D reveal that individuals who received EM have significantly higher odds of being unsuccessful on community supervision. These findings align with those of the PSM analyses performed in Tables 3 and 4. Finally, as an added check for the robustness of the findings we examined inverse probability of treatment weights (IPTW). Unlike traditional logistic regression, IPTW adjusts the analysis by using a weight of the treatment effect (e.g., receiving EM). Appendix E and F reveal that individuals who received EM have significantly higher odds of being unsuccessful on community supervision. Across each of our checks for the robustness of the findings presented in Tables 3 and 4, the takeaway is that placement on EM increases the odds of being unsuccessful on community supervision, which supports our final conclusion of the study.

Disclosure statement

No potential conflict of interest was reported by the author(s).

References

Aos, S., Miller, M., & Drake, E. (2007). Evidence-based public policy options to reduce future prison construction, criminal justice costs, and crime rates. *Federal Sentencing Reporter*, *19*(4), 275–290.

Bales, W., Mann, K., Blomberg, T., Gaes, G., Barrick, K., Dhungana, K., & McManus, B. (2010). *A quantitative and qualitative assessment of electronic monitoring*. Office of Justice Programs, National Institute of Justice. https://jrsa.org/events/conference/presentations-10/Bill_Bales_2.pdf

Bartles, L., & Martinovic, M. (2017). Electronic monitoring: The experience in Australia. *European Journal of Probation*, *9*(1), 80–102. https://doi.org/10.1177/2066220317697658

Belur, J., Thorton, A., Tompson, L., Manning, M., Sidebottom, A., & Bowers, K. (2020). A systematic review of the effectiveness of the electronic monitoring of offenders. *Journal of Criminal Justice*, *68* (2020), 1–18. https://doi.org/10.1016/j.jcrimjus.2020.101686

Blumstein, A. (2002). Prisons: A policy challenge. In J. Q. Wilson & J. Petersilia (Eds.), *Crime: Public policies for crime control* (pp. 451–482). ICS Press.

Bonta, J., Wallace-Capretta, S., & Rooney, J. (2000a). Can electronic monitoring make a difference? An evaluation of three Canadian programs. *Crime & Delinquency*, *46*(1), 61–75. https://doi.org/10.1177/0011128700046001004

Bonta, J., Wallace-Capretta, S., & Rooney, J. (2000b). A quasi-experimental evaluation of an intensive rehabilitation supervision program. *Criminal Justice and Behavior*, *27*(3), 312–329. https://doi.org/10.1177/0093854800027003003

Bouchard, J., & Wong, J. S. (2018). The new panopticon? Examining the effect of home confinement on criminal recidivism. *Victims & Offenders*, *13*(5), 589–608. https://doi.org/10.1080/15564886.2017.1392387

Brown, T. M., McCabe, S. A., & Wellford, C. F. (2007). *Global positioning system (GPS) technology for community supervision: Lessons learned (no. 219376).* Noblis. https://www.ncjrs.gov/pdffiles1/nij/grants/219376.pdf

Finn, M. A., & Muirhead Steves, S. (2002). The effectiveness of electronic monitoring with violent male parolees. *Justice Quarterly*, *19*(2), 293–312. https://doi.org/10.1080/07418820200095251

Gendreau, P., Goggin, C., Cullen, F. T., & Andrews, D. A. (2000). The effects of community sanctions and incarceration on recidivism. *Forum on Corrections Research*, *12*(2), 10–13.

Gies, S. V., Gainey, R., Cohen, M. I., Healy, E., Yeide, M., Bekelman, A., & Bobnis, A. (2013). *Monitoring high-risk gang offenders with GPS technology: An evaluation of the California supervision program final report.* US Department of Justice, National Institute of Justice.

Gies, S., Gainey, R., & Healy, E. (2016). Monitoring high-risk sex offenders with GPS. *Criminal Justice Studies*, *29*(1), 1–20. https://doi.org/10.1080/1478601X.2015.1129088

Guo, S., & Fraser, M. W. (2010). *Propensity score analysis: Statistical methods and applications.* SAGE Publications.

Hawkes, A. L., Sellbom, M., & Gilmour, F. E. (2023). Under surveillance: Does global positioning system monitoring of offenders reduce recidivism? *Criminology & Criminal Justice*, 0(0. https://doi.org/10.1177/17488958231188414

Hernán, M. A., & Robins, J. M. (2020). *Causal inference: What if.* Chapman & Hall/CRC.

Kilgore, J. (2018). Toward a research and action agenda for electronic monitoring in the United States. *Journal of Community Corrections, Summer* 27(4) , 7–21. https://www.civicresearchinstitute.com/online/article_abstract.php?pid=9&iid=1346&aid=8795

King, G., & Nielsen, R. (2019). Why propensity scores should not be used for matching. *Political Analysis*, *27*(4), 435–454. https://doi.org/10.1017/pan.2019.11

Lab, S. P. (2020). *Crime prevention: Approaches, practices, and evaluation* (10th ed.). Routledge.

Lilly, J. R. (2006). Issues beyond empirical EM reports. *Criminology and Public Policy*, *5*(1), 93–102. https://doi.org/10.1111/j.1745-9133.2006.00105.x

MacKenzie, D. L. (1997). Criminal Justice and Crime Prevention. In L. W. Sherman, D. Gottfredson, D. MacKenzie, J. Eck, P. Reuter, & S. Busway (Eds.), *Preventing crime: What works, what doesn't, what's promising: Areport to the United States Congress* (pp. 9–76). U.S. Department of Justice, National Institute of Justice.

Morris, N., & Tonry, M. H. (1990). *Between prison and probation: Intermediate punishments in a rational sentencing system.* Oxford University Press.

Omori, M. K., & Turner, S. F. (2015). Assessing the cost of electronically monitoring high-risk sex offenders. *Crime and Delinquency*, *61*(6), 873–894. https://doi.org/10.1177/0011128712466373

Padgett, K. G., Bales, W. D., & Blomberg, T. G. (2006). Under surveillance: An empirical test of the effectiveness and consequences of electronic monitoring. *Criminology & Public Policy*, *5*(1), 61–91. https://doi.org/10.1111/j.1745-9133.2006.00102.x

Petersilia, J., & Turner, S. (1992). An evaluation of intensive probation in California. *The Journal of Criminal Law and Criminology*, *82*(3), 610–658. https://doi.org/10.2307/1143747

Pew Charitable Trusts. (2016). *Use of electronic offender-tracking devices expands sharply.* https://www.pewtrusts.org/en/research-and-analysis/issue-briefs/2016/09/use-of-electronic-offender-tracking-devices-expands-sharply

Renzema, M., & Mayo-Wilson, E. (2005). Can electronic monitoring reduce crime for moderate to high-risk offenders? *Journal of Experimental Criminology*, *1*(2005), 215–237. https://doi.org/10.1007/s11292-005-1615-1

Rosenbaum, P. R., & Rubin, D. B. (1984). Reducing bias in observational studies using subclassification on the propensity score. *Journal of the American Statistical Association*, *79*(387), 516–524.

SCRAM Systems. (2024, February 5). *SCRAM CAM® bracelet alcohol ankle monitor – SCRAM systems*. https://www.scramsystems.com/monitoring/scram-continuous-alcohol-monitoring/

Sugg, D., Moore, L., & Howard, P. (2001). *Electronic monitoring and offending behaviour: Reconviction results for the second year of trials of curfew orders*. Home Office.

Tonry, M. (1996). *Sentencing matters*. Oxford University Press.

Travis, J., Western, B., & Redburn, S. (2014). *The growth of incarceration in the United States: Exploring causes and consequences*. National Academies Press.

Yeh, S. S. (2010). Cost-benefit analysis of reducing crime through electronic monitoring of parolees and probationers. *Journal of Criminal Justice*, *38*(5), 1090–1096. https://doi.org/10.1016/j.jcrimjus.2010.08.001

Zhang, J., Kang-Brown, J., & Kotler, A. (2024). *People on electronic monitoring*. Vera Institute of Justice.

Index

Note: Figures are indicated by *italics*. Tables are indicated by **bold**.

FSC
www.fsc.org
MIX
Papier | Fördert gute Waldnutzung
FSC® C083411

Kolibri 360 GmbH
Ferdinand-Jühlke-Straße 7
99095 Erfurt, Deutschland
produktsicherheit@kolibri360.de